HARDPRESS.NET
HOME OF HARD-TO-FIND BOOKS

Poetry for Schools
by Eliza Robbins

POETRY FOR SCHOOLS;

DESIGNED FOR

READING AND RECITATION.

THE

WHOLE SELECTED FROM THE BEST POETS

IN THE

ENGLISH LANGUAGE.

Robbins

BY THE AUTHOR OF AMERICAN POPULAR LESSONS.

" Not marble nor the gilded monuments
Of princes, shall outlive this powerful rhyme."
Shakspeare.

NEW-YORK :

PUBLISHED BY WHITE, GALLAHER AND WHITE.
Elliott & Palmer, Printers.

1828.

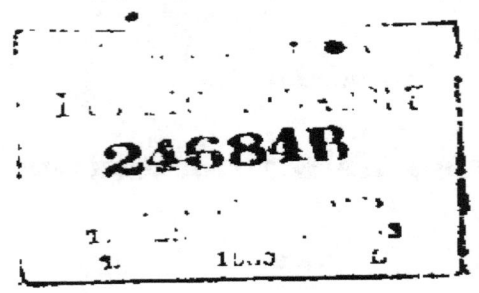
Southern District of New-York, ss.

BE IT REMEMBERED, That on the 23d day of January, in the fifty-second year of the Independence of the United States of America, White, Gallaher & White, of the said District, have deposited in this office, the title of a Book, the right whereof they claim as proprietors, in the words following, *to wit :*

"Poetry for Schools; designed for Reading and Recitation. The whole selected from the best poets in the English language. By the Author of American Popular Lessons.

'Not marble, nor the gilded monuments
Of princes, shall outlive this powerful rhyme.' "

In conformity to the Act of the Congress of the United States, entitled, "An Act for the encouragement of learning, by securing the copies of maps, charts, and books to the authors and proprietors of such copies, during the times therein mentioned;" And also, to an Act entitled, "An Act, supplementary to an Act, entitled An Act for the encouragement of learning, by securing the copies of maps, charts, and books, to the authors and proprietors of such copies, during the times therein mentioned, and extending the benefits thereof to the arts of designing, engraving, and etching historical and other prints."

F. J. BETTS,
Clerk of the Southern District of New-York.

TO MY OWN PUPILS,

AND

TO THE CHILDREN OF THOSE PARENTS

WHOSE APPROBATION HAS ENCOURAGED AND WHOSE JUDG-
MENT HAS ASSISTED ME IN THE COMPILATION OF

CHILDREN'S BOOKS,

THIS VOLUME IS OFFERED,

IN THE HOPE THAT IT MAY BE USEFUL TO THEM.

INTRODUCTION.

THE superfluity of school-books which already exists, seems to make any further multiplication of them absurd, unless new ones should be better than the old; and it is somewhat presumptuous to suppose that a better than so many existing compilations can be furnished—but as an instructer of young persons, I have felt the want of elementary books different from those in common use, and therefore I have composed them.

All that is new to a pupil stands in need of illustration, for without it his mind is rather overburthened than enriched by his acquirements. Oral instruction may furnish an enlightened commentary upon what is contained in school-books; still it would diminish the labour of instruction if school-books themselves should not only afford the principal matter of instruction, but lead the young to inquiry, and supply the helps which the understanding requires in order to make the finest writers intelligible, and it appears to me that ordinary school-books are wholly deficient in this respect.

It is a matter of self-gratulation to many, that they were early made acquainted with the finest passages of English poetry, that these passages were safely stored in the memory before the imagination or the heart could be affected by their beauty, and that, when the higher powers have been cultivated in after life, they could discover their inspiration and enjoyments to have grown not only from nature but knowledge.

This is certainly true of many who have read Shakspeare and Milton as *tasks*, or because they loved the *sound of their words*—and that this fondness for the *sound* of poetry or eloquence does exist in young minds, before the subjects of either can be comprehended, may sometimes be observed. The writer has seen a boy of seven years listen to the pages of Burke with fixed and delighted attention, and has known a little girl two years younger as much excited and gratified by the reading of fine poetry—yet in both instances it was not a genuine comprehension of beauty, but an influence of sympathetic affection. A parent's tastes, and animated pleasure, imparted this lively interest to the full-toned periods of the orator, and the magic numbers of the poet—and these early indications of taste and enthusiasm are rare. The greater part of young per-

sons do not love literature, because they do not
understand it—do not *begin at the beginning.* In
our common schools we make our children read
disputes upon the comparative excellence of Rea-
son and Revelation,* and require them to recite
Pope's Messiah, the Dialogue between Brutus
and Cassius, and a multitude more of difficult
passages from the poets. I never knew a boy who
could explain the first lines of the Messiah, or
who could tell the matter of dispute between the
complotters of Cæsar's death—and only because
boys are not instructed in elementary facts in re-
lation to those pieces, or any others of this cha-
racter. How repugnant this mode of cultivating
literary taste is to some highly endowed minds, is
happily expressed by one whose memory, and
whose genius, in its creations, will endure for ever.

*   *   *   *   " I abhorr'd
Too much, to conquer for the poet's sake,
The drill'd dull lesson, forced down word by word
In my repugnant youth, with pleasure to record

Aught that recals the daily drug which turn'd
My sickening memory ; and though Time hath taught
My mind to meditate what then it learn'd,
Yet such the fixed inveteracy wrought

* See English Reader, Dialogue between Locke and Bayle.

By the impatience of my early thought
That, with the freshness wearing out before
My mind could relish what it might have sought
If free to choose, I cannot now restore
Its health ; but what it then detested, still abhor."

In a note upon these lines this high authority expresses all that I would say upon this subject.

"I wish," says Lord Byron, "to express that we become tired of the task before we can comprehend the beauty; that we learn by rote before we can get by heart; that the freshness is worn away, and the future pleasure and advantage deadened and destroyed, by the didactic anticipation, at an age when we can neither feel nor understand the compositions which it requires an acquaintance with life, as well as Latin and Greek, to relish, or to reason upon. For the same reason we never can be aware of the fulness of some of the finest passages of Shakspeare, ('To be or not to be,' for instance,) from the habit of having them hammered into us at eight years old, as an exercise, not of mind but memory: so that when we are old enough to enjoy them, the taste is gone, and the appetite palled. In some parts of the Continent, young persons are taught from more common authors, and do not read the best classics till their maturity."

In conformity to these views, and my own experience in relation to education, I have endeavoured to prepare a school-book after this suggestion; and in order to compose it, I resorted to the purest fountains of English verse, and took what I found suitable to my humble purpose. I left the more elevated and sublime portions of the poets who supplied me, and appropriated to my selection such passages only as I believed would, with a little exposition, be useful and agreeable to young readers. As a bird does not lead her new-fledged offspring to the skies in her first flight with them, so I would dictate short excursions to the unformed faculties of the human mind, that young readers, feeling their own power and felicity as they proceed, may at length be able and willing, without assistance, to ascend " the brightest heaven of invention."

In the modes of education in present fashion, civil and political history is presented to young minds at an early period of study, but literary history—the peaceful influence of mind upon mind —is wholly neglected; and those who are initiated in the most remarkable passages of Shakspeare, ilton, and other great authors, are taught nothing at school of these memorable men and their contemporaries. It is a debt that posterity owes

to genius, to attach the memory of the man to his
works, and to keep him and his contemporaries
in the view of succeeding ages.   I had only suf-
ficient space simply to introduce authors and their
relations to contemporary society, but I intended
to suggest this relation, to awaken inquiry, to
give my readers some acquaintance with the his-
tory of English poets and poetry, and also to show
them the relations of English poetry to the rest of
their intellectual pursuits.   I hope my purpose
will be effected, and that Poetry for Schools will
be acceptable to teachers and pupils.

New-York, Jan. 1828.

◆

NATURE OF POETRY.

WHATEVER exists, is divided into *mind* and *matter*. Philosophers do not accurately define the difference of mind and matter, but the body of animals, or living beings, which appears to die, and the " insensible clod" which we tread upon, are composed of *matter*. Every creature endowed with animal life, is, in some degree, " instinct with spirit"—endowed with some consciousness of wants, and some sense of supply and of enjoyment—this is *intelligence*. Intelligence, *in man*, is called Mind.

The minds of men are very different—some are wise, and others are foolish—some minds acquire very great knowledge, and others only understand a few facts. Boys at school call others who are easily puzzled in arithmetic, or who are incapable of learning long lessons, *dunces.* Those who are capable of thinking with attention, who acquire knowledge readily, and who accurately remember what they have learned, are said to possess *abilities ;* and one, who, besides learning his tasks with facility, can compose verses, or write a story of his own invention, possesses *genius.* Some *men* excel others, as the *boy* of genius excels the dunce. The genius and the dunce grow to be men, but they always remain the *genius* and the *dunce.*

Genius is, properly, the talent of discovery—the talent in one mind of conceiving, and of displaying to others, something previously unthought of. *Genius* is a capability to produce much advantage and pleasure to mankind. *Genius* may be very differently employed by different individuals. Columbus was a man of genius. He mani-

2

fested his genius when he meditated in one hemisphere, of our globe upon another which had never been explored, when he devised means to navigate unknown seas, and when he persevered in his great enterprize till he had accomplished it. Mr. Fulton, the mechanician, who applied the steam engine to navigation, was a man of genius. Benjamin West, the painter, was a man of genius. He painted many fine pictures, and among others, the subjects of which were taken from the gospel, "Christ healing the sick." In this picture Mr. West represented the benevolence of Jesus in his gracious countenance, a variety of diseases in those who surrounded him, and the emotions of desire, hope, and gratitude, in those who expected to be, or who had been, restored to health. The power to do all this so much surpasses the powers of common men that it serves for a clear illustration of *genius*.

Bonaparte, who conquered in many battles, and obtained the first magistracy in France by his power of controlling others, and after dethroning kings in Europe, gave kingdoms to his brothers, and who, after having slain his thousands, and tens of thousands, devised wise and practical improvements in the condition of those he permitted to live, was a man of great genius, though he is only to be admired and imitated so far as he effected or intended good to mankind. But there is another order of genius—men, who having ceased to live, still speak, who are known and honoured for their thoughts, when their actions are forgotten, and with whom we may be familiar, though we should never see them. These are the authors of books, who have recorded their beautiful ideas, that others may be better, and wiser, and happier, than they could be without the intelligence supplied from these divine minds. Shakspeare, who wrote the plays, which almost every reader of the English language possesses, and Milton, the author of Paradise Lost, were men of this class of genius.

We should be thankful to God that such men have ever lived. They exalt our nature, and procure for us pleasures which we could not enjoy if some minds did not differ from others in glory.   If we could not enrich our understandings with the thoughts of others, we should be like savages, in ignorance—or like bees and beavers: men of no age would be more cultivated or improved than their ancestors who lived centuries before them.

The body has different functions : eyes for seeing, ears for hearing, &c.   The mind also has its different operations.   After we have been instructed in the nature of different objects, and have been taught their names, and the proper use of our senses, we learn to distinguish one substance from another. and we remember the qualities of these various substances : thus, if a lighted lamp and a rose are set before us, we instantly comprehend that the lamp is an invention of art, and the rose a production of nature ; that the lamp is for use, and the rose for ornament; that the lamp flame diffuses light and heat, and that the rose delights us by its beauty and its fragrance.

The different properties of these objects are comprehended by the *mind*, though they were first perceived by the senses of sight and smell.   This consciousness of the presence of the lamp and the rose. given to the mind by the sight and smell, is called a *perception*.   We receive from the presence of these objects a certain feeling that they indeed exist, and are before us.   This exhibition to our minds, of the lamp and the rose, we call a *demonstration*, or *certainty*.   We understand that the lamp and t'.e rose are not alike—we then *distinguish* or *compare* them, and comprehend the different qualities of the two things. When we reflect, as we must, upon the different properties of these objects, we exert the power of comparing things, which is *judgment*.

But suppose we did not *see* either of these objects, and should read the following passages of poetry :

" How far the little candle throws its beams !"

Shakspeare.

Or,

" I will show you what is beautiful : it is a rose fully

blown. See, how she sits upon her mossy stem, like the queen of all the flowers. Her leaves glow like fire, and the air is filled with her sweet odour."

In reading the former passage, we should immediately remember, that in some dark night, while we were yet far from a house, we clearly perceived the light of a candle, and we know the light to have proceeded from that candle to our eyes. We first knew this by a *perception* of the light, and we comprehend that the light was a candle flame, and not another thing, by our *judgment*. When we *read* of the extended reach of the candle beams, we know that the fact mentioned is true, because it has been *demonstrated* to us at a former time. The present certainty of formerly acquired knowledge, is the *memory* of that knowledge. As we know *how far the little candle throws its beams*, so we also know that the properties of the *rose* are well described. With our eyes shut, and far from the candle or the rose, we comprehend the properties of both objects—we perceive them with the "mind's eye," as Shakspeare says. This *mind's eye* is the *imagination*. Before the imagination can be employed upon absent objects, that is, before we can think about, or reflect upon absent objects, we must exert the powers of Perception, Judgment, and Memory.

It is, then, by an effort of memory and of imagination that we form an idea of absent objects ; and by *imagination* we comprehend what is written in books, or represented in pictures which exhibit beautiful *images*. The imagination of an ignorant person is not powerful—he thinks almost always of objects before his eyes ; but the imagination of a fine poet is a noble faculty. The poet, or the artist, comprehends and feels more than other men, and he makes others feel, in some measure, as he feels. The imagination of him who writes a fine poem, or a tale, produces *invention*, or the combination and composition of something new to others. The imagination of a well instructed person, who perhaps can *invent* nothing, produces *taste*—which is a power of taking pleasure in something beautiful and elegant that may be presented to us.

This same *taste*, or enjoyment of the beautiful, must exist in the mind of the writer of a poem or tale, or in the mind of an artist, as well as in that of a person who delights in reading a poem, or beholding a good picture. The *sympathy of taste* makes the poet write—he expects to be admired, and the same sympathy makes other persons admire and enjoy the works of genius.

All that is written in books is *literature.* Literature is written language : it is divided into *prose* and *poetry*. *Quadrupeds have four feet*, is a prose sentence.

> " Full many a flower is born to blush unseen,
>   And waste its sweetness on the desert air,"

is *poetry*. Poetry is generally written in *verse*. Verse is a certain measure or quantity of sound, expressed in words, at regular times, during the whole of a poem. This measure, or metre, consists of a certain number of syllables in the printed lines of a poem.

" Heroic metre, which is the most usual kind, consists of lines of ten syllables. *Pope's and Milton's works are chiefly written in this metre ; but Pope wrote in rhyme, and Milton chiefly in blank verse :—

> ' Soft as the wily fox is seen to creep,
>   Where bask on sunny banks the simple sheep.'—*Pope*.

Each of these lines consists of ten syllables ; and the last words of each of them, '*creep*' and '*sheep*,' rhyme to each other ; that is to say, resemble each other in sound.

> ' Ye mists and exhalations that now rise .
>   From hill or steaming lake, dusky or gray,
>   Till the sun paints your fleecy skirts with gold.'—*Milton*.

" Each of these lines also consists of ten syllables ; but though they are not in rhyme, we easily distinguish them from prose. The difference consists in the choice of words, and in their arrangement, as may be perceived by reading the same words in an order different from that in which they are at present placed. The ear will feel that

* Pope and Milton are English poets.
2*

the cadence or sound is unlike verse; and the understanding will know that the sense is conveyed in words different from those used in history or in a newspaper. For instance, the following passage cannot be mistaken for prose:—' Ye exhalations and mists that now rise from steaming lake, or gray or dusky hill, till the sun paints with gold your fleecy skirts.'

"All verses are not written in lines of ten syllables; some are written in eight, and some few in twelve ; indeed we meet with lines in poetry of every number of syllables from three to fourteen."

In poetry, words are not used *literally*, as, for the most part, in prose. *Snow is white*, expresses what is *literally true*.—The words, *snow is white*, exactly express what we know to be true, but, *the golden sun diffuses his beams over the face of nature*, is an expression altogether *figurative*. We understand not that the sun is gold, but that his yellow lustre resembles the appearance of gold. These words only signify that the sun shines upon the surface of the earth, and the objects which are upon the earth. *Truth* describes something which really exists, as *God made the world*. *Fiction* describes something which might exist, or has been supposed to exist, yet is not now really in existence. One of Gay's Fables begins,

" Remote from cities lived a swain,"

and proceeds to relate a conversation of a shepherd and a philosopher. There have been many shepherds and philosophers ; but probably no particular shepherd and philosopher ever met, and held the conversation which Gay describes, yet a shepherd and philosopher *might* talk together in that manner. Gay's Shepherd and Philosopher is a *Fable* or *Fiction*. It is proper to distinguish between *fiction* and a *lie*. A *Fiction* is an *avowed invention*—a *Lie* is a false declaration intended to deceive.

English poetry includes the inventions of English poets, and their translations from other languages : from Greek and Latin, and from the modern languages of Europe, besides a few from the oriental or Asiatic languages.

Our poetry, (for whatever is written in the English language properly belongs to 'the Americans who speak it,) is divided into many kinds : the Sacred, Classical, Romantic, Dramatic, &c. *Sacred poetry* relates to serious subjects, to the scriptures, and to the praise of God. Milton's Paradise Lost, and Watts' Hymns, are *sacred poetry*, and so are many parts of the Old Testament. *Classical poetry* is that which has been translated from Greek and Latin. Pope's translation of Homer's Iliad, and Dryden's translation of Virgil, are *classical poetry*. *Romantic poetry*, or *metrical romance*, relates a tale in verse: as, The Lady of the Lake, by Sir Walter Scott. *Dramatic poetry* is composed of poems in dialogue, or discourse of persons, which relate a story : Shakspeare's Lear, and the tragedy of Douglas, are of this class.

In order to understand the greater part of poetry, it is necessary to know something of Mythology and Classical Fable. A young reader may get this information from the Classical Dictionary, a book in very common use. Poetry which relates to fictions taken from the north of Europe, alludes often to *Scandinavian Mythology*, or to the superstitions of the more northern nations of Europe. The writers of Romantic poetry have supplied notes to their works, which make their *text* very clear.

The Epic Poem, relates a long history of some great event. It has what is called the beginning, middle, and end of the action. The *beginning* is the cause of what follows ; the *middle* relates the progress or carrying-on of the action ; the *end* is its *catastrophe*, or finishing. Homer's Iliad is an Epic poem—the story related in it is a war between the princes of Greece and those of Troy. The *cause* of the war was the elopement of Helen, a Grecian princess, with a young Trojan. The war itself consisted of a series of engagements or battles between the Greeks and Trojans, which are described by Homer in many successive books of the Iliad ; and the *catastrophe*, or end of the poem, is the death of Hector, the Trojan prince, who alone could defend Troy ; and the destruction of that city by the Greeks, must be supposed immediately to follow.

When a long tale in verse relates some *private history*, which includes but a small number of persons in the action, it is *Metrical Romance.*

The Ode was perhaps originally designed to be sung. It is a poem usually addressed to some real or ideal personage, or it celebrates some distinguished individual. Gray's Ode to Spring, is addressed to the season of Spring, upon the supposition that she is a female, endowed with the capacity of knowing what is addressed to her, and of answering the prayer of the poet. Dryden's Alexander's Feast, is an ode which celebrates the music of the ancients, but it was first written to be recited or sung on *St. Cecilia's Day.* St. Cecilia is a Catholic Saint, the supposed inventress of the harp. A painter has represented her attended by St. Peter and St. Paul, with an *angel* hovering over them, listening to the music she made, which was to represent, that it was believed she drew angels from Heaven. Mr. Dryden writes thus of her :—

"At last divine Cecilia came,
   Inventress of the vocal frame ;
The sweet enthusiast, from her sacred store
   Enlarged the former narrow bounds,
   And added length to solemn sounds,
With nature's mother-wit, and art unknown before.
   Let old Timotheus yield the prize,
   Or both divide the crown ;
   He raised a mortal to the skies,
   She drew an angel down."

Dryden represents in Alexander's Feast, that after his conquest of Persia, Alexander of Macedon celebrated his victory in a great festival at Persepolis ; that upon this occasion Timotheus played upon the *lyre,* a stringed instrument in use among the Greeks, and sang various kinds of airs. Timotheus began his songs, by proclaiming that Alexander was the *son of Jove,* the supreme god of the Greeks ; and Alexander, in his weak folly, believed him. In this sense Timotheus " raised a mortal to the skies." Some centuries after Timotheus lived, it is said that St. Cecilia " enlarged the bounds" of ancient music, by the invention of the harp—an instrument with more strings, and capable of producing a greater variety of sounds than the ancient lyre.

It was customary among the Greeks for musicians, or poets who excelled all others to receive a wreath, or crown at the public festivals, as a mark of admiration from those who heard them, and as the reward of their excellence. Timotheus might have received such a crown, but Dryden commands him to resign to St. Cecilia, or to divide it with her, because she surpassed him in his art.

If, in prose writing, an author should speak of two persons living at different periods of time, as *contemporaries* or existing together, it would be called an *anachronism*, or disregard of time—but poets are sometimes allowed to speak thus, and their liberty to exceed the limits of strict truth, is *poetic license.*

The Elegy is a melancholy poem, written upon some subject which of itself excites the feeling of sadness. The most popular and most beautiful *elegy* in our language, is Gray's, upon a *country churchyard*. It celebrates no distinguished individual, but was composed under a deep feeling that it is appointed to all men, once to die, and, that each " in his narrow bed for ever laid," all men are *equal*, or in the same condition. A tender sorrow for the fate of the dead, and a veneration for those moral and intellectual capacities for excellence and happiness, which God dispenses without respect to fortune or power, seem to have inspired this most exquisite production. The young cannot comprehend all its beauty and truth, but in mature life, it is impossible that he who feels for all that live, should not be affected by this sweet picture of the lot of mortality, and the virtues of humble life.

The Ballad is a narrative song. Ballads are usually composed among a rude people in the early ages of society, and after society becomes more highly civilized, some writers imitate the old ballads ; but in highly polished communities ballads are too simple to please as new and original,—they must, to be interesting, refer to the manners of a past age. The Children in the Wood is a pretty ballad, and very well known.

The Eclogue is a narrative, or a descriptive poem, meant to exhibit the particular manners of some few individuals in a country. The Eclogue is often a conversation. Collins's Eclogues are much read—one of them, Hassan the Camel Driver. will be found in this collection.

Satire is, in its best character, a moral lecture in verse —a censure upon something which is respected without deserving to be so—of some *person* who is generally approved, or of some prevailing *conduct* which is allowed without much blame. Satire endeavours to make its subject, whatever it is, contemptible. Satire is sometimes wholesome correction of what is wrong, and sometimes it is mean malignity—the spirit which a writer of talents expresses against some person whom he unworthily hates. Juvenal's Satires from the Latin are translated into English—they describe the corrupt manners of the people in Rome, during the reigns of the emperors Nero, Domitian, and Trajan. Pope's and Young's Satires are, among English poetry, of this description—they attack follies and persons, ridiculous in their time. Satire is like a caricature, it diverts when first known, but unless it is very just and happy, it soon ceases to give pleasure.

The Epitaph is designed for a memorial of the dead, and is generally a few verses inscribed upon a tombstone. The following one has been much admired.

"ON THE COUNTESS OF PEMBROKE.

"Underneath this marble hearse
Lies the subject of all verse.
Sidney's sister, Pembroke's mother.
Death, ere thou hast killed another
Fair, and learned. and good as she,
Time shall throw a dart at thee."—*Ben Jonson.*

This epitaph expresses very high praise. Before another so exalted by all merit as this lady was, should die, Death himself would cease to number his victims, for she surpassed all who should live after her But this is *hyperbole*, or exaggeration. These lines are pretty, and *epigrammatic*, that is, the words have a variety of meaning, unexpectedly and happily presented to the mind of the reader—but they are wanting in *simplicity*. Simplicity is a single purpose.—The epitaph not only praises Lady Pembroke, it intimates the dignity of her brother, Sir Philip Sidney, and of her son, the earl of Pembroke, and it disparages the rest of her sex by comparison with her;—still it is,—(as we sometimes apply this word to expressive language,)—*very happy*; it conveys much in a few words. One of Mr. Pope's epitaphs is a very pure and beautiful tribute to a good woman.

"EPITAPH ON MRS. CORBET.

" Here rests a woman good without pretence,
  Blest with plain reason, and with sober sense.
  No conquest she but o'er herself desired,
  No art essayed, but not to be admired.
  Heaven, as its purest gold, by tortures tried—
  The saint sustained it, but the *woman* died."

The *simplicity* of this epitaph is perfectly obvious.

The Epigram is a few verses expressing a perspicuous and pointed meaning, and it usually conveys a brief satire. *Mild* William Clarke, grandfather to Dr. Clarke, the traveller, composed an epigram on seeing the inscription which is engraved over the vault, or family tomb, of the Dukes of Richmond.—The inscription is *Domus ultima*—in English, the *last house*, and the *epigram*, the following:—

" Did he who thus inscribed the wall
  Not read or not believe Saint Paul,
  Who says there is, where'er it stands,
  Another house not made with hands—
  Or may we gather from these words
  That house is not a house of Lords ?"

The writer here intimates that something which suggests the idea of eternal life, ought to be written over the place of the body's interment. St. Paul says, in the New Testament, and alluding to the immortality of the soul, there is a " a house not made with hands, eternal in the heavens."——Our Saviour says, " in my father's house are many mansions,"——many places suitable to be assigned to my followers in their future state of existence. Mr. Clarke, who was a Christian, instantly thought, on seeing the tomb of the Lords of Richmond, of those other mansions of the dead ; and because this noble race thus appeared to regard the grave as their last rest, he means at once to satirize and reprove their seeming unbelief, by insinuating, that, perhaps the heavenly habitation mentioned by Paul would not suit the pride of Lords, or that Lords, though they enjoy high honours on earth, might be excluded from an inheritance in heaven.

Besides, the kinds of poetry, that have been mentioned, there are the *mock-heroic*, and the *pastoral*. The *mock-heroic* gives a fanciful importance to trivial things. The commencement of Cowper's Task is *mock-heroic*. The poet describes the progressive elegance of *seats* used at different times in Britain. The whole passage is sprightly and amusing.

" Time was, when clothing sumptuous or for use,
Save their own painted skins, our sires had none.
As yet black breeches were not ; satin smooth,
Or velvet soft, or plush with shaggy pile :
The hardy chief upon the rugged rock
Wash'd by the sea, or on the gravelly bank
Thrown up by wintry torrents roaring loud,
Fearless of wrong, reposed his weary strength.
Those barbarous ages past, succeeded next
The birthday of invention ; weak at first,
Dull in design, and clumsy to perform.
Jointstools were then created ; on three legs
Upborne they stood. Three legs upholding firm
A massy slab, in fashion square or round.
On such a stool immortal Alfred sat,
And sway'd the sceptre of his infant realms :
And such in ancient halls and mansions drear

May still be seen ; but perforated sore,
And drill'd in holes, the solid oak is found,
By worms voracious eating through and through.
　　At length a generation more refined
Improved the simple plan ; made three legs four,
Gave them a twisted form vermicular,
And o'er the seat, with plenteous wadding stuff'd,
Induced a splendid cover, green and blue,
Yellow and red, of tapestry richly wrought
And woven close, or needlework sublime.
There might you see the piony spread wide,
The full-blown rose, the shepherd and his lass,
Lapdog and lambkin with black staring eyes,
And parrots with twin cherries in their beak.
　　Now came the cane from India smooth and bright
With Nature's varnish ; sever'd into stripes,
That interlaced each other, these supplied
Of texture firm a lattice-work, that braced
The new machine, and it became a chair.
But restless was the chair ; the back erect
Distress'd the weary loins, that felt no ease ;
The slippery seat betray'd the sliding part
That press'd it, and the feet hung dangling down,
Anxious in vain to find the distant floor.
　　These for the rich : the rest, whom Fate had placed
In modest mediocrity, content
With base materials, sat on well-tann'd hides,
Obdurate and unyielding, glassy smooth,
With here and there a tuft of crimson yarn,
Or scarlet crewel, in the cushion fix'd,
If cushion might be call'd, what harder seem'd
Than the firm oak, of which the frame was form'd.
　　No want of timber then was felt or fear'd
In Albion's happy isle.　The lumber stood
Ponderous and fix'd by its own massy weight.
But elbows still were wanting ; these, some say,
An alderman of Cripplegate contrived ;
And some ascribe the invention to a priest,
Burly, and big, and studious of his ease.

But, rude at first, and not with easy slope
Receding wide, they press'd against the ribs,
And bruised the side ; and, elevated high,
Taught the raised shoulders to invade the ears.
 Long time elapsed or ere our rugged sires
Complain'd, though incommodiously pent in,
And ill at ease behind. The ladies first
'Gan murmur, as became the softer sex.
Ingenious Fancy, never better pleased
Than when employ'd to accommodate the fair,
Heard the sweet moan with pity, and devised
The soft settee ; one elbow at each end
And in the midst an elbow it received.
United yet divided, twain at once.
So sit two kings of Brentford on one throne ;
And so two citizens, who take the air,
Close packed and smiling, in a chaise and one.
But relaxation of the languid frame,
By soft recumbency of outstretch'd limbs,
Was bliss reserved for happier days. So slow
The growth of what is excellent ; so hard
To attain perfection in this nether world.
Thus first Necessity invented stools,
Convenience next suggested elbow-chairs,
And Luxury the accomplishe'd SOFA last."

 Pastoral poetry, as the name indicates, describes the shepherd's life, and indeed many modes of rural occupation and pleasure. In America we have no persons professedly devoted to the care of flocks, but in Asia and Europe, from time immemorial, this mode of life has been followed by considerable numbers. It is necessarily lonely and quiet, and disposes the mind to reflection. When Moses was a shepherd in Midian, he saw the vision of God ; when the shepherds, mentioned by St. Luke, were " keeping watch over their flock by night, the glory of the Lord shone round about them." There is something peculiarly innocent and interesting in the occupation of shepherds ; and the state of their minds, detached from the common business of life, may be supposed to be highly favourable to poetic thought ; but, notwithstand-

ing this presumption, *Pastoral poetry* is out of date—
little read, and, at present, not at all written. Many
English poets from Chaucer to Shenstone have written
Pastorals. Ambrose Phillips, a contemporary of Pope,
wrote pastorals better than he wrote any thing else. As
a specimen of this species of poetry, an extract from
Phillips's Pastorals is subjoined. Two shepherds meet
annually to bewail the loss of one of their young com-
peers; one of them, Angelot, here rehearses the praises
of the dead Albino:

" Thus yearly circling, by-past times return ;
And yearly, thus, Albino's death we mourn.
Sent into life, alas ! how short thy stay :
How sweet the rose ! how speedy to decay !
Can we forget, Albino dear, thy knell,
Sad-sounding wide from every village bell ;
Can we forget how sorely Albion moan'd,
That hills, and dales, and rocks, in echo groan'd,
Presaging future woe, when for our crimes,
We lost Albino, pledge of peaceful times,
Fair boast of this fair island, darling joy
Of nobles high, and every shepherd boy ?
No joyous pipe was heard, no flocks were seen,
Nor shepherd found upon the grassy green,
No cattle graz'd the field, nor drank the flood,
No birds were heard to warble through the wood.
In yonder gloomy grove outstretch'd he lay
His lovely limbs upon the dampy clay ;
On his cold cheek the rosy hue decay'd,
And o'er his lips the deadly blue display'd :
Beating around him lie his plaintive sheep,
And mourning shepherds come, in crowds, to weep.
Young Buckhurst comes : and, is there no redress ?
As if the grave regarded our distress !
The tender virgins come, to tears yet new,
And give, aloud, the lamentations due.
The pious mother comes, with grief opprest :
Ye trees and conscious fountains, can attest
With what sad accents and what piercing cries,

She fill'd the grove, and importun'd the skies,
And every star upbraided with his death,
When, in her widow'd arms, devoid of breath,
She clasp'd her son : nor did the nymph, for this,
Place in her darling's welfare all her bliss,
Him teaching, young, the harmless crook to wield
And rule the peaceful empire of the field.

As milk-white swans on streams of silver show,
And silvery streams to grace the meadows flow,
As corn the vales, and trees the hills adorn,
So thou, to thine, an ornament was born.
Since thou, delicious youth, didst quit the plains,
Th' ungrateful ground we till with fruitless pains,
In labour'd furrows sow the choice of wheat,
And, over empty sheaves, in harvest sweat ;
A thin increase our fleecy cattle yield ;
And thorns, and thistles, overspread the field.
How all our hope is fled like morning-dew !
And scarce did we thy dawn of manhood view.

Who now shall teach the pointed spear to throw,
To whirl the sling, and bend the stubborn bow,
To toss the quoit with steady aim, and far,
With sinewy force, to pitch the massy bar :
Nor dost thou live to bless thy mother's days,
To share her triumphs, and to feel her praise,
In foreign realms to purchase early fame,
And add new glories to the British name.
O, peaceful may thy gentle spirit rest ;
The flowery turf lie light upon thy breast ;
Nor shrieking owl, nor bat, thy tomb fly round,
Nor midnight goblins revel o'er the ground !"

Poetry is *descriptive* when it exhibits the appearances of nature, as in Mr. Bryant's Green River—*humorous* when it would excite laughter, as in Byrom's Three Black Crows—*pathetic* when it induces the feelings of sadness and pity.—Gray's Elegy is *pathetic.* When humorous poetry excites contempt for any object by assuming dignity of style in representing it, we call it *burlesque.*

It may be remarked that poetry does not consist merely

of *measured words*, but of *poetic ideas*. Common business, whatever relates to gaining money, and to supplying the mere wants of the body, is not poetical. Whatever employs the imagination without regard to bodily wants—God and his works, the mind and its pleasures, great actions of good men, the appearance of the heavens and the beauty of the earth, and the hopes and probable enjoyments of another life, are poetical subjects. There is a proper manner or style of writing upon these subjects, more dignified and more refined than that which we use in ordinary writing : this is the *poetic style*, and it admits of ornaments which are explained by Rhetoric. *Grammar* informs us how to speak and write with *propriety*, *Rhetorick* instructs us to do both with *elegance*.

Rules do not convey exact ideas of a just and beautiful style of writing : they are useful, but not sufficient. Good examples set before a writer, and good sense and good taste on his part, are necessary to make him write well ; and the careful and intelligent reading of the best books in his own language, is the best help which any young person can find to exalt and multiply his own ideas, or to create the power of expressing them with effect upon others.

The *genius* of a man determines whether he shall be a fine poet, an original artist, or an eloquent orator ; but genius does not determine whether whatever he does shall be done well or ill—his education, his habits, and his own will, determine that. Industry and application of mind, are the means of improving all the faculties. Taste consists in the knowledge of what is beautiful and proper, and in the love of it. If a young person be careless how he speaks and writes, if his desire of excellence be no higher than to *spell well*, and to be amused by books, he has no chance of any high enjoyments derived from literature. A gentleman really accomplished, capable of sustaining any eminence with honour, must know how to converse and to write well, and to form a

3*

correct judgment of the abilities of others in these respects.

A person accustomed to books, and desirous of expressing his thoughts well in writing or discourse, must know what is proper and elegant in the style of writing which he attempts, and also the style of conversation suited to his associates. Perhaps there is no mortification more frequently felt than that of an embarrassed speech—a want of self-satisfying power to give ready utterance to one's thoughts. This may be obviated by careful and early study, and by a habit of committing our ideas to writing. We ought to know what terms are suitable to ordinary discourse. A person who reads much becomes *pedantic* or *bombastical,* if he does not learn that the subjects and language of his books are somewhat distinct from the topics which spring up in common conversation —but his conversation will be corrupted if he does not bear in mind the corrections which vulgar speech may take from an intimacy with good authors; and his written compositions will not attain their suitable elegance unless he *knows what is proper.*

What is proper, is the style which the best writers have agreed to consider proper. The *models* of what is proper must be known—we must read poetry and prose to know them. We are not obliged exactly to imitate any style of writing—if we understand and love what we read, our minds will be conformed to the spirit of our reading; and if we have talents we may improve upon the manner of others. No artist could have formed the statue of a *god* who had never seen a *man,* but having seen and studied the human figure, images far surpassing the beauty of any individual man have been formed. Books are in every house; instruction lifts up her voice every where—we have nothing to do but to read, to listen, to think of these things, and to elevate ourselves above "the vulgar flight of low desire," to be all that we ought to be.

Poetry is so happily adapted to our faculties that its construction catches the ear instantly, it fastens upon the mind, assimilates our thoughts to its suggestions, and is held more tenaciously in the memory than any other part of our knowledge which is not connected with the mere preservation of life. The pleasure it affords as a luxury of imagination is incalculable, and as a purifying influence upon the heart and life, its moral benefit is beyond estimation. We cannot love things high and holy, and things mean and unworthy, at the same time. Poetry utters the oracles of God—she is the voice of wisdom : let us seek for instruction from her inspiration. She is the handmaid of religion—her flights are upward, and her dwelling place is Heaven—let us follow whither she will lead us, there is the throne of the Almighty and there is the intelligence of angels ; there will be the last growth of our minds, and there the highest felicity of our nature.

FIGURES OF SPEECH.

Figures of speech are properly ornaments of written language, embellishments of thought, and illustrations of fact—*associated ideas* brought before the mind of a writer or speaker, and exhibited to other minds, in order to set off or adorn some primary object of thought : thus,

"The rose, with feeble streak
So *slightly tinged* the maiden's cheek,
That you had said her hue was pale," &c.
Rokeby, Canto iv.

The *primary*, or first idea in this example, is the delicate glow of Matilda's cheek ; the *associated idea* is the pale red of a faintly coloured rose. The idea of the rose serves to convey to the mind of a reader the idea of the tint of Matilda's cheek, by *inducing a comparison* between the two objects—that is, by making him think of both at the same time. Figures of speech are very impressive illustrations of ideas, when the figure is suitable to the *primary* idea. From the print of an elephant, as he may sometimes be seen in books, one who had never seen an elephant, could not form a just notion of his size ; but if the figure of a *man*, in proper proportion, should be placed near that of the elephant in the print, the relative size of the elephant would be obvious, and a tolerably correct notion of it might be formed, by comparing the two objects. The figure of the man serves for an illustration : in a similar way, the image or thought presented to the mind by a figure of speech, *illustrates*, or makes plain, some original or fore-mentioned idea.

A *simile*, or comparison, is a figure of speech. It shows one thing, or circumstance, to be like another. The latter subject of the comparison, illustrates the former part. Here is a simile taken from Parnell's Hermit :—

" Then pleased and thankful from the porch *they go*,
And, but the landlord, none had cause of woe :
His cup was vanished ; for, in secret guise,
The younger guest purloined the glittering prize.
As one who spies a serpent in his way,
Glistening and basking in the summer ray,
Disordered stops to shun the danger near,
Then walks with faintness on, and looks with fear—
So seemed the sire, when, far upon the road,
The shining spoil his wily partner showed."

The propriety of this *simile*, detached from the story to which it belongs, is not quite clear. *From the porch they go*—who go ? an old hermit and a young man, his companion, who are travelling on foot. The time is morning, and they have just left the hospitable mansion of a rich man, to whom they were strangers, but in whose house they had fared sumptuously the night before. Wine was presented to them in a valuable silver cup, which the younger, at his departure, stole, and soon after showed to the hermit. The virtuous old man, struck with the dishonesty and ingratitude of the youth, regards him with the same horror which he would have felt at the sight of a venomous snake, suddenly discovered in his path. The danger of being attended by a wicked companion, and the detestation felt by the good at a treacherous action, are highly suggested by the image of the danger any would be in, and all would regard with terror, at the sudden appearance of such a frightful reptile.

A *Metaphor* is an expression used as a simile ; but it substitutes one thing for another, and speaks of illustration as being the thing compared with it : thus—*God is the rock of ages*, is a Metaphor. The meaning of this is, *God is like a rock*—a firm immoveable foundation for human trust in every age. We readily understand this species of comparison. Here is a fine metaphor from the poetry of Thomas Moore :

> * * * " the fresh buoyant sense of Being
> That bounds in youth's yet careless breast,
> Itself a star not borrowing light
> But in its own glad essence bright."

Metonymy is a figure in which one name *is put for* another, on account of some relation between the thing *named*, and that *understood*, or some resemblance between the original meant to be expressed, and the individual whose name is substituted for his : as, we call a wise man a Franklin, and a base one a Catiline. Such a Metonymy as these is a sort of comparison. When the name of a *place* is used to convey the idea of its inhabitants, the expression is Metonymy : as, when we say " the resources of Britain are immense," we mean, the resources of the people of Britain.

Cicero says—

" To omit Greece, which always claimed the pre-eminence for eloquence ; and Athens, the inventress of all sciences, where the art of speaking was invented and perfected ; in this city of ours, no studies have prevailed more than that of eloquence."

Here the words Greece and Athens stand to denote the inhabitants of those places ; and it is this usage of the city or country for the inhabitants that forms the *metonymy*.

A *Synecdoche* puts the whole for a part, or a part for the whole, as,

"_Thy growing virtues justify'd my cares,
  And promised comfort to my _silver hairs_."

Pope's Homer.

The _silver hairs_ signify the _old age_ of the speaker.

An _Hyperbole_ is a figure that goes beyond the bounds of strict truth, and represents things as greater or smaller, better or worse, than they really are.

Sir Walter Scott says of Ellen, in the Lady of the Lake:

" E'en the light hare-bell lift its head
  Elastic from her airy tread."

This is Hyperbole. Ellen was lively and light, but her foot-prints must have broken the tender herb. However, we understand this to be poetic license, and admire the delicate illustration of her slight form and animated motion.

Irony is common to poetry and prose—it is an expression of one idea, when we would convey the idea of its opposite extreme : thus, in common conversation, in order to ridicule his choice, we say, when we think a friend has preferred an inferior to a better thing, "_I admire your taste._" In Scott's Rokeby two assassins are described watching their intended victims. One of them approaches a young man whom he fears, and when he discovers who he is, suddenly withdraws ; upon this his companion _laughs grimly_, and says,

"_A trusty mate_ art thou, to fear
  A single arm, and aid so near."

This is Irony. An expressive example of irony may be found in the XVIII. Chapter of I. Kings. But the whole passage must be read, that the irony may be obvious.

The false prophets of Israel had taught the people the idolatries of Syria, but Elijah, the prophet of God, was instructed to convince them of their folly. In compliance with the request of Elijah, Ahab, king of Israel, called together an assembly of the people, and of the prophets of Baal, their idol, and Elijah proceeded to expose their crime in the manner thus described :

" So Ahab sent unto all the children of Israel, and gathered the prophets together unto mount Carmel. And Elijah came unto all the people, and said, How long halt ye between two opinions? if the Lord be God, follow him : but if Baal, then follow him. And the people answered him not a word. Then said Elijah unto the people, I, even I only, remain a prophet of the Lord ; but Baal's prophets are four hundred and fifty men. Let them therefore give us two bullocks ; and let them choose one bullock for themselves, and cut it in pieces, and lay it on wood, and put no fire under : and I will dress the other bullock, and lay it on wood, and put no fire under : and call ye on the name of your gods, and I will call on the name of the Lord : and the God that answereth by fire, let him be God. And all the people answered and said, It is well spoken.

"And Elijah said unto the prophets of Baal, Choose you one bullock for yourselves, and dress it first : for ye are many ; and call on the name of your gods, but put no fire under. And they took the bullock which was given them, and they dressed it, and called on the name of Baal from morning even until noon, saying, O Baal, hear us. But there was no voice, nor any that answered. And they leaped upon the altar which was made. And it came to pass at noon, that Elijah mocked them, and said, *Cry aloud :* for he is a god ; either he is talking, or he is pursuing, or he is in a journey, or peradventure he sleepeth, and must be awaked. And they cried aloud, and cut themselves after their manner with knives and lancets, till the blood gushed out upon them. And it came to pass, when mid-day was past, and they prophesied until the time of the offering of the evening sacrifice, that there was neither voice, nor any to answer, nor any that regarded."

Interrogation is asking a question. When the interrogation is made in writing, or public speaking, and no reply is expected, it is used to induce the hearer to reflect with attention, and answer to his own reason, if the speaker's argument be not just and forcible.

When Habakkuk, the Hebrew prophet, forewarns his countrymen of God's *vindictive justice*, that is, his punishment of their sins, which had been revealed to him, and of which he speaks as if it were past, he says :

" Was the Lord displeased against the *rivers ?*
Was thy wrath against the *sea ?*"

The obvious anwer would be, No—God is not displeased with the *rivers*, nor angry against the *sea ;* but he wounds the head of the wicked, and as a whirlwind, he scatters the nations that offend.

Exclamation is little more than a cry, a sudden, broken expression of surprise, pleasure, contempt, indignation, or pain. The Duke, in Shakspeare's Twelfth Night, relieving his melancholy with music, exclaims :

" That strain again ! it had a dying fall !
Oh, it came o'er my ear like the sweet south,
That breathes upon a bank of violets,
Stealing and giving odour."

This example of *exclamation* from Shakspeare, expresses *rapture*—unexpected, lively delight. The next from Cicero expresses sorrow for his banishment, and pleasure at the idea of his honourable return to Rome :

" Oh mournful day to the senate and all good men !
calamitous to the senate, afflictive to me and my family ;
but to posterity glorious, and worthy of admiration !"

Pro Sext. chap. 12.

Thus the *exclamation* adapts itself to the passion which adopts it.

Climax is the enumeration of many particulars in one period or whole sense, intended to produce one effect of persuasion or conviction in the minds to which it is addressed. In *climax* or *gradation* the most important idea of the whole assemblage is the first mentioned. From the beginning to the end of the climax it is proper that each particular enumerated should rise in dignity of sense above the preceding.

Mr. Walker in his Rhetorical Grammar gives an example of Climax from the Spectator:

"Mr. Addison has a beautiful climax of circumstances arising one above another, when he is describing the treatment of Negroes in the West Indies, who sometimes, upon the death of their masters, or upon changing their service, hang themselves upon the next tree.

'Who can forbear admiring their fidelity, though it expresses itself in so dreadful a manner? What might not that savage greatness of soul, which appears in these poor wretches on many occasions, be raised to, were it rightly cultivated? and what colour of excuse can there be for the contempt with which we treat this part of our species? That we should not put them upon the common foot of humanity; that we should only set an *insignificant fine* upon *the man who murders them,* nay, that we should, as much as in us lies, cut them off from the prospects of happiness in another world as well as in this, and deny them that which we look upon as the proper means for attaining it?' "

Here Mr. Addison first mentions the virtues of the poor negroes, and then contrasts the cruel treatment of white men with their deserts. This cruel treatment in fact is this: *We*—Mr. Addison meant the Europeans, but his remarks apply to some Americans of the present age—*We,* says he in *effect,* deny them to possess the understandings of men; we consider them brute animals; we do not punish their murderers; and we not only deprive them of liberty and the sympathies that exist between man and man in this world, but we refuse to consider them as immortal beings, and withhold from them the knowledge necessary to their salvation.——It is very plain that the last articles of this passage—the *immortal soul,* and its final happiness in heaven—are considerations of greater magnitude, in regard to the negro character, the abuse it has suffered, and the redress that the author here claims for it, than any he had previously detailed.

4

This example is not taken from poetry, but Climax is a figure which often occurs in poetry. *Anticlimax* is often used as a word to denote a foolish representation of things, which exaggerates the unimportant, and gives the least regard to the more important particulars under consideration.

Apostrophe is an abrupt address to the absent. It sometimes partakes of the character of personification : as St. Paul, in holy rapture, exclaims,

"Oh Grave ! where is thy victory ? Oh Death ! where is thy sting ?"

" This figure," says Walker, "is seldom used ; but when, in a violent commotion, the speaker turns himself on all sides, and appeals to the living and the dead, to angels and to men, to rocks, groves, and rivers, for the justice of his cause, or calls upon them to sympathize with his joy, grief, or resentment."

The Minstrel, in Scott's Lay, breaks out, at the thought of his beloved country, into this *apostrophe :*

" O Caledonia, stern and wild,
　Meet nurse for a poetic child !
　Land of brown heath and shaggy wood,
　Land of the mountain and the flood,
　Land of my sires ! what mortal hand
　Can e'er untie the filial band
　That knits me to thy rugged strand !"

Personification is the investing of qualities, or things inanimate, with the character of persons, or the introducing of dead or absent persons as if they were alive and present. This is at once one of the boldest and finest figures in rhetoric. Poets are prodigal in their use of this figure.

The following example of the figure of personification is from Milton's Comus. The poet personifies Virtue, Wisdom, and Contemplation :

" Virtue could see to do what virtue would
By her own radiant light, though sun and moon
Were in the flat sea sunk. And Wisdom's self
Oft seeks to sweet retired solitude,
Where with her best nurse, Contemplation,
She plumes her feathers, and lets grow her wings,
That in the various bustle of resort
Were all too ruffled, and sometimes impair'd."

Cowper has personified *Winter*, as the

————" King of intimate delights,
Fire-side enjoyments, homeborn happiness"——
and has introduced him in a very picturesque description :
thus :

" O Winter, ruler of the inverted year,
Thy scatter'd hair with sleet-like ashes fill'd,
Thy breath congeal'd upon thy lips, thy cheeks
Fringed with a beard made white with other snows
Than those of age, thy forehead wrapp'd in clouds,
A leafless branch thy sceptre, and thy throne
A sliding car, indebted to no wheels,
But urged by storms along its slippery way,——
I love thee, all unlovely as thou seem'st,
And dreaded as thou art !"

Allegory is a prolonged use of figures, so connected in
sense as to form a parable or fable. Gray's Ode to
Adversity is an allegory.

" ODE TO ADVERSITY.

" Daughter of Jove, relentless power,
Thou tamer of the human breast,
Whose iron scourge and torturing hour
The bad affright, afflict the best !
Bound in thy adamantine chain,
The proud are taught to taste of pain,
And purple tyrants vainly groan
With pangs unfelt before, unpitied and alone.

When first thy sire to send on earth
Virtue, his darling child, design'd,

To thee he gave the heav'nly birth,
  And bade to form her infant mind.
Stern rugged nurse! thy rigid lore
With patience many a year she bore:
What sorrow was, thou bad'st her know,
And from her own she learn'd to melt at others' woe.

Scar'd at thy frown terrific, fly
  Self-pleasing Folly's idle brood,
Wild laughter, noise, and thoughtless joy,
  And leave us leisure to be good.
Light they disperse ; and with them go
The summer friend, the flattering foe ;
By vain prosperity receiv'd,
To her they vow their truth, and are again believ'd.

Wisdom in sable garb array'd,
  Immers'd in rapturous thought profound,
And Melancholy, silent maid,
  With leaden eye that loves the ground,
Still on thy solemn steps attend :
Warm Charity, the general friend,
With Justice, to herself severe,
And Pity, dropping soft the sadly-pleasing tear.

Oh, gently on thy suppliant's head,
  Dread Goddess, lay thy chast'ning hand !
Not in thy Gorgon terrors clad,
  Not circled with the vengeful band
(As by the impious thou art seen)
With thundering voice, and threatening mien,
With screaming horror's funeral cry,
Despair, and fell Disease, and ghastly Poverty :

Thy form benign, oh Goddess ! wear,
  Thy milder influence impart,
Thy philosophic train be there
  To soften, not to wound my heart.
The generous spark extinct revive,
Teach me to love, and to forgive,
Exact my own defects to scan,
What others are to feel, and know myself a man."

Mr. Gray has thus personified **Misfortune or Adversity.** He has represented her as the daughter of the supreme deity ; but employed to " affright the bad, and afflict the best men"——" Whom he loveth, he chasteneth," or purifieth, say the Hebrew Scriptures. Perhaps this excelent poet had this passage in his mind when he wrote this stanza. " Sweet are the uses of Adversity," says Shakspeare, and so has Gray represented them.——" By the sadness of the countenance, the heart is made better," says Solomon. Taught by our sufferings, we learn to pity others ; we abandon our follies, and gain leisure to be good. When we are in affliction, the sordid, and the frivolous, who shared the pleasures of our prosperity, forsake us ; but our virtues——wisdom, meditation, charity, justice, and pity, remain with us, and console us. The poet, having asserted this, changes the form of his verses to *apostrophe*, and entreats the goddess, as he terms Adversity, to spare him from the severest inflictions of her hand, and to purify and exalt his heart. Young persons should commit these fine verses to memory.

Antithesis is a figure by which words and ideas very different or contrary are contrasted or placed together, that they may mutually set off and illustrate each other.

In Blair's Sermon on Gentleness the annexed example of Antithesis may be found :

"As there is a worldly *happiness* which God perceives to be no more than disguised *misery; as there are worldly *honours* which in his estimation are *reproach:* so there is a worldly *wisdom* which in his sight is *foolishness.* Of this worldly wisdom the characters are given in the Scriptures, and placed in contrast with those of the wisdom which is from above. The one is the wisdom of the *crafty;* the other that of the *upright:* the one terminates in *selfishness;* the other in *charity:* the one is full of *strife and bitter envyings;* the other of *mercy and of good fruits.*"

The antithetical words of this passage are printed in italics——*Happiness* and *misery, honour* and *reproach, wisdom* and *foolishness,* are ideas in direct opposition——and

4*

the remaining antitheses of the period are, it is presumed, quite as clear.

The preceding definitions are not as full as might be, but they are simple, and necessary to be understood in order to read poetry with good taste and satisfaction. There must be elementary books in common use, which give more critical and elaborate instances of the artificial structure of poetic diction.

HISTORY OF ENGLISH POETRY.

Young persons at all instructed in modern history know, that the English language is formed from several more ancient languages. The Romans carried the Latin into Britain half a century before the birth of Christ. About four hundred years after, the Saxons, a warlike people from Germany, succeeded the Romans as masters of England, and introduced and established their speech with their dominion. The language of England for several centuries was what is called the Anglo-Saxon, but this was superseded, in great measure, by the Norman French. In 1066, William, Duke of Normandy, in France, conquered England, and established his power over the country. He brought with him a multitude of followers whom he distributed over the kingdom, and caused the ministration of religion and the laws to be announced in the Norman French. This language gradually combined itself with the previous dialect of England, and our English language, by slow degrees, has been drawn from these sources.

The Anglo-Saxons were not wholly without literature; they had wandering minstrels who sung verses, and in their convents some of the priests composed in rhyme. The Normans brought to England their own poetry, which consisted chiefly of songs, satires, morality, and rhyming chronicles. But in the twelfth century, the crusades, or religious war, carried on by the Europeans in Palestine, furnished romantic adventures which the poets rehearsed in verse ; and at the same time, narrative poems from scripture and classical subjects began to appear in England. In the thirteenth century it became customary for the minstrels to "sing devotional strains to the harp on Sundays, for the edification of the people, instead of the verses on gayer subjects which were sung at public entertainments."

The first original poem of any extent in the English language is ascribed to Robert Langlande, a priest. It describes the Christian life, and the abuses of religion under the authority of the Pope. It is to the honour of poetry that among the first efforts of her power over a partially civilized people she should fearlessly utter the dictates of truth, unbought and undismayed by arbitrary princes, and selfish priests. "The mind," says Mr. Campbell, speaking of Langlande, "is struck with his rude voice, proclaiming independent and popular sentiments, from an age of slavery and superstition, and thundering a prediction in the ear of papacy, which was doomed to be literally fulfilled at the distance of nearly two hundred years. His allusions to cotemporary life afford some amusing glimpses of its manners.".

The earliest English poet whose remains are still preserved to popular readers is Geoffrey Chaucer. He died in 1400. It would not be suitable to the design of this little sketch to descant upon a poet whose works few young persons would have the patience to read. But matured readers with a little pains may make the obsolete language of Chaucer intelligible. The very lively pictures which his writings afford of the manners and sentiments peculiar to his time, and which abound in them, are interesting to minds that love to look far back into the dim region of the past, and behold there, stars of mind that shine for ever and ever.

Civil wars and religious persecutions during two centuries after the death of Chaucer silenced the muse in England. Some obscure names of this period attached to poetry may be drawn from oblivion by the antiquaries, but the poetical feeling and genius of England are regarded by Mr. Campbell to have been at that time almost extinct.

In the fifteenth century printing was introduced into Britain. The desire of knowledge is excited in the public mind by the means of obtaining it, and it would seem that divine providence has adjusted the productiveness of genius, to the estimation in which talent is held. Whenever the people become eager for instruction or for entertainment, Wisdom is heard crying in the streets, and the sweet strains of Poetry seem to mingle in the common air that we breathe. In the sixteenth century the Scriptures were given freely to the people of England, learning was cultivated, and poetry revived ; and as society was improved, genius was developed and honoured. Of this influence of society upon poetic genius, Mr. Campbell says :

"Poets may be indebted to the learning and philosophy of their age, without being themselves men of erudition or philosophers. When the fine spirit of truth has gone abroad, it passes insensibly from mind to mind, independent of its direct transmissions from books ; and it comes home in a more welcome shape to the poet, when caught from his social intercourse with his species, than from solitary study."

Lord Surrey lived in the reign of Henry VIII, and was the inventor of *blank verse*. In the reign of queen Elizabeth, and of her successor, James I. lived Shakspeare, Ben Jonson and Spenser. Spenser, the author of the Faery Queen, is now very much praised, and very little read. His subject is partly *allegorical*, and partly in representation of persons of his own age ; and on account of this confusion and obscurity in his poetry, it may be, that Spenser is more studied by poets than by general readers. Jonson is hardly more popular, but " every body's Shakspeare" now in universal estimation wears, and will wear in the eyes of all posterity, his laurels fresh and green as ever. Shakspeare's appearance as a dramatist can be traced back to 1589, and the Faery Queen was published in 1590.

English Poetry comprehends the Drama.—Mysteries, Moralities, and Interludes, are names of the dramatic representations known in England previous to Shakspeare's time. The Mysteries were religious shows exhibited under the sanction of the ministers of religion to the people. The Resurrection of Lazarus, and the Sepulture of our Lord, were among these representations : they were in fashion in England four hundred years, and went out of vogue in the middle of the sixteenth century. Surely, not only taste but piety has made great advances in the *community of the English language* (if such an expression is allowable) since such subjects could be acceptable under the form of public amusements.

The Moralists dramatized moral subjects, and sometimes represented discoveries in science. An Interlude on the nature of the four elements, and The Tracts of America lately discovered and the manners of the natives, is recorded among the last of these entertainments.

Greek and Latin tragedies were translated into English as soon as 1566. During the last twenty years of the sixteenth century, play-writers by profession became common, but their names and works have now, for the most part, become insignificant. Ben Jonsons's plays exhibit much learning and wit—they are still read, but are not exhibited upon the stage. Among his works are specimens of that poetic and tasteful drama, the Masque. Milton's Comus is a masque, and Percy's Masque, by Mr. Hillhouse, which was written about 1820 in America, is a masque.

Poetic translation commenced in England about 1560. The poetry of Virgil, Ovid, and soon afterwards of Homer, were translated into English verse near this time. Dr. Johnson commences his Lives of the Poets with the life of Cowley, and classes him with Donne, Waller, and some other poets who had lived during the preceding century: these were the *metaphysical poets*. Their works exist in old books, but they are only known to very curious readers.

Shakspeare stands at the head of English poets, and next in eminence is the divine Milton: Milton died in 1674, at the age of 62. In his early life Milton felt that he was born for posterity and all time, and in the consciousness of his great endowments, his elevated mind was little disturbed by the neglect of his contemporaries. For almost a century after the publication of his minor works, they were little known: and Paradise Lost, which appeared in print in 1669, after its author had become blind to external things, attracted little of the admiration which it has since called forth.

Among British poets next to Milton, in the order of time, comes Dryden. Gray describes Milton and Dryden in these lines :

* * * "He, that rode sublime
Upon the seraph wings of Ecstacy,
The secrets of th' Abyss to spy.
He pass'd the flaming bounds of Place and Time,
The living Throne, the sapphire-blaze,
Where Angels tremble while they gaze,
He saw ; but, blasted with excess of light,
Clos'd his eyes in endless night.——
Behold where Dryden's less presumptuous car
Wide o'er the fields of Glory bear
Two coursers of etherial race,
With necks in thunder cloth'd, and long-resounding pace.

Hark, his hands the lyre explore !
Bright-ey'd Fancy, hovering o'er,
Scatters from her pictur'd urn
Thoughts that breathe, and words that burn."

Dryden's plays and poems are not much read, though Alexander's Feast still retains its popularity, and almost every school-boy can repeat it. Dryden died in 1690.

Pope died in 1744. For a whole century Mr. Pope was perhaps the most popular of English poets ; and though his moral and religious sentiments were censured by the rigidly righteous, still they passed into the principles and common talk of most readers. "As Pope says," is a phrase which is often prefixed in conversation to a multitude of pointed remarks which are found in Mr. Pope's writings, and that are readily applied by almost every mind to the practical wisdom of daily life.

"Whate'er by nature is in *worth* denied
   She gives in large recruits of needful pride."

"Trust not thyself—thy own defects to know
   Make use of every friend, and every foe."

" True wit is nature to advantage dressed—
What oft was thought, but ne'er so well expressed."

" 'Tis not a lip, or eye, we beauty call,
But the joint force and full result of *all*."

" Man, like the generous vine, supported, lives—
The strength he gains is from the embrace he gives."

" Reason's whole pleasure, all the joys of sense,
Lie in three words, Health, Peace, and Competence."

Such are a few of those couplets which are become almost common-place, but which express important principles with admirable simplicity and plainness.

The force and independence of Mr. Pope's sentiments, the purity of motives from which his principles spring, and to which they tend, the delightful harmony of his versification, and sometimes, the beauty of his descriptions, have made him the almost universal favourite that he is among English readers. Within a few years a *controversy* has been carried on, among some distinguished poets and critics, concerning the pre-eminence of Pope as a poet. But the argument is not interesting to young readers ; however, those who feel any veneration for the author of that beautiful version of the Lord's prayer— " Father of All," &c.—will be pleased to know, that among those who exalted the fame of that eminent person were the late Lord Byron, and Thomas Campbell.

Among the contemporaries of Pope, were several poets much in fashion during their lives, and some of whose works are yet popular. Of these Addison, Swift, Gay, and Parnell deserve to be mentioned. The respective characters of these writers, and their works, may be learned from sources more ample than this brief notice of English poetry and poets.

After the death of Pope, Thomson, Collins, Shenstone, Akenside, Gray, and Goldsmith, were much and deservedly admired as English poets. Goldsmith, the last in the order in which they are mentioned, died in 1774 ; but the genius of each, differing, as they do, from one another in glory, is "essentially immortal," still exerts its sweet influence, and gathers increase of honours from successive years.

Cowper died in 1800. His poetry is in every house. It is without spot or blemish—inspired by the genius of Christianity—full of humanity and piety—tender and holy as the writer's heart, and beautiful as the rural sights and sounds which delighted his pure nature. Since Cowper—Rogers, Walter Scott, Southey, Crabbe, Campbell, Byron, Moore, and Wordsworth, have appeared in the world. Collectively they have produced a vast increase of wealth in the treasury of our intellectual riches. Mr. Rogers is moral and sentimental. The others are peculiarly original, and the inventive talent of each is employed upon materials furnished principally by the varieties of human passions and manners, as they have existed in different ages and countries.

The inexhaustible storehouse of history, or the observation of local character, has supplied subjects to these admirable minds which are in unison with general sympathies; and in no period since the existence of our language has such extended homage been paid to living poets, as in the present century. The legends of Scotland are made familiar and inexpressibly interesting, all over the world, by the minstrelsy of Scott—the valleys of America are brought out of obscurity by the genius of Campbell— the "gorgeous east" glitters in the pictured pages of Moore.—

" Woods that wave o'er Delphi's steep,
 Isles that crown the Egean deep,
 Fields that cool Illysus laves,"

have again breathed their inspiration, and the British name of Byron is now associated with the birth place of all the muses. The talent of Southey has celebrated the chivalry of Spain; and the rural life of England, in all its forms of good and evil, has been recorded for ever by the masterly hands of Crabbe and Wordsworth.

5

Nothing like criticism upon the several works of these authors, can be useful to young readers. Read first, judge afterwards.   All that is contained in this volume, is collected to inspire love for the pursuit of literature, and to make it agreeable by making it intelligible.   Young persons are here introduced to a community of the most venerable and gifted minds that ever lived, and they are invited to assimilate their moral nature, by purity of heart and of thought, to this goodly fellowship;—and to the repositories of their heavenly fancies, repairing "as to their fountain," thence to draw light that shall not grow dim with age, but shine brighter and brighter to the perfect day of their intellectual progress.

Various changes that the language has undergone are exhibited by English poetry.   Our language has not always been written as it now is.   English grammars and dictionaries were not in general use till the latter half of the last century; before that time, however, good English writers *nearly agreed* in their orthography and grammatical construction, and from their practice, in respect to orthography and grammar, our rules are principally taken.   Here are four specimens of English poetry, written at different times.   The first is from Chaucer:—

———— " Emilie, that fayrer was to sene
Than is the lilie upon his stalk grene,   ·
And fresher than the May with floures newe,
(For with the rose colour strof hire hewe,
I n'ot which was the finer of hem two.)
Ere it was day, as she was wont to do,
She was arisen, and all redy dight :
For May wol have no slogardie a-night.
The season priketh every gentil herte,   ·
And maketh him out of his sleep to sterte,
And sayth, arise, and do thin observance."
Chaucer's Knighte's Tale, verses 1037—1048.

If a school boy should alter these verses after his own habits, and preserve the words as nearly as possible, he would write them thus :

———— " Emilie, that fairer was to see
Than is the lily upon his stalk green,
And fresher than the May with flowers new,
(For with the rose colour strove her hue,
I know not which was finer of them two.)
Ere it was day, as she was wont to do,
She was arisen, and already drest :
For May will have no sluggishness of night.
The season pricketh every gentle heart,
And maketh him out of his sleep to start,
And saith, arise, and do thine observance."

Spenser published the Faery Queene in 1570, one hundred and seventy years after Chaucer died. The following description of a fine lady's ornaments and equipage is taken from the Faery Queene:

" Hee had a faire companion of his way,
A goodly lady clad in *scarlet* red,
Purfled with gold and pearle of rich assay ;
And like a Persian mitre on her head
She wore with crowns and owches garnished ;
The which her lavish lovers to her gave.
The wanton palfrey all way overspread
With tinsel trappings woven like a wave,
Whose bridle hung with golden bells and bosses brave."
Faery Queene, Canto II. *verse* 13.

This is not so simple a description, not so easy to be understood, nor does it present so beautiful an image, as that of the sweet Emilie—rising with the dawn, and going forth among the flowers in May,—"herself the fairest flower," as the poet Milton afterwards said of Eve in Paradise. Chaucer's lady is lovely in herself, but Spenser's goodly fair one is thought much less of than the splendour with which she is attired and mounted. A fine woman dressed in a robe of scarlet, adorned with pearls and gold richly wrought, wearing a splendid crown, and governing a noble horse, himself covered with cloth of silver, and reined with a glittering and tinkling bridle, may be looked at for a moment with pleasure, but not for the same length of time, or with the same satisfaction as she must be regarded, whose beauty is the expression of gracefulness, modesty, and kindness.

The next specimen shows the progress of our language, and teaches the very lesson that a moral comparison between the preceding ones may do. It was written but a few years after that of Spenser. The author, Ben Jonson, died 1616.

" Give me a look, give me a face
    That make simplicity a grace.
    Robes loosely flowing, hair as free :
    Such sweet neglect more taketh me
    Than all the adulteries of art,—
    They strike my eyes and not my heart."

The following specimen, written in 1821, is like the orthography of that which preceded it two hundred years:

" 'Tis eve, the soft, the purple hour,
    The dew is glistening on the bower ;
    The lily droops its silver head,
    The violet slumbers on its bed ;
    Heavy with sleep the leaflets close,
    Veiling thy bloom, enchanting rose,
    Still gazing on the western ray
    The last sweet worshipper of day."—*Croly.*

English poetry is not confined to the *British dominions*—our western world has produced a poet whose memory will be proof " 'Gainst death, and all oblivious enmity"—whose verses embellish these pages, and whose talent we should cherish with sentiments of pride and pleasure.

EDMUND SPENSER.

Spenser is the earliest English poet whose writings afford any specimens suitable to this collection. English History furnishes an interesting and useful subject of study to the young scholar, if it afford him just views of

English *mind*. If history describes those only who have conquered certain armies, who have devastated countries, or who have built towns and forts, it informs us of little that is useful and improving. But it is delightful to learn from history that wise men have arisen in a nation after long periods of general ignorance—delightful to read the works which during centuries have made one generation of men after another, wiser and better,—delightful to turn from the barbarous triumphs of mad ambition and physical force to the dominion of intellect, and to enrich the understanding by the talent of others, who have refined and exalted society ever since they came into being.

Queen Elizabeth succeeded to the throne of Brittain in 1558. Elizabeth was attached to the Protestant faith, made it the national religion, cultivated learning herself, and cherished genius in others. Shakspeare lived in her reign, and paid homage to this maiden queen. He styles her, "a fair star, throned in the west;" and makes one, speaking of her infancy, say,

—————————————— "Sheba was never
More covetous of wisdom, and fair virtue,
Than this pure soul shall be—————————
————————————Truth shall nurse her;
Holy and heavenly thoughts still counsel her."

"In the reign of Elizabeth," says Campbell, "the English *mind* put forth its energies in every direction, exalted by a purer religion, and enlarged by new views of truth. This was an age of loyalty, adventure, and generous emulation. The chivalrous character was softened by intellectual pursuits, while the genius of chivalry itself still lingered, as if unwilling to depart, and paid his last homage to a warlike and female reign. A degree of romantic fancy remained in the manners and superstitions of the people; and allegory might be said to parade the streets in their public pageants and festivals. Quaint and pedantic as those allegorical exhibitions might often be, they were nevertheless more expressive

5*

of erudition, ingenuity, and moral meaning, than they had
been in former times.

The philosophy of the highest minds still partook of a
visionary character. A poetical spirit infused itself into
the practical heroism of the age ; and some of the wor-
thies of that period seem less like ordinary men, than
like beings called forth out of fiction, and arrayed in the
brightness of her dreams. They had ' High thoughts
seated in a heart of courtesy.' The life of Sir Philip
Sidney was poetry put into action."

Three very memorable individuals adorned this reign,
Spenser, Sir Philip Sidney, and Sir Walter Raleigh. The
latter two are more properly *subjects of verse* than poets,
though their verses are found in collections of English
poetry, but Spenser stands without a rival in his own style
of poetic invention.

Spenser was born in London about the middle of the
sixteenth century. He passed some time; after leaving
the university of Cambridge where he was educated, in a
state of rustic obscurity in the North of England, but there
his mind was furnished with those natural images that
abound in his works. He was afterwards introduced to
Sir Philip Sidney, and once resided with him at Pens-
hurst in Kent. By the influence of Sidney, Spencer pro-
cured the place of Secretary to the Lord Lieutenant of
Ireland, and subsequently, a grant from the Queen of
land in that country, in which he remained for several
years.

Spenser's residence at Kilcolman, an ancient castle of
the earls of Desmond, commanded a view of above half
the breadth of Ireland, and must have been a most roman-
tic and pleasant situation.—The river Mulla, which Spen-
ser has so often celebrated, ran through his grounds. In
this retreat he was visited by Sir Walter Raleigh, at that
time a captain in the Queen's army. His visit occasioned
the first resolution of Spenser to prepare the first books
of the Faery Queen for immediate publication. Spenser

has commemorated this interview, and the inspiring influence of Raleigh's praise, under the figurative description of two shepherds tuning their pipes, beneath the alders of the *Mulla*;—a fiction with which the mind, perhaps, will be much less satisfied, than by recalling the scene as it really existed.

When we conceive of Spenser reciting his compositions to Raleigh, in a scene so beautifully appropriate, the mind casts a pleasing retrospect over that influence which the *enterprize* of the discoverer of Virginia, and the *genius* of the author of the Faery Queen, have respectively produced on the fortune and language of England. "The fancy might even be pardoned for a momentary superstition, that the Genius of their country hovered unseen over their meeting, casting her first look of regard on the poet, that was destined to inspire her future Milton, and the other on the maritime hero, who paved the way for colonizing distant regions of the earth, where the language of England was to be spoken, and the poetry of Spenser to be admired."

In 1597, a rebellion against the British government broke out in Ireland, and occasioned the precipitate flight of Spenser with his family to England. Spenser died at London, January, 1599. He was buried, according to his own desire, near the tomb of Chaucer; and the most celebrated poets of the time (Shakspeare was probably of the number) followed his hearse, and threw tributary verses into his grave.

SIR PHILIP SIDNEY.

Sir Philip Sidney was the most celebrated man of his age.—The question immediately occurs—for what?—"Traits of character will distinguish great men independent of their pens or their swords," remarks Mr. Campbell. "The contemporaries of Sidney knew the man: and foreigners, no less than his own countrymen, seem to have felt, from his personal influence and conversation, an homage for him, that could only be paid to a commanding intellect guiding the principles of a noble heart."

He spent part of his short life in the court of Queen

Elizabeth, and another very brilliant portion of it in military service upon the continent. As a courtier, a scholar, a traveller, and a soldier, he commanded the admiration of Europe, and all England wore mourning at his death. This event happened in 1580, when he was only 32 years of age. His writings are obsolete, but we sometimes hear of Sir Philip Sidney's Arcadia. This is an incomplete romance which he left. Miss Lucy Aikin says of the Arcadia, that "fervour of eloquence," "nice discrimination of character," and "purity of thought," "stamp it for the offspring of a noble mind."

"His death," continues Miss Aikin, "was worthy of the best parts of his life ; he showed himself to the last devout, courageous, and serene. His wife, the beautiful daughter of Walsingham; his brother Robert, to whom he had performed the part rather of an anxious and indulgent parent than of a brother ; and many sorrowing friends, surrounded his bed. Their grief was, beyond a doubt, sincere and poignant, as well as that of the many persons of letters and of worth who gloried in his friendship, and flourished by his bountiful patronage."

Such a man's name and example should still serve to kindle in the bosom of youth the animating glow of virtuous emulation. Lord Thurlow, a late Lord Chancellor of England, wrote a pretty sonnet on Sidney's picture.

" The man that looks, sweet Sidney, in thy face,
   Beholding there love's truest majesty,
And the soft image of departed grace,
   Shall fill his mind with magnanimity :
There may he read unfeign'd humility,
   And golden pity, born of heav'nly brood,
Unsullied thoughts of immortality,
   And musing virtue, prodigal of blood :
Yes in this map of what is fair and good,
   This glorious index of a heav'nly book,
Not seldom, as in youthful years he stood,
   Divinest Spenser would admiring look ;
And, framing thence high wit and pure desire,
Imagin'd deeds, that set the world on fire!

SIR WALTER RALEIGH.

Sir Walter Raleigh was born at Hayes Farm in Devonshire, 1552, and was beheaded in London, 1618. He is memorable for his understanding, his knowledge, and his enterprising spirit. During the reign of Elizabeth, Raleigh performed many honourable services in the British navy, and fitted out, and sometimes accompanied, ships of discovery which explored the coasts of North and South America. After the accession of James I. of England, who was Elizabeth's successor, Raleigh was indicted and tried for treason, upon the charge of attempting to place Lady Arabella Stuart upon the throne of England; and though he was not condemned, he suffered fifteen years of imprisonment. When Raleigh was liberated, he obtained a commission from the King, and commanded an expedition against Guiana, in South America. In this enterprize he was unsuccessful, though he committed some depredations upon the Spaniards who were in possession of the country. On his return to England he was tried upon the former accusation, and sentenced to death. The sentence was immediately executed, and a life of singular vicissitudes, in which the prosperity was adorned by eminent accomplishments, and the adversity sustained by admirable fortitude, was thus cruelly terminated.

SPENSER.

UNA AND THE REDCROSS KNIGHT.

" The heavenly Una and her milk-white lamb."—*Wordsworth.*

" A gentle knight* was pricking on the plain,
  Yclad† in mighty arms and silver shield,
  Wherein old dints of deep wounds did remain,
  The cruel marks of many a bloody field;
  Yet arms till that time did he never wield;
  His angry steed did chide his foaming bit,
  As much disdaining to the curb to yield:

* Riding.   † Attired.

Full jolly knight he seem'd, and fair did sit,
As one for knightly jousts* and fierce encounters fit.

But on his breast a bloody cross he bore,
The dear remembrance of his dying Lord,
For whose sweet sake that glorious badge he wore,
And dead (as living) ever him ador'd :
Upon his shield the like was also scor'd,†
For sovereign hope, which in his help he had :
Right faithful true he was in deed and word ;
But of his cheer did seem too solemn sad :
Yet nothing did he dread ; but ever was ydrad.‡

Upon a great adventure he was bound,
That greatest Gloriana to him gave,
That greatest glorious queen of fairy lond,
To win him worship, and her grace to have,
Which of all earthly things he most did crave ;
And ever as he rode his heart did yearn
To prove his puissance in battle brave
Upon his foe, and his new force to learn ;
Upon his foe, a dragon horrible and stern.

A lovely lady rode him fair beside,
Upon a lowly ass more white than snow ;
Yet she much whiter, but the same did hide
Under a veil, that wimpled§ was full low,
And over all a black stole‖ she did throw,
As one that inly mourn'd ; so was she sad,
And heavy sat upon her palfry slow ;
Seemed in heart some hidden care she had,
And by her in a line a milk-white lamb she led.

So pure an innocent, as that same lamb,
She was in life and every virtuous lore,
And by descent from royal lineage came
Of ancient kings and queens, that had of yore

* Contests of skill at arms.   † Engraved.   ‡ Dreaded.
§ Drawn closely.   ‖ Robe.

Their sceptres stretcht from east to western shore,
And all the world in their subjection held;
Till that infernal fiend with foul uproar
Forewasted all their land and them expell'd:
Whom to avenge, she had this knight from far compell'd.

Behind her far away a dwarf did lag,
That lazy seem'd in being ever last,
Or wearied with bearing of her bag
Of needments at his back.   Thus as they past
The day with clouds was sudden overcast,
And angry Jove an hideous storm of rain
Did pour into his leman's lap so fast,
That every wight to shroud it did constrain,
And this fair couple eke to shroud themselves were fain.

Enforc'd to seek some covert nigh at hand,
A shady grove not far away they spied,
That promis'd aid the tempest to withstand;
Whose lofty trees, yclad with summer's pride,
Did spread so broad, they heaven's light did hide,
Not pierceable with power of any star:
And all within were paths and alleys wide,
With footing worn, and leading inward far:
Fair harbour, that them seems; so in they entred are.

And forth they pass, with pleasure forward-led,
Joying to hear the birds' sweet harmony,
Which therein shrouded from the tempest's dread,
Seem'd in their song to scorn the cruel sky.
Much can they praise the trees so strait and high,
The sailing Pine, the Cedar proud and tall,
The vine-prop Elm, the Poplar never dry,
The builder Oak, sole king of forests all,
The Aspin good for staves, the Cypress funeral,

The Laurel, meed of mighty conquerors
And poets sage, the Fir that weepeth still,
The Willow, worn of forlorn paramours,
The Yew, obedient to the bender's will,

The Birch for shafts, the Sallow for the mill,
The Myrrh sweet bleeding in the bitter wound,
The warlike Beech, the Ash for nothing ill,
The fruitful Olive, and the Plantain round,
The carver Holme, the Maple seldom inward sound:

Led with delight they thus beguile the way,
Until the blustering storm is overblown,
When, weening* to return, whence they did stray,
They cannot find that path which first was shown,
But wander to and fro in ways unknown,
Furthest from end then, when they nearest ween,
That makes them doubt their wits be not their own:
So many paths, so many turnings seen,
That which of them to take, in divers doubts they been.

These verses are easily comprehended. Every young person should know something of chivalry. That institution once had great influence upon the manners and happiness of Europe. The situation of Una, and the nature of her protector's character and office, will not be understood without some acquaintance with the meaning of chivalry.

CHIVALRY.

The origin of Chivalry was briefly this :—France, Spain, England, Germany, Italy and Holland, once belonged to the Roman Empire; but armies from the North of Europe invaded these more southern countries, overthrew the Roman power, and at different times took possession of the places they conquered. When they made themselves masters of a country, the great leaders of the armies took large tracts of land, and their followers, that is the soldiers they commanded, together with such of the original inhabitants of the countries as they permitted to live, became the vassals of these great men.

* Presuming.

These poor people were not acquainted with the useful arts or comforts of life that we enjoy, but they could take care of cattle, cultivate the soil in a rude and imperfect manner, could help to erect the castles and churches of their masters, and could follow him to battle. This latter service, together with a great part of the cattle and corn which they could procure from the cultivation of the soil, they gave to their lords. The lords always kept many of their vassals in their houses or castles; and usually went out with a considerable number of them as attendants. This was partly for show, and partly for safety. These followers were called Retainers, and when they went abroad with their master formed his Retinue. The more people a great lord had about his person, the better was he guarded, and the more was he feared.

In the present happier age of the world, when every man has his own business, and property, and leisure, and enjoyments, no great man has any right to the services of so many of his fellow-men; nor has he any need of them, for he has nothing to fear from the violence of others—he is protected by the laws of his country, and what is better, by the humanity of all men who have learned, in some measure, to respect one another's lives and property, and to know, in order that all may be happy, all must be safe, and protected by each other.

But a thousand years ago men lived very differently. The lands which had been seized by the great lords of Europe, were not exactly bounded, each proprietor or landholder did not precisely know how much belonged to himself: so that the owners of property which lay together often claimed the same; and as there were not courts of justice to inquire into and settle their rights, they and their vassals fought about them. Many of the richer and more powerful lords, wanting to become still more rich and powerful, and having no sense of religion, of justice, or mercy—none of the fear of God or love of man—murdered their neighbours, set fire to their houses, carried off their property, and claimed their lands : on

6

these occasions the ladies were often treated in a barbarous manner.

A remarkable instance of this may be found in Shakspeare's Tragedy of Macbeth. Macbeth, a Scottish nobleman, invited Duncan, king of Scotland, to his castle, and there murdered him, that he might be king instead of Duncan. On the murder of the king, his two sons fled from Scotland in fear of their lives. Macduff, a Scotch lord, followed Malcolm, one of the young princes, into England; upon which the usurper Macbeth was so enraged, that he vowed to revenge himself upon Macduff for this desertion. In order to do this, Macbeth resolved upon killing Macduff's innocent family, which he had left behind, and he accordingly gave orders for this cruel act. It is described nearly thus:—After the bloody work was done, Rosse, a friend of the unfortunate family, escaped into England to inform Macduff of it. He found him talking to Malcolm, and after preparing his mind, relates the event.

"*Rosse.* Your castle is surprised, your wife and babes
Savagely slaughtered!
Malcolm. Merciful heaven!
Macduff. My children too?
Rosse. Wife, children, servants, all
That could be found.
Macd. And I must be from thence!—
My wife kill'd too?
Rosse. I have said.
Mal. Let us make *medicines of our great revenge,*
To cure this deadly grief.
Macd. *He* has no children!—All my pretty ones?
Did you say all?
Rosse. All.
Macd. What, all my pretty chickens and their dam?"
                    Macbeth, Act IV. *Scene* 3.

You will observe that Malcolm proposes to make amends for this cruel injury by some " great revenge," that is, by some act of equal cruelty to the murderers of

Macduff's wife and children. This was the way in which people at that time usually endeavoured to satisfy themselves, but they only continued a strife which the descendants of both parties felt bound never to forget nor forgive, and which many long years after the first offence, was given, caused fresh quarrels, murders, and destruction of property.

In this state of violence and danger, many people lived in constant and great fear, and were always prepared to expect, and to defend themselves against an enemy. The rich lived in strong castles, surrounded by walls and gates, a watch was kept to look out for the approach of their foes, and, before the discovery of gunpowder, and the use of firearms, the knights—that is, the gentlemen-soldiers—used generally to wear *armour*.

Then, as at all times, there were good men—some who were not weak and timid, or ferocious and cruel, who could not see the acts of these barbarians without indignation against them, and compassion for the unfortunate victims of their cruelty. The distress of the ladies, above all, inspired the just and the generous with a desire to serve them, and to save them from the dreadful calamities to which they were exposed. Many noblemen and brave soldiers devoted themselves to the redress of injuries inflicted upon all good persons, and particularly upon the young and the beautiful of the female sex. These formed what is called the order of Chivalry.

The young men who composed the order of Chivalry could not be admitted into it, unless they possessed strength and courage, and were distinguished by truth and honour; and this being known, made ambitious youth desirous to be so distinguished, that they might be worthy to assert justice, and to defend innocence, that they might become objects of admiration and praise, and form at once the protectors and ornaments of society. To be all this, it was necessary that they should not only be fearless and powerful, but that they should also be pleasing and interesting: that they should perfectly understand the use of arms to prevail over their enemies, and be masters of every graceful accomplishment to inspire the affection of their friends. Many arts of little use at this time were *then necessary*, and these arts exhibited much grace and skill. The management of fiery horses, the throwing of the pike, (a sharp instrument used in ancient war,) and the exercise of the bow, were taught to young men with as much and more pains than dancing, fencing, and music now require. Horsemanship, archery, &c. require great presence of mind and great strength of body, and show elegance of person and quickness of thought to the utmost advantage.

For a long time Chivalry did much good, but at length it went out of use, because laws were made and enforced that compelled people to live peaceably together, so that the arts that belonged to Chivalry only served for amusement, and Knights or Champions used to practice a sort of mock fighting, as a mere trial of strength and skill, not intending to kill one another, but to spare the life of him who should be proved the weakest; and the most beautiful lady present at the encounter, used to give a prize to the victorious knight. These public spectacles were at last given up, but not all at once, for so late as the year 1600, and afterwards, we read of young gentlemen who were taught all the exercises of Chivalry.

These remarks do not refer exclusively to the preceding extract from Spenser, but they also serve to explain other pieces in this collection. The distressed condition of Una exemplifies the sufferings to which the young and beautiful were exposed in a rude age, and the devotedness of her attendant is a further illustration of the sentiments and services of a disinterested knight-errant, in behalf of endangered innocence.

THE FABLE OF THE OAK AND THE BRIAR.

" There grew an aged tree on the green,
A goodly Oak sometimes had it been,
With arms full strong and largely display'd,
But of their leaves they were disarray'd :
The body big and mightily pight,
Throughly rooted, and of wondrous height ;
Whilom* had been the king of the field,
And mochel mast† to the husband did yield,
And with his nuts larded many swine,
But now the gray moss marred his rine,
His bared boughs were beaten with storms,
His top was bald, and wasted with worms,
His honour decay'd, his braunches sere.‡
 Hard by his side grew a bragging Breere,
Which proudly thrust into th' element,
And seemed to threat the firmament :
It was imbellisht with blossoms fair,
And thereto age wonted to repair ;
The shepherd's daughters to gather flowres,
To paint their garlands with his colowres ;
And in his small bushes used to shroud,
The sweet nightingale singing so loud,
Which made this foolish Breere wex so bold,
That on a time he cast him to scold,
And sneb the good Oak, for he was old.
 Why stand'st there (quoth he) thou brutish block ?
Nor for fruit nor for shadow serves thy stock ;
Seest how fresh my flowres been spread,
Died in lily white and crimson red,
With leaves engrained in lusty green,
Coloures meet to cloath a maiden queen ?
Thy waste bigness but cumbers the ground,
And dirks the beauty of my blossoms round :
The mouldy moss, which thee accloyeth,
My cinnamon smell too much annoyeth :

* Formerly.   † Many acorns.   ‡ Dry.
6*

Wherefore soon I rede* thee hence remove,
Lest thou the price of my displeasure prove.
So spake this bold Breere with great disdain,
Little him answer'd the Oak again,
But yielded, with shame and grief adaw'd,†
That of a weed he was over-craw'd.‡

　　It chaunced after upon a day,
The husband-man's self to come that way,
Of custom to surview his ground,
And his trees of state in compass round :
Him when the spightful Breere had espyed,
He causeless complained, and loudly cried
Unto his lord, stirring up stern strife :

　　O my liege Lord ! the god of my life,
Please you pond§ your suppliant's plaint,
Caused of wrong and cruell constraint,
Which I your poor vassal daily endure ;
And but your goodness the same recure,
Am like for desperate dole‖ to die,
Through felonous force of mine enemy.

　　Greatly aghast with this piteous plea,
Him rested the good man on the lea,
And bad the Breere in his plaint proceed.
With painted words then gan this proud weed
(As most used ambitious folk)
His colour'd crime with craft to cloke.

　　Ah, my Sovereign ! lord of creatures all,
Thou placer of plants both humble and tall,
Was not I planted of thine own hand,
To be the primrose of all thy land,
With flowring blossoms to furnish the prime,
And scarlet berries in sommer-time ?
How falls it then that this faded Oak,
Whose body is sere, whose branches broke,
Whose naked arms stretch unto the fire,
Unto such tyranny doth aspire,
Hindring with his shade my lovely light,
And robbing me of the sweet sun's sight ?

* Advise.　† Dejected.　‡ Triumphed over.　§ Consider.　‖ Grief.

So beat his old boughs my tender side,
That oft the bloud springeth from woundes wide ;
Untimely my flowers forced to fall,
That been the honour of your coronal ;*
And oft he lets his canker-worms light
Upon my branches, to work me more spight ;
And of his hoary locks down doth cast,
Wherewith my fresh flowrets been defast :
For this, and many more such outrage,
Craving your godlyhead to assuage
The rancorous rigour of his might ;
Nought ask I, but onely to hold my right,
Submitting me to your good sufferaunce,
And praying to be guarded from grievaunce.
   To this this Oak cast him to reply
Well as he couth ; but his enemy
Had kindled such coles of displeasure,
That the good man nould† stay his leisure,
But home him hasted with furious heat,
Encreasing his wrath with many a threat ;
His harmful hatchet he hent‡ in hand,
(Alas ! that it so ready should stand !)
And to the field alone he speedeth,
(Aye little help to harm there needeth)
Anger nould let him speak to the tree,
Enaunter his rage mought cooled be,
But to the root bent his sturdy stroke,
And made many wounds in the waste Oak.
The axe's edge did oft turn again,
As half unwilling to cut the grain,
Seemed the senseless iron did fear,
Or to wrong holy eld did forbear ;
For it had been an antient tree,
Sacred with many a mystery,
And often crost with the priests' crew,
And often hallowed with holy-water dew ;
But like fancies weren foolery,
And broughten this Oak to this misery ;

* Wreath of flowers, chaplet.   † Would not.   ‡ Took.

For nought might they quitten him from decay,
For fiercely the good man at him did lay.
The block oft groaned under his blow,
And sighed to see his near overthrow.
In fine, the steel had pierced his pith,
Then down to the ground he fell forthwith.
His wondrous weight made the ground to quake,
Th' earth sunk under him, and seem'd to shake :
There lieth the Oak pitied of none.
  Now stands the Breere like a lord alone,
Puff'd up with pride and vain pleasance ;
But all this glee had no continuance :
For eftsoons* winter 'gan to approach,
The blustering Boreas did encroach,
And beat upon this solitary Breere,
For now no succour was seen him neere.
Now 'gan he repent his pride too late,
For naked left and disconsolate,
The biting frost nipt his stalk dead,
The watry wet weighed down his head,
And heaped snow burdened him so sore,
That now upright he can stand no more ;
And being down is trod in the durt
Of cattel, and brouzed, and sorely hurt.
Such was th' end of this ambitious Breere,
For scorning eld——"

                    * Not long after.

SHAKSPEARE.

"I speak this truth, thou art of poets, king."—*Thurlow*.

This dramatic poet is justly esteemed by those who speak the English language, as the most interesting writer in the world. There are few so highly endowed as to be able to comprehend the wealth and magnitude of of Shakspeare's genius, in all its variety and comprehension, but there are none perhaps within even the remotest influences of English literature, that have not felt the power of this mighty master in some of those numerous passages of his works which have passed into the popular mind. The best furnished and most profound intellects meet with congenial thoughts in Shakspeare; and all human experience, from the monarch's to the labourer's lot, is recorded and expressed by his immortal muse, so that every mind may find its own feelings and circumstances somewhere illustrated by his inspiration.

From the accounts which are preserved of Shakspeare's early life it appears that he had few advantages of direct instruction, though the knowledge contained in books popular at that time in England, lent him its little light; and the talent "that Nature did him give," supplied in him every defect of human learning, and enabled him to leave an inheritance of thought to future ages, which nothing but the dissolution of "the great globe itself" can annihilate. Dryden says of him, "He was a man who, of all modern and, perhaps, ancient poets, had the largest and most comprehensive soul. All the images of nature were still present to him, and he drew them not laboriously, but luckily. When he describes any thing, you more than see it, you feel it too. He needed not the spectacles of books to read nature; he looked inwards and found her there." But,

————————————'Tis wonderful,
That an invisible instinct should frame him
To poetry *unlearned*; honour *untaught;*
Civility not seen in other; knowledge

That wildly grew in him, yet yielded crops
As though it had been sown.

Shakspeare was born at Stratford upon Avon in War-
wickshire, 1564.   The documents of his life are very
imperfect   Rowe, the   poet, published a   memoir of
him a century after his death.   From this it appears that
Shakspeare removed himself to London, and that he was
an actor as well as a writer of plays.   Shakspeare how-
ever returned to Stratford, purchased a house there, and
died in that town.   In the church of Stratford a monu-
ment to his memory still remains.   The following inscrip-
tion on this monument is engraved beneath a bust of
Shakspeare :

" Stay, passenger, why goest thou so fast ?
Read, if thou can'st, whom envious death has plac'd
Within this monument—Shakspeare : with whom
Quick nature died; whose *name* doth deck this tomb
Far more than cost ; since all that he hath writ
Leaves living art, but art to serve his wit.
     Obit A. D. 1616—Ætatis 53. die 23 April."

Shakspeare's thirty-five plays were first collected and
published in 1623, in folio.   The title page of this folio
was embellished by an engraving, which was said to be a
likeness of the author, and attached to it were these lines
by Ben Jonson, addressed to the reader :

" This figure that thou seest here put,
  It was for gentle Shakspeare cut,
  Wherein the graver had a strife
  With nature to outdo the life :
  O, could he but have drawn his wit
  As well in brass, as he hath hit
  His face ; the print would then surpass
  All that was ever writ in brass.
  But since he cannot—reader, look
  Not on his picture, but his book."

From 1709, when Rowe published Shakspeare's plays,
to the present time, (1827,) they have been often

published, and are disseminated throughout the reading world of our language ; and the more they are studied, the more are they admired and enjoyed. The fine arts have derived importan taid from Shakspeare. The stage has been exalted, literature has been illustrated and adorned by him, his scenes have been delineated an infinite number of times by the pencil, and they embellish almost every house and every library.

Every fine poet since Shakspeare's time has paid homage to the commanding genius of this great man.

Milton's Sonnet to Shakspeare is among the most interesting tributes to his memory :

" What needs my Shakspeare for his honour'd bones
The labour of an age in piled stones,
Or that his hallow'd reliques should be hid
Under a satr-ypointing pyramid ?
Dear son of memory, great heir of fame,
What need'st thou such weak witness of thy name?
Thou in our wonder and astonishment
Hast built thyself a live-long monument.
For whilst to the shame of slow endeavouring art
Thy easy numbers flow, and that each heart
Hath from the leaves of thy unvalued book
Those Delphic lines with deep impression took ;
Then thou our fancy of itself bereaving,
Dost make us marble with too much conceiving ;
And so sepulcher'd, in such pomp dost lie,
That kings for such a tomb would wish to die."

English, Roman, and Grecian History, furnish part of the subjects of Shakspeare's plays ; and some of his plots are taken from Italian romances that had been translated into English ; but upon what foundation soever he built, the superstructure is perfectly original and eminently beautiful.

" Though Shakspeare's poetry is the delight and pride of all who speak our language, it is in general too abstruse and difficult for foreigners and young persons.

It exhibits the most lively pictures of external nature,

and the most perfect representations of human passions. But his language is frequently obscure, from its containing many words and phrases which are now out of common use ; besides, his writings relate so much to the passions of men, and the concerns of princes and politicians, that a person must have what is called a knowledge of the world, and must have had some experience of the effects of human passions, before he can perceive the beauties, or have a relish for the excellencies of Shakspeare." Parts of King John, and of Henry IV. are in some measure free from these difficulties ; and are selected for the purpose of introducing the style and manner of Shakspeare to young readers.

Shakspeare wrote dramatic pieces upon the history of England ; they are now called *plays*, though formerly they were called *histories* ; each of them takes in several years ; and they carry the imagination of the spectator from England to France, and back again, many times in the space of one night. King John is one of these dramas."

KING JOHN.

John, surnamed *Sans Terre*, or *Lackland*, was the fourth son of Henry II. King of England. John succeeded to the throne upon the death of his brother, Richard I. Arthur, Duke of Brittany, was the son of Geoffrey, John's elder brother ; and, according to the laws of England, was the legal successor of his uncle Richard. The unfortunate Arthur, it is supposed, was murdered by the command of John, but the manner of his death is unknown. Philip, King of France, was Arthur's maternal uncle, and publicly accused John of murdering his nephew ; but John declared that Arthur fell from the walls of a castle where he was confined, into a river which flowed below, and thus lost his life. Shakspeare has made a most affecting scene of John's cruelty to the poor youth. That, and the subsequent passages, from Shakspeare's play of King John, which complete Arthur's history, follow in this place.

KING JOHN, ACT IV. SCENE I.

HUBERT, *the assassin, employed to put out the young prince's eyes.* ARTHUR, *and attendants.* Scene, *a room in the Castle.*

Hubert. Heat me these irons hot; and look thou stand
Within the arras: when I strike my foot
Upon the bosom of the ground, rush forth:
And bind the boy, which you shall find with me,
Fast to the chair: be heedful: hence, and watch.

1 *Attend.* I hope, your warrant will bear out the deed.

Hub. Uncleanly scruples! Fear not you: look to't.—
[*Exeunt Attendants.*
Young lad, come forth; I have to say with you.
Enter ARTHUR.

Arth. Good morrow, Hubert.

Hub. Good morrow, little prince.

Arth. As little prince (having so great a title
To be more prince,) as may be.—You are sad.

Hub. Indeed, I have been merrier.

Arth. Mercy on me!
Methinks, no body should be sad but I:
Yet, I remember, when I was in France,
Young gentlemen would be as sad as night,
Only for wantonness. By my christendom,
So I were out of prison, and kept sheep,
I should be as merry as the day is long;
And so I would be here, but that I doubt
My uncle practises more harm to me:
He is afraid of me, and I of him:
Is it my fault that I was Geoffrey's son?
No, indeed, is't not: And I would to heaven,
I were your son, so you would love me, Hubert.

Hub. If I talk to him, with his innocent prate
He will awake my mercy, which lies dead:
Therefore I will be sudden, and despatch. [*Aside.*

Arth. Are you sick, Hubert? you look pale to-day:
In sooth, I would you were a little sick:

7

That I might sit all night, and watch with you:
I warrant, I love you more than you do me.
   Hub. His words do take possession of my bosom.——
Read here, young Arthur.   [*Showing the paper.*]   How
      now, foolish rheum !   [*Aside.*
Turning dispiteous torture out of door !
I must be brief; lest resolution drop
Out at mine eyes, in tender womanish tears.——
Can you not read it ? is it not fair writ ?
   Arth. Too fairly, Hubert, for so foul effect :
Must you with hot irons burn out both mine eyes ?
   Hub. Young boy, I must.
   Arth. And will you?
   Hub. And I will.
   Arth. Have you the heart? When your head did but ake,
I knit my handkerchief about your brows,
(The best I had, a princess wrought it me,)
And I did never ask it you again :
And with my hand at midnight held your head ;
And, like the watchful minutes to the hour,
Still and anon cheer'd up the heavy time ;
Saying, What lack you ? and, Where lies your grief?
Or, What good love may I perform for you ?
Many a poor man's son would have lain still,
And ne'er have spoke a loving word to you ;
But you at your sick service had a *prince.*
Nay, you may think, my love was crafty love,
And call it cunning ; Do, an if you will :
If heaven be pleas'd that you must use me ill,
Why, then you must.——Will you put out mine eyes ?
These eyes, that never did, nor never shall,
So much as frown on you ?
   Hub. I have sworn to do it ;
And with hot irons must I burn them out.
   Arth. Ah, none, but in this iron age, would do it !
The iron of itself, though *heat* read hot,
Approaching near these eyes, would drink my tears,
And quench his fiery indignation,
Even in the matter of mine innocence :

Nay, after that, consume away in rust,
But for containing fire to harm mine eye.
Are you more stubborn-hard than hammer'd iron?
An if an angel should have come to me,
And told me, Hubert should put out mine eyes,
I would not have believed no tongue, but Hubert's.
 Hub. Come forth. Do, as I bid you do. [*Stamps.*
  Re-enter Attendants, with cord, irons, &c.
 Arth. O, save me, Hubert, save me! my eyes are out,
Even with the fierce looks of these bloody men.
 Hub. Give me the iron, I say, and bind him here.
 Arth. Alas, what need you be so boist'rous rough?
I will not struggle, I will stand stone-still.
For heaven's sake, Hubert, let me not be bound!
Nay, hear me, Hubert! drive these men away,
And I will sit as quiet as a lamb ;
I will not stir, nor wince, nor speak a word,
Nor look upon the iron angerly :
Thrust but these men away, and I'll forgive you,
Whatever torment you do put me to.
 Hub. Go, stand within ; let me alone with him.
 1 *At.* I am best pleas'd to be from such a deed. [*Exe.*
 Arth. Alas, I then have chid away my friend ;
He hath a stern look, but a gentle heart :——
Let him come back, that his compassion may
Give life to yours.
 Hub. Come, boy, prepare yourself.
 Arth. Is there no remedy?
 Hub. None, but to lose your eyes.
 Arth. O heaven!——that there were but a mote in yours,
A grain, a dust, a gnat, a wand'ring hair,
Any annoyance in that precious sense !
Then, feeling what small things are boist'rous there,
Your vile intent must needs seem horrible.
 Hub. Is this your promise? go to, hold your tongue.
 Arth. Hubert, the utterance of a brace of tongues
Must needs want pleading for a pair of eyes :
Let me not hold my tongue ; let me not, Hubert!
Or, Hubert, if you will, cut out my tongue,

So I may keep mine eyes; O, spare mine eyes;
Though to no use, but still to look on you!
Lo, by my troth, the instrument is cold,
And would not harm me.
    Hub. I can heat it, boy.
    Arth. No, in good sooth; the fire is dead with grief,
Being create for comfort, to be us'd
In undeserv'd extremes: See else yourself;
There is no malice in this burning coal;
The breath of heaven hath blown his spirit out,
And strew'd repentant ashes on his head.
    Hub. But with my breath I can revive it, boy.
    Arth. And if you do, you will but make it blush,
And glow with shame of your proceedings, Hubert:
Nay, it, perchance, will sparkle in your eyes;
And, like a dog, that is compell'd to fight,
Snatch at his master that doth *tarre* him on.
All things, that you should use to do me wrong,
Deny their office: only you do lack
That mercy, which fierce fire, and iron, extends,
Creatures of note, for mercy-lacking uses.
    Hub. Well, see to live; I will not touch thine eyes
For all the treasure that thine uncle owes:
Yet am I sworn, and I did purpose, boy,
With this same very iron to burn them out.
    Arth. O, now you look like Hubert! all this while
You were disguised.
    Hub. Peace: no more. Adieu;
Your uncle must not know but you are dead:
I'll fill these dogged spies with false reports.
And, pretty child, sleep doubtless, and secure,
That Hubert, for the wealth of all the world,
Will not offend thee.
    Arth. O heaven!—I thank you, Hubert.
    Hub. Silence; no more: Go closely in with me;
Much danger do I undergo for thee.   [*Exeunt.*

I hope your warrant will bear out the deed. I hope you
act in this bloody business, by some higher authority
than your own cruelty or selfishness. It is necessary
that poor men, in the service of arbitrary princes, should
act their wicked wills. If you do as you are commanded,
you are not so guilty as if you devised of your own heart
such horrible deeds; but if you do this without some
such justification—dread the punishment due to your
cruelty. All this is *implied* in this passage.

Heat.—*Heated* is the modern participle. "The par-
ticiple *heat,* though now obsolete, was in use in our au-
thor's time. So in the sacred writings: 'He command-
ed that they should heat the furnace one seven times
more than it was wont to be *heat.*' *Dan.* iii. 19."

Tarre—stimulate, set on.

SCENE III. ARTHUR *on the castle wall.*

Arth. The wall is high; and yet will I leap down:
Good ground, be pitiful, and hurt me not!—
There's few, or none, do know me; if they did,
This ship-boy's semblance hath disguis'd me quite.
I am afraid; and yet I'll venture it.
If I get down, and do not break my limbs,
I'll find a thousand shifts to get away:
As good to die, and go, as die, and stay.
Oh me! my uncle's spirit is in these stones:—
Heaven take my soul, and England keep my bones!

Enter PEMBROKE, SALISBURY, *and* BIGOD,

Sal. This is the prison: What is he lies here?

[*Seeing* ARTHUR.

Pem. O death, made proud with pure and princely
beauty!
The earth hath not a hole to hide this deed.

Sal. Murder, as hating what himself hath done,
Doth lay it open, to urge on revenge.

Big. Or, when he doom'd this beauty to a grave,
Found it too precious-princely for a grave.

Sal. Sir Richard, what think you? Have you beheld,

7*

Or have you read, or heard? or could you think?
Or do you almost think, although you see,
That you do see? could thought, without this object,
Form such another? This is the very top,
The height, the crest, or crest unto the crest,
Of murder's arms: this is the bloodiest shame,
The wildest savag'ry, the vilest stroke,
That ever wall-ey'd wrath, or staring rage,
Presented to the tears of soft remorse.

    Pem. All murders past do stand excus'd in this.—
It is a bloody work;
The graceless action of a heavy hand,
If that it be the work of any hand.

    Sal. If that it be the work of any hand?—
We had a kind of light, what would ensue
It is the shameful work of Hubert's hand;
The practice, and the purpose, of the king:—
From whose obedience I forbid my soul,
Kneeling before this ruin of sweet life,
And breathing to his breathless excellence
The incense of a *vow*, a *holy vow*;
Never to taste the pleasures of the world,
Never to be infected with delight,
Nor conversant with ease and idleness,
Till I have set a glory to this hand,
By giving it the *worship of revenge*.

    Pem. Big. Our souls religiously confirm thy words.

    Revenge, to a certain extent, is the love of justice. It has been shown, in the brief sketch which was given of the origin and principal object of Chivalry, that its purpose was not only to defend innocence, but to punish those who should injure the weak and unprotected. The Knights of that age, not only made a vow to serve God, and the interests of humanity, when they were *initiated*, but, on setting out upon a special enterprize, they solemnly devoted themselves to the work before them.—In conformity to this practice, Salisbury kneels beside the dead body of Arthur, and vows never to take pleasure or rest till he has punished the wretches who wrought his death.

HENRY IV.

Henry, Duke of Lancaster, surnamed Bolingbroke, was son of John of Gaunt, duke of Lancaster, third son of Edward III., king of England. Richard II. was the predecessor of Henry IV. Richard was the rightful king, but he had no talent for government, and during his reign all England was in a state of confusion and civil warfare. Richard was, in consequence of his mis-government, deposed and thrown into prison. He was a son of Edward, called from the black armour which he wore, the Black Prince. The Black Prince was the eldest son of Edward III., the duke of Clarence was his second son, and John of Gaunt the third. When Richard was deposed, a descendant of the duke of Clarence, Mortimer, duke of York, was the legal successor to the throne, but Henry Bolingbroke set aside Mortimer's claim, and caused himself to be crowned King. Henry IV. died March, 1413, in the 14th year of his reign.

At the age of twenty-five Henry V. succeeded his father. During his short reign of nine years he exhibited such qualities as are much admired in a rude age. He possessed great personal courage, a spirit of military enterprise, talent for command, and patient perseverance in the accomplishment of his purposes. According to history, his deportment was singularly graceful and dignified, and his power of self-government even more extraordinary than his control of other men.

Shakspeare, in the last act of Henry IV. has given a very touching scene—it is the closing one of the king's life, in which he gives his latest counsel to the Prince of Wales. The king being ill, has his crown displaced from his head, and falls asleep. At this moment the prince enters the apartment of his father, and perceiving his condition, tenderly laments it, but removes the crown, and swears to maintain his right to it. The king awakes, eagerly demands who has taken away the crown, and seeing prince Henry, requests to be left alone with him, and they then confer together thus :

HENRY IV. *and* PRINCE HENRY.

K. Hen. Come hither to me, Harry.

P. Hen. I never thought to hear you speak again.

K. Hen. Thy wish was father, Harry, to that thought:
I stay too long by thee, I weary thee.
Dost thou so hunger for my empty chair,
That thou wilt needs invest thee with mine honours
Before thy hour be ripe? O foolish youth!
Thou seek'st the greatness that will overwhelm thee.
Stay but a little; for my cloud of dignity
Is held from falling with so weak a wind,
That it will quickly drop: my day is dim.
Thou hast stol'n that, which, after some few hours,
Were thine without offence; and, at my death,
Thou hast seal'd up my expectation:
Thy life did manifest, thou lov'dst me not,
And thou wilt have me die assured of it.
Thou hid'st a thousand daggers in thy thoughts;
Which thou hast whetted on thy stony heart,
To stab at half an hour of my life.
What! can'st thou not forbear me half an hour!
Then get thee gone; and dig my grave thyself;
And bid the merry bells ring to thine ear,
That thou art crowned, not that I am dead.
Let all the tears that should bedew my hearse,
Be drops of balm, to sanctify thy head:
Only compound me with forgotten dust;
Give that, which gave thee life, unto the worms.
Pluck down my officers, break my decrees;
For now the time is come to mock at form,
Harry the fifth is crown'd:—Up, vanity!
Down, royal state! all you sage counsellors, hence!
And to the English court assemble now,
From every region, apes of idleness!
Now, neighbour confines, purge you of your scum:
Have you a ruffian, that will swear, drink, dance,
Revel the night; rob, murder, and commit
The oldest sins the newest kind of ways?

Be happy, he will trouble you no more:
England shall double gild his treble guilt;
England shall give him office, honour, might:
For the fifth Harry from curb'd licence plucks
The muzzle of restraint, and the wild dog
Shall flesh his tooth in every innocent.
O my poor kingdom, sick with civil blows!
When that my care could not withhold thy riots,
What wilt thou do, when riot is thy care?
O, thou wilt be a wilderness again,
Peopled with wolves, thy old inhabitants!

    P. Hen. O, pardon me, my liege! but for my tears,
The moist impediments unto my speech,   [*Kneeling.*
I had forestall'd this dear and deep rebuke,
Ere you with grief had spoke, and I had heard
The course of it so far. There is your crown;
And He that wears the crown immortally,
Long guard it yours! If I affect it more,
Than as your honour, and as your renown,
Let me no more from this obedience rise,
(Which my most true and inward-duteous spirit
Teacheth,) this prostrate and exterior bending!
Heaven witness with me, when I here came in,
And found no course of breath within your majesty,
How cold it struck my heart! if I do feign,
O, let me in my present wildness die;
And never live to show th' incredulous world
The noble change that I have purposed!
Coming to look on you, thinking you dead,
(And dead almost, my liege, to think you were,)
I spake unto the crown, as having sense,
And thus upbraided it. *The care on thee depending,*
Hath fed upon the body of my father;
Therefore, thou, best of gold, art worst of gold.
And thou, most fine, most honour'd, most renown'd,
Hast eat thy bearer up. Thus, my most royal liege,
Accusing it, I put it on my head;
To try with it,—as with an enemy,
That had before my face murdered my father,—

The quarrel of a true inheritor.
But if it did infect my blood with joy,
Or swell my thoughts to any strain of pride;
If any rebel or vain spirit of mine
Did, with the least affection of a welcome,
Give entertainment to the might of it,
Let God for ever keep it from my head!
And make me as the poorest vassal is,
That doth with awe and terror kneel to it!
   K. Hen. O my son!
Heaven put it in thy mind, to take it hence,
That thou might'st win the more thy father's love,
Pleading so wisely in excuse of it.
Come hither, Harry, sit thou by my bed;
And hear, I think, the very latest counsel
That ever I shall breathe. Heaven knows, my son,
By what by-paths, and indirect, crook'd ways,
I met this crown; and I myself know well,
How troublesome it sat upon my head:
To thee it shall descend with better quiet,
Better opinion, better confirmation;
For all the soil of the achievement goes
With me into the earth. It seem'd in me,
But as an honour snatch'd with boist'rous hand;
And I had many living, to upbraid
My gain of it by their assistances;
Which daily grew to quarrel, and to bloodshed.
What in me was purchas'd,
Falls upon thee in a more fairer sort;
So thou the garland wear'st successively.
Yet, though thou stand'st more sure than I could do,
Thou art not firm enough, since griefs are green;
And all thy friends, which thou must make thy friends,
Have but their stings and teeth newly ta'en out;
By whose fell working I was first advanc'd,
And by whose power I well might lodge a fear
To be again displac'd: which to avoid,
I cut them off; and had a purpose now
To lead out many to the Holy Land;

Lest rest, and lying still, might make them look
Too near unto my state.   Therefore, my Harry,
Be it thy course, to busy giddy minds
With foreign quarrels ; that action, hence borne out,
May waste the memory of the former days.
More would I, but my lungs are wasted so,
That strength of speech is utterly denied me.
How I came by the crown, O God, forgive !
And grant it may with thee in true peace live !
  P. Hen. My gracious liege,
You won it, wore it, kept it, gave it me ;
Then plain, and right, must my possession be :
Which I, with more than with a common pain,
'Gainst all the world will rightfully maintain.

  What in me was purchas'd, &c.—The royal dignity
which I possess was obtained by artifice—it is not my
right, and I have held it precariously, and in fear.   *Thou
the garland wear'st successively.*—The crown devolves
to thee from thy father—thy *hereditary right* is establish-
ed, and thou art secure in it.

HENRY V.

  The noble change that he had *purposed,* as he bound his
brows with the crown of his dying father, was exempli-
fied in Prince Henry when he became King of England.
One circumstance of his public conduct, which is finely
exhibited by Shakspeare, is illustrative of his respect for
the constitution and laws of his kingdom, and as an ex-
ample of his disinterestedness and veneration for justice,
does honour to his memory.
  "Henry the Fifth, when Prince of Wales, was wild, and
in the disgraceful society of Sir John Falstaff, Poins, and
other idlers, committed several offences against the laws.
Some of his attendants had been taken up by the officers
of justice, for a riot, and were brought before the chief
justice, Sir William Gascoigne.   While they were in
court, prince Henry came, and rudely demanded that
they should be released. The chief justice refused. The

prince insulted, and, it is supposed, even struck the judge. The chief justice with great dignity kept his seat upon the bench, and in the authoritative tone of a man, to whom the execution of the laws is intrusted, rebuked the prince, and ordered him to be taken into custody. To this the prince, recollecting his duty, becomingly submitted."

It is related by an old historian that Prince Henry, being ordered to prison, "doing reverence" to the judge, departed, and went to the King's Bench, as he was commanded. One of his attendants, displeased at this indignity, (as he deemed it,) offered to the prince, and thinking to incense the King against the chief justice, repaired to his majesty with the whole affair. The King, on hearing the circumstance, paused for a moment, and then, lifting his eyes and clasped hands to Heaven, exclaimed, " O merciful God! how much, above all other men, am I indebted to thine infinite goodness; especially that thou hast given me a judge who feareth not to minister justice, and also a son who can suffer worthily and obey justice."

"After the death of his father, when Henry became king, the nation expected he would give himself up to amusement and intemperance; but on the contrary, he immediately assumed the deportment and conduct of a wise monarch, and, dismissing from his presence his former companions, instead of disgracing the chief justice who had committed him, he thanked him for the firmness and dignity with which he had executed the laws, and conferred great favours upon him."

KING HENRY, *the Princes his brothers, and the* CHIEF JUSTICE.

Ch. Just. Good morrow; and heaven save your majesty!

King. This new and gorgeous garment, majesty,
Sits not so easy on me as you think.——
Brothers, you mix your sadness with some fear;
This is the English, not the Turkish court.

——————————— good brothers—be assured,
I'll be your father and your brother too;
Let me but bear your love, I'll bear your cares.

P. John, and the others. We hope no other from your
majesty.

King. You all look strangely on me :—and you most;
You are, I think, assur'd I love you not.

Ch. Just. I am assur'd, if I be measur'd rightly,
Your majesty hath no just cause to hate me.

King. No!
How might a prince of my great hopes forget
So great indignities you laid upon me?
What! rate, rebuke, and roughly send to prison
Th' immediate heir of England? Was this easy?
May this be wash'd in Lethe, and forgotten?

Ch. Just. I then did use the person of your father:
The image of his power lay then in me:
And, in th' administration of his law,
Whiles I was busy for the commonwealth,
Your highness pleased to forget my place,
The majesty and power of law and justice,
The image of the king whom I presented,
And struck me in my very seat of judgment:
Whereon, as an offender to your father,
I gave bold way to my authority,
And did commit you. If the deed were ill,
Be you contented, wearing now the garland,
To have a son set your decrees at nought;
To pluck down justice from your awful bench;
To trip the course of law, and blunt the sword
That guards the peace and safety of your person;
Nay, more; to spurn at your most royal image,
And mock your workings in a second body.
Question your royal thoughts, make the case yours;
Be now the father, and propose a son:
Hear your own dignity so much profan'd,
See your most dreadful laws so loosely slighted,
Behold yourself so by a son disdain'd;
And then imagine me taking your part,

S

And, in your power, soft silencing your son:
After this cold considerance, sentence me;
And, as you are a king, speak in your state,—
What I have done, that misbecame my place,
My person, or my liege's sovereignty.
   King. You are right, justice, and you weigh this well;
Therefore, still bear the balance, and the sword:
And I do wish your honours may increase,
Till you do live to see a son of mine
Offend you, and obey you, as I did.
So shall I live to speak my father's words;—
Happy am I, that have a man so bold,
That dares do justice on my proper son:
And not less happy, having such a son,
That would deliver up his greatness so
Into the hands of justice.—You did commit me;
For which, I do commit into your hand
Th' unstain'd sword that you have us'd to bear;
With this remembrance,—That you use the same
With the like bold, just, and impartial spirit,
That you have done 'gainst me. There is my hand;
You shall be as a father to my youth:
My voice shall sound as you do prompt mine ear;
And I will stoop and humble my intents
To your well-practis'd, wise directions.——
And, princes all, believe me, I beseech you;—
My father's gone into his grave, and in
His tomb lie all my wild affections;
And with his spirit sadly I survive,
To mock the expectation of the world;
To frustrate prophecies; and to raze out
Rotten opinion, who hath writ me down
After my seeming. The tide of blood in me
Hath proudly flow'd in vanity, till now:
Now doth it turn, and ebb back to the sea;
Where it shall mingle with the state of floods,
And flow henceforth in formal majesty.
Now call we our high court of parliament:
And let us choose such limbs of noble counsel,

That the great body of our state may go
In equal rank with the best govern'd nation ;
That war, or peace, or both at once, may be
As things acquainted and familiar to us ;—
In which you, father, shall have foremost hand.
                    [*To the Lord Chief Justice.*

This is the English, not the Turkish court.—Brothers,
why should you fear me ?—You are not in the despotic
country of Turkey, where a monarch, through fear that
his brothers should kill him, in order that one of them
may usurp the throne, to secure his own life takes
theirs. You are in Britain, where our knowledge and laws
make me your protéctor ; and the institutions we live un-
der induce me to trust as well as to defend you.

· Mr. Edgeworth, in Poetry Explained, has rendered
the reply to the King into the following prose :—When
the King asks, Was this *easy* ? Can it be *easily* forgot-
ten ? the judge's remonstrance signifies, "I then repre-
sented the person of your father (who is supposed to be
present in this court of justice ;) his power was then in
me, and whilst I was administering the laws, and busy
for the common-weal (for the common good,) your high-
ness forgot my office—forgot the power and majesty of
the laws and of justice—you forgot your father, whom I
represented, and struck me on the bench of justice ;
whereupon I boldly exerted my authority, and sent you
to a prison.

"If you think this wrong, you must be contented when,
now you wear the garland, (the crown,) to have your son
set your decrees at nought, to have him pull down the
authority of your judgment-seat, to trip and stop the cur-
rent course of law, and to take off the edge and power of
the sword of justice, which guards the peace and safety of
your person ; nay more, you must submit to have your
son affront your own royal image, represented and act-
ing in the person of your judge, whom you substitute in
your place.

"Question your royal thoughts; make the case your own; suppose yourself a father, and that you had a son; suppose you heard your dignity scorned, and that you saw your laws disdained; then imagine me taking your part, and by your power, inherent in me, silencing your son. After having brought these images before your mind, and after cool consideration, pass sentence upon me: and as you are a king, speak not as a private person, but in the dignity of your public capacity, and declare what I have done unbecoming of my office, my person, or your sovereignty."

Your highness.——Highness is now a title of honour or respect, addressed in England to the sons and daughters of the king; formerly it was also used in addressing the king or queen."

" *The garland.*——Shakspeare, in two or three places, calls the crown the garland."

"*Liege's sovereignty.*——Liege properly means a person to whom a certain duty or obedience is owing. Formerly, after the conquest of England by William the Conqueror, when the land of the kingdom was divided amongst his followers, or vassals, in the same manner that lands were usually divided upon the continent, every man, instead of paying rent in money for the land which he held, was bound to supply the person from whom he held it, with a certain number of armed men, on horseback, or on foot. The person to whom he owed this service, was called his liege lord. Persons who were themselves princes, frequently had liege lords over them; in particular, the emperor of Germany had a great number of princes and dukes for his vassals, who were all bound to him as their liege lord."

"*Therefore still bear the balance and the sword.*——The chief justice of the king's bench has neither a balance (a pair of scales,) nor a sword, carried before him; but the allegorical figure of Justice is represented in painting and statuary by a female figure blindfold, to show that Justice should not respect the persons of people; with a balance in her left hand, to denote that she weighs carefully before she determines; and with a sword in her right hand, to denote that Justice can punish offenders with the sword of the law. The Roman magistrates had axes surrounded with rods, carried before them, as emblems of punishment; the rods to punish smaller offences, the axe to punish greater crimes with death. Though the judges have not swords carried before them, yet the king of England, who is the head of the law, and who is represented by the chief justice of the king's bench, has the sword of state carried before him on days of ceremony."

" 'And, princes all, believe me, I beseech you;
My father's gone into his grave; and in
His tomb lie all my wild affections.'

'And, princes, believe me, my father has carried my wildness and youthful follies into his grave with him, for all my former affections or propensities lie there; and his sedate spirit lives in me, to disappoint the expectation which the world has of my being a dissipated monarch, and to contradict prophesies and opinions which were formed from my former conduct.' "

MILTON.

" Thy soul was like a star and dwelt apart :
    Thou hadst a voice whose sound was like the sea ;
    Pure as the naked heavens, majestic, free,
    So didst thou travel on life's common way,
    In cheerful godliness ; and yet thy heart
    The lowliest duties on herself did lay."—*Wordsworth.*

Milton, who is rightly classed among the most exalted of British poets, was the son of a gentleman in the middle rank of society, but the moral dignity of his character would have done honour to any station.   For abjuring the Roman Catholic, and professing the Protestant faith, the elder Milton was disinherited by his father, and compelled to make his way in the world by industry and integrity only ; but his ability in business secured to him a complete estate, and the happy turn of his mind rendered a moderate fortune sufficient.   From the childhood of the poet, his father discerned his extraordinary endowments, and trained him with suitable care and skill.   Milton was at first educated by a private tutor, then sent to a public school in London, and, at a proper age, was entered at the university of Cambridge.   After his collegiate studies were finished, he spent a few years in a delightful rural retirement at Horton in Buckinghamshire, and at the age of thirty repaired to the continent of Europe.   All the influences of domestic culture, of self-application, and of foreign travel, tended to give the highest finish to the character of a man on whom nature had bestowed the most beautiful countenance, and the most sublime soul.

During his residence in France and Italy, Milton's virtues and accomplishments gained him the friendship of some of the most gifted men of the age.   He lived, in respect to his own country, at a period of political trouble ; but he was neither " a bigot of the iron time" of Cromwell, nor a sycophant in the licentious court of Charles II.   He was a true republican, and Cromwell, had distinguished him : consequently, after the Stuart ascended the throne, he fell into obscurity and neglect. But what was infinitely more afflictive, he was totally deprived of sight at the age of forty-two years.   The happiness of this great man depended little upon fortune. His intellectual and moral worth gave dignity to his condition, and he was not forsaken of honourable friendships when he was removed from active life. His divine complacency, and the consolations that sustained his spirit, are exhibited by his own declarations.

A person engaged in a controversy with Milton, enraged at the zeal with which he supported the cause of civil and religious liberty, reproached him with his blindness, as a retribution of God upon the principles which he defended. Upon this occasion, the poet made the following reply to his accuser :

" I do not regard my lot either with weariness or compunction ; I continue in the same sentiments fixed and immoveable. I do not think God displeased with me, neither is he displeased ; on the contrary, I experience and thankfully acknowledge his paternal clemency and benignity towards me in every thing that is of the greatest moment ; specially in this, that he himself consoling and encouraging my spirit, I acquiesce without a murmur in his sacred dispensations. It is through his grace that I find my friends, even more than before, kind and officious towards me—that they are my consolers, honourers, visiters, and assistants. Those who are of the highest consideration in the republic, finding that the light of my eyes departed from me, not being slothful and inactive, but while I was with constancy and resolution placing myself in the foremost post of danger for the defence of sacred liberty, do not on their part desert me. Nor is it an occasion of anguish to me, though you count it miserable, that I am fallen in vulgar estimation into the class of the blind, the unfortunate, the wretched, and the helpless ; since my hope is, that I am thus brought nearer to the mercy and protection of the universal father.

" There is a path, as the apostle teaches me, through weakness to a more consummate strength ; let me therefore be helpless, so that in my debility the better and more immortal part of our human nature may be more effectually displayed : so that amidst my darkness, the

light of the divine countenance may shine forth more
bright—then shall I be at once helpless, and yet of giant
strength : blind, yet of vision most penetrating : thus may
I be in this helplessness carried on to fulness of joy, and
in this darkness surrounded with the light of eternal
day."—*Translated from the Latin of Milton, Defensio
Secunda.*

The more powerful of Milton's poems may be found
in different collections of poetry, as well as in his entire
works ; such passages as were suitable to this book are
here inserted.   Cowper has translated from Milton's
Latin poetry some endearing verses to the poet's father—
they are an affecting acknowledgment of the benefits he
had derived from that exemplary parent.

TO MY FATHER.

————"Thou hatest not the gentle Muse,
My father! for thou never badst me tread
The beaten path, and broad, that lead'st right on
To opulence, nor didst condemn thy son
To the insipid clamours of the bar,
To laws voluminous, and ill observ'd ;
But, wishing to enrich me more, to fill
My mind with treasure, led'st me far away
From city-din to deep retreats, to banks
And streams Aonian: and, with free consent,
Didst place me happy at Apollo's side.
I speak not now, on more important themes
Intent, of common benefits, and such
As nature bids, but of thy larger gifts,
My Father! who, when I had open'd once
The stores of Roman rhetoric, and learn'd
The full-ton'd language of the eloquent Greeks,
Whose lofty music grac'd the lips of Jove,
Thyself did'st counsel me to add the flow'rs
That Gallia boasts, those too, with which the smooth
Italian his degen'rate speech adorns,
That witnesses his mixture with the Goth ;
And Palestine's prophetic songs divine.

To sum the whole, whate'er the heav'n contains,
The earth beneath it, and the air between,
The rivers and the restless deep, may all
Prove intellectual gain to me, my wish
Concurring with thy will; science herself,
All cloud remov'd, inclines her beauteous head,
And offers me the lip, if, dull of heart,
I shrink not, and decline her gracious boon.

Go now, and gather dross, ye sordid minds,
That covet it; what could my Father more?
What more could Jove himself, unless he gave
His own abode, the heav'n, in which he reigns?
More eligible gifts than these were not
Apollo's to his son, had they been safe,
As they were insecure, who made the boy
The world's vice-luminary, bade him rule
The radiant chariot of the day, and bind
To his young brows his own all-dazzling wreath.
I therefore, although last and least, my place
Among the learned in the laurel grove
Will hold, and where the conqu'ror's ivy twines,
Henceforth exempt from the unletter'd throng
Profane, nor even to be seen by such.
Away, then, sleepless Care, Complaint, away,
And, Envy, with thy "jealous leer malign!"
Nor let the monster Calumny shoot forth
Her venom'd tongue at me. Detested foes!
Ye all are impotent against my peace,
For I am privileg'd, and bear my breast
Safe, and too high, for your viperian wound.

But thou! my Father, since to render thanks
Equivalent, and to requite by deeds
Thy liberality, exceeds my power,
Suffice it, that I thus record thy gifts,
And bear them treasur'd in a grateful mind!
Ye too, the favourite pastime of my youth,
My voluntary numbers, if ye dare

To hope longevity, and to survive
Your master's funeral, not soon absorb'd
In the oblivious Lethæan gulf,
Shall to futurity perhaps convey
This theme, and by these praises of my sire
Improve the Fathers of a distant age!"

The boy, the world's vice-luminary.—In mythology it is related that Apollo, or the Sun, permitted his son Phaëton to drive the celestial coursers, which according to the fable, bear the sun round the earth, and that the unpractised charioteer would have set the world on-fire, had he not been precipitated into the river Po.

Lethæan gulf.—Those who tasted the waters of Lethe forgot the past.

Milton's minor pieces were written before he was thirty : the Paradise Lost was published when he had attained the age of sixty years. Comus, L'Allegro, and Penseroso, are delightful, but Paradise Lost has a power and elevation in it, a variety, and sublimity of excellence, which have given to Milton that rank as a sacred poet which belongs to him only. But his fame was not awarded to him while he lived—his place in society was humble, and he was never distinguished during his life but by a few of his more discerning contemporaries.

"He stood alone," says Mr. Campbell, "and aloof above his times, the bard of immortal subjects, and, as far as there is perpetuity in language, of immortal fame. The very choice of those subjects bespoke a contempt for any species of excellence that was attainable by other men. There is something that overawes the mind in conceiving his long deliberated selection of that theme —his attempting it when his eyes were shut upon the face of nature—his dependence, we might almost say, on supernatural inspiration, and in the calm air of strength with which he opens Paradise Lost, beginning a mighty performance without the appearance of an effort. Taking the subject all in all, his powers could nowhere else have enjoyed the same scope. It was only from the height of this great argument that he could look back upon eternity past, and forward upon eternity to come, that he could survey the abyss of infernal darkness, open visions of Paradise, or ascend to heaven and breathe empyreal air."

The subject of Paradise Lost, is taken from that portion of the Hebrew Scriptures which relates to our first parents. It supposes, what many Christians admit to be true in theology, that God placed the first human pair in a happy condition, and promised that they and all their posterity should remain for ever in that happy state, provided they would obey God; but that, if they would disobey the divine commands, they should be punished. They disobeyed God, were driven out of Paradise, and they and all their descendants were, thenceforth, made liable to sin, sorrow, and death.

Satan, a malignant spirit, tempted the first woman to break the prohibition of God, *she* tempted her husband, and *both*, in consequence of their weakness, were driven out from Eden, their primitive dwelling place, and destined to "labour and sorrow," in some other region. The only alleviation which their expulsion from Paradise admitted, was the promise of God, that "one greater man" than Adam should restore his descendants to the moral image of God, which they had forfeited, and likewise reconcile them to God's government and will.

SENTENCE PRONOUNCED ON ADAM AND EVE.

In the XIth Book of the Paradise Lost, Adam and Eve, after they had broken the divine command, are represented as lamenting their offence, when Michael, a spirit sent from God, descends to them, and commands them to leave their native Paradise. Perceiving his approach, Adam to Eve

———————————————"thus spake :

Eve, now expect great tidings, which perhaps
Of us will soon determine, or impose
New laws to be observed; for I descry
From yonder blazing cloud that veils the hill

One of the heav'nly host, and by his gait,
None of the meanest, some great potentate
Or of the thrones above, such majesty
Invests him coming ; yet not terrible,
That I should fear, nor sociably mild,
As Raphael, that I should much confide,
But solemn and sublime, whom not t' offend,
With rev'rence I must meet, and thou retire.
      He ended ; and the Archangel soon drew nigh.
Not in his shape celestial, but as man
Clad to meet man ; over his lucid arms
A military vest of purple flow'd,
Livelier than Melibœan, or the grain
Of Sarra, worn by kings and heroes old
In time of truce ; Iris had dipt the woof ;
His starry helm unbuckled show'd him prime
In manhood where youth ended ; by his side
As in a glist'ring zodiac hung the sword,
Satan's dire dread, and in his hand the spear.
Adam bow'd low : he kingly from his state
Inclin'd not, but his coming thus declar'd :
      Adam, heav'n's high behest no preface needs :
Sufficient that thy pray'rs are heard, and death,
Then due by sentence when thou didst transgress,
Defeated of his seizure many days
Giv'n thee of grace, wherein thou may'st repent,
And one bad act with many deeds well done
Mayst cover : well may then thy Lord appeas'd
Redeem thee quite from Death's rapacious claim ;
But longer in this Paradise to dwell
Permits not ; to remove thee I am come,
And send thee from the garden forth to till
The ground whence thou wast taken, fitter soil.
      He added not, for Adam at the news
Heart-struck with chilling gripe of sorrow stood,
That all his senses bound ; Eve, who unseen
Yet all had heard, with audible lament
Discover'd soon the place of her retire."

A military vest, &c.—This magnificent attire of the archangel is compared with that of Asiatic kings, who in ancient times endeavoured in their warfare to astonish their enemies by their splendour, as well as to overcome them by their military prowess.

Iris had dipt the woof.—The *woof* of any texture is composed of the transverse threads which interlace the threads that form the *warp* of the woven substance. *Iris* is the goddess of the rainbow, which exhibits all the prismatic colours, and consequently the most pure and vivid hues in nature.

THE DEPARTURE FROM PARADISE.

The archangel fulfils the commission with which God had intrusted him with peculiar tenderness to our first parents. They are not driven into an untried condition of existence without gracious preparation. Michael "ascends in the visions of God" with Adam, and foreshows to him the degeneracy and misery of his posterity, but to console him for these tremendous prospects, he reveals to him " salvation by Jesus Christ"—the reformation of a " perverted world," and the commencement of a kingdom,

" Founded in righteousness and peace and love,
 To bring forth fruits, joy and eternal bliss."

Thus enlightened and encouraged, Adam submissively replies to his celestial visitant—

" Greatly instructed I shall hence depart,
Greatly in peace of thought, and have my fill
Of knowledge, what this vessel can contain ;
Beyond which was my folly to aspire.
Henceforth I learn, that to obey is best,
And love with fear the only God, to walk
As in his presence, ever to observe
His providence, and on him sole depend ;
Merciful over all his works, with good

9

Still overcoming evil, and by small
Accomplishing great things, by things deem'd weak
Subverting worldly strong, and worldly wise
By simply meek : that suffering for truth's sake
Is fortitude to highest victory,
And to the faithful, death the gate of life—
Taught this by his example whom I now
Acknowledge my Redeemer ever blest.
    To whom thus also th' angel last replied.
This having learn'd, thou hast attain'd the sum
Of wisdom ; hope no high'r, though all the stars
Thou knew'st by name, and all th' ethereal pow'rs,
All secrets of the deep, all Nature's works,
Or works of God in heav'n, air, earth, or sea,
And all the riches of this world enjoy'dst,
And all the rule, one empire ; only add
Deeds to thy knowledge answerable, add faith,
Add virtue, patience, temperance, add love,
By name to come, call'd Charity, the soul
Of all the rest : then wilt thou not be loath
To leave this Paradise, but shalt possess
A Paradise within thee, happier far.
    Let us descend now therefore from this top
Of speculation ; for the hour precise
Exacts our parting hence ; and see, the guards,
By me encamp'd on yonder hill,—expect
Their motion, at whose front a flaming sword
In signal of remove, waves fiercely round ;
We may no longer stay : go, waken Eve ;
Her also I with gentle dreams have calm'd
Portending good, and all her spirits compos'd
To meek submission : thou at season fit
Let her with thee partake what thou hast heard,
Chiefly what may concern her faith to know :
That ye may live, which will be many days,
Both in one faith unanimous though sad,
With cause, for evils past, yet much more cheer'd
With meditation on the happy end.
    He ended, and they both descend the hill ;

Descended, Adam to the bow'r where Eve
Lay sleeping ran before, but found her wak'd ;
And thus with words not sad she him receiv'd.

Whence thou return'st, and whither went'st, I know,
For God is also in sleep, and dreams advise,
Which he hath sent propitious, some great good
Presaging, since with sorrow and heart's distress
Wearied I fell asleep : but now lead on ;
In me is no delay ; with thee to go,
Is to stay here ; without thee here to stay,
Is to go hence unwilling ; thou to me
Art all things under heav'n, all places thou,
Who for my wilful crime art banish'd hence.
This further consolation yet secure
I carry hence ; though all by me is lost,
Such favour I unworthy am vouchsaf'd,
By me the promis'd seed shall all restore.

So spake our mother Eve, and Adam heard
Well pleas'd, but answer'd not ; for now too nigh
Th' archangel stood, and from th' other hill
To their fix'd station, all in bright array
The cherubim descended ; on the ground
Gliding meteorous, as evening mist
Ris'n from a river o'er the marish glides,
And gathers ground fast at the lab'rer's heel
Homeward returning. High in front advanc'd,
The brandish'd sword of God before them blaz'd
Fierce as a comet ; which with torrid heat,
And vapour as the Lybian air a dust,
Began to parch that temp'rate clime ; whereat
In either hand the hast'ning Angel caught
Our lingering parents, and to th' eastern gate
Led them direct, and down the cliff as fast
To the subjected plain ; then disappear'd.

They looking back, all th' eastern side beheld
Of Paradise, so late their happy seat,
Wav'd over by that flaming brand, the gate
With dreadful faces throng'd and fiery arms :
Some natural tears they dropt, but wip'd them soon :
The world was all before them, where to choose

Their place of rest, and Providence their guide:
They hand in hand, with wand'ring steps and slow,
Through Eden took their solitary way.

PARTHIA.

The subject of Paradise Regained may be found in the fourth chapter of the gospel of St. Matthew—it is what is commonly called the Temptation of Christ. When this event occurred, our Saviour had attained the age of thirty years, and was about to begin that moral revolution in the world, which his teaching and example afterwards accomplished. From the gospel history it appears that at this time an evil spirit counselled him to assume the state of a temporal prince; but to have done this he must have accommodated himself to prevailing vices and institutions wholly incompatible with his high office, and as he came into the world in the name of the Lord his God, he resolved to serve him only, and not the Prince of this world.

The tempter "taking him into an exceeding high mountain, showed him all the kingdoms of the world, and the glory of them." The most remarkable nations then existing were the Parthians, the Greeks and Romans. Parthia, on the ancient maps, was the country immediately east of Syria, and south of the Caspian sea, and contained at that time a populous and powerful state. Among the kingdoms which, according to Milton, passed under the survey of Jesus, was Parthia, and he has described its warfare—military prowess, or mere physical force, being the chief distinction of that barbarous nation.

——————————————— "There
Artaxata, Teredon, Ctesiphon,
Turning with easy eye thou may'st behold.
All these the Parthian, now some ages past,
By great Arsaces led, who founded first
That empire, under his dominion holds
From the luxurious kings of Antioch won.
And just in time thou com'st to have a view

Of his great power; for now the Parthian king
In Ctesiphon hath gather'd all his host
Against the Scythian, whose incursions wild
Have wasted Sogdiana; to her aid
He marches now in haste. See, though from far,
His thousands, in what martial equipage
They issue forth, steel bows, and shafts, their arms,
Of equal dread in flight, or in pursuit;
All horsemen, in which fight they most excel :
See how in warlike muster they appear,
In rhombs and wedges, and half-moons, and wings.
   He look'd, and saw what numbers numberless
The city-gates out-pour'd, light armed troops
In coats of mail and military pride ;
In mail their horses clad, yet fleet and strong,
Prancing their riders bore, the flower and choice
Of many provinces from bound to bound,
He saw them in their forms of battle rang'd,
How quick they wheel'd, and flying behind them shot
Sharp sleet of arrowy showers against the face
Of their pursuers, and overcame by flight ;
The field all iron cast a gleaming brown :
Nor wanted clouds of foot, nor on each horn
Cuirassiers all in steel for standing fight,
Chariots or elephants endors'd with towers
Of archers, nor of lab'ring pioneers
A multitude with spades and axes arm'd
To lay hills plain, fell woods, or valleys fill,
Or where plain was, raise hill, or overlay
With bridges rivers proud, as with a yoke ;
Mules after these, camels and dromedaries,
And wagons fraught with utensils of war.
   Such forces met not, nor so wide a camp,
When Agrican with all his northern powers
Besieg'd Albracca, as romances tell,
The city of Gallaphorne, from whence to win
The fairest of her sex Angelica
His daughter, sought by many prowest knights

9*

Both Paynim, and the peers of Charlemagne:
Such and so numerous was their chivalry."

Agrican with all his northern powers, &c.—This and
the five following lines furnish a comparison between
some fictitious army and that of Parthia. Charlemagne
was Emperor of the Franks, since called the French, and
a great promoter of the civilization of Europe. He lived
A. D. 800, but the French romance writers composed
many fictions concerning his achievements, and to one
of these Milton refers in this place.

Prowest knights.—Courageous and strong knights.

Paynim.—Pagan.

ROME.

Milton had been at Rome. Her ruins still testify her
former magnificence, and he doubtless felt all that the
contemplation of her departed glory inspires. The time
he describes was in the reign of Tiberius, the successor of
Augustus. The city of Rome had been increasing in
riches and splendour for eight centuries, and for three of
these centuries the Roman arms had been carried beyond
the limits of Italy. The commerce of Rome extended
from Britain to India; and the inhabitants of this vast
metropolis, computed to be several millions, consisted,
like Jerusalem, of *every nation under heaven,* that is, of
people from all countries then civilized. This is suffi-
ciently plain from the animated description given of Rome
by Milton :

" He brought our Saviour to the western side
Of that high mountain, whence he might behold
Another plain, thence in the midst
Divided by a river, of whose banks
On each side an imperial city stood,
With tow'rs and temples proudly elevate
On sev'n small hills, with palaces adorn'd,
Porches and theatres, baths, aqueducts,
Statues and trophies, and triumphal arcs,

Gardens and groves presented to his eyes,
Above the height of mountains interpos'd.
  The city which thou seest no other deem
Than great and glorious Rome, queen of the earth
So far renown'd, and with the spoils enrich'd
Of nations; there the capitol thou seest
Above the rest lifting his stately head
On the Tarpeian rock, her citadel
Impregnable; and there mount Pálatine,
Th' imperial palace, compass huge and high
The structure, skill of noblest architects,
With gilded battlements, conspicuous far,
Turrets and terraces, and glitt'ring spires:
Many a fair edifice besides, more like
Houses of God, thou may'st behold
Outside and inside both, pillars and roofs,
Carv'd work, the hand of fam'd artificers
In cedar, marble, ivory, or gold.
  Thence to the gates cast round thine eye, and see
What conflux issuing forth, or ent'ring in,
Pretors, proconsuls to their provinces
Hasting, or to return, in robes of state;
Lictors and rods, the ensigns of their power,
Legions and cohorts, turms of horse and wings;
Or embassies from regions far remote,
In various habits on the Appian road,
Or on th' Emilian, some from farthest south,
Syene, and where the shadow both way falls,
Meroe Nilotic isle, and more to west,
The realm of Bocchus to the Black-moor sea;
From th' Asian kings and Parthian among these,
From India and the golden Chersonese,
And utmost Indian isle Taprobane,
Dusk faces with white silken turbans wreath'd
From Gallia, Gades, and the British west,
Germans and Scythians, and Sarmatians north
Beyond Danubius to the Tauric pool.
  All nations now to Rome obedience pay,
To Rome's great Emperor, whose wide domain

In ample territory, wealth and power,
Civility of manners, arts and arms,
And long renown, thou justly may'st prefer
Before the Parthian; these two thrones except,
The rest are barb'rous, and scarce worth the sight,
Shar'd among petty kings too far remov'd;
These having shown thee, I have shown thee all
The kingdoms of the world, and all their glory."

The reader who has been instructed in history, knows that this splendour has in the course of years passed away, and that though travellers still resort to Rome for the gratification of curiosity, yet the monuments of its former greatness form the present attraction to it. Under the Emperors, such bloody civil wars raged at Rome, that it became an unsafe and unhappy residence; the arts of peace were neglected, and its population insensibly diminished. The Goths and other barbarians devastated the empire; and in A. D. 476 Rome was abandoned its by last Emperor. Then Genseric and Alaric, two barbarian generals, with their infatuated armies, took and ravaged the city of the Cæsars. But they did not entirely demolish it—it ever retained its name, and after its conquerors grew weary of destruction, civilization sprung up from its ashes.

In A. D. 800 Charlemagne, who included Italy in his dominions, yielded the city to the *Pope*, formerly the Bishop of Rome. From that time Rome became the capital of a new dominion—that of the Catholic religion; and the fine arts of painting, sculpture, and architecture, have attained to high perfection in modern Rome. Still Rome continually decays, and its present population little exceeds 100,000. Mr. Pope describes Rome thus:

" See the wild waste of all-devouring years!
  How Rome her own sad sepulchre appears,
  With nodding arches, broken temples spread
  The very tombs now vanish'd like their dead!
  Imperial wonders rais'd on nations spoil'd,
  Where mix'd with slaves the groaning martyr toil'd:

Huge theatres, that now unpeople'd woods,
Now drain'd a distant country of her floods :
Fanes, which admiring gods with pride survey ;
Statues of men scarce less alive than they !
Some felt the silent stroke of mould'ring age,
Some hostile fury, some religious rage.
Barbarian blindness, Christian zeal conspire,
And Papal piety, and Gothic fire.
Perhaps, by its own ruins sav'd from flame,
Some buried marble half preserves a name ;
That name the learn'd with fierce disputes pursue,
And give to Titus old Vespasian's due."

*Barbarian blindness, Christian zeal conspire,
And Papal piety, and Gothic fire.——*

These several causes contributed to the destruction of
Rome.   The Goths with undiscerning fury, burnt, bat-
tered down, and buried many beautiful works of ancient
arts ; and the Catholic Christians, finding among the
buildings of Rome many heathen temples and many
statues of ancient gods and heroes, thought it their duty
to destroy those remains of Paganism.

Some buried marble half preserves a name.

It has become desirable among the curious and the
learned to recover and identify as much as possible of
the buried sculpture of ancient Rome.   Much of this has
been disinterred, and many disputes among connoisseurs
have originated in the doubtful character of these mar-
bles.

The most animated and touching commemoration of
ruined Rome is by Lord Byron.   This great poet visited
that city within a few years of this time, and his imagina-
tion, saddened in all its views by affliction, has formed a
most striking picture of the desolation of that great
Babylon.——

"Oh Rome! my country! city of the soul!
  The orphans of the heart must turn to thee,
  Lone mother of dead empires! and control
  In their shut breasts their petty misery.
  What are our woes and sufferance? come and see
  The cypress, hear the owl, and plod your way
  O'er steps of broken thrones and temples, Ye!
  Whose agonies are evils of a day—
A world is at our feet as fragile as our clay.

  The Niobe of nations! there she stands,
  Childless and crownless, in her voiceless wo;
  An empty urn within her wither'd hands,
  Whose holy dust was scatter'd long ago;
  The Scipios' tomb contains no ashes now;
  The very sepulchres lie tenantless
  Of their heroic dwellers: dost thou flow,
  Old Tiber! through a marble wilderness?
Rise, with thy yellow-waves, and mantle her distress.

  The Goth, the Christian, Time, War, Flood, and Fire,
  Have dealt upon the seven-hill'd city's pride;
  She saw her glories star by star expire,
  And up the steep barbarian monarchs ride,
  Where the car climb'd the capitol; far and wide
  Temple and tower went down, nor left a site:—
  Chaos of ruins! who shall trace the void,
  O'er the dim fragments cast a lunar light,
And say, 'here was, or is,' where all is doubly night?

  The double night of ages, and of her,
  Night's daughter, Ignorance, hath wrapt and wrap
  All round us; we but feel our way to err:
  The ocean hath his chart, the stars their map,
  And Knowledge spreads them in her ample lap;
  But Rome is as the desert, where we steer
  Stumbling o'er recollections; now we clap
  Our hands, and cry 'Eureka!' it is clear—
When but some false mirage of ruin rises near.

Alas! the lofty city! and alas!
The trebly hundred triumphs! and the day
When Brutus made the dagger's edge surpass
The conqueror's sword in bearing fame away!
Alas, for Tully's voice, and Virgil's lay,
And Livy's pictur'd page!—but these shall be
Her resurrection; all beside—decay.
Alas, for Earth, for never shall we see
That brightness in her eye she bore when Rome was free!"

The Niobe of nations.—This metaphor alludes to a well-known classical fable. Niobe, a princess of Lydia, had twelve beautiful children, six sons and six daughters. Latona, the mother of Diana and Apollo, had only those two children, but Niobe boasted that herself and her beautiful children were more proper objects of worship than Latona and her children. To punish this insolence, Apollo and Diana destroyed Niobe's sons and daughters; and Niobe, overwhelmed by her misfortune, was changed to stone, and became the source of a rivulet. This account of Niobe is taken from Homer. Achilles, in the twenty-fourth book of the Iliad, says to Priam, who is mourning the death of his son Hector,

"But now the peaceful hours of sacred night
Demand refection, and to rest invite :
Nor thou, O father! thus consum'd with wo,
The common cares that nourish life, forego.
Not thus did Niobe, of form divine,
A parent once, whose sorrows equall'd thine :
Six youthful sons, as many blooming maids,
In one sad day beheld the Stygian shades ;
These by Apollo's silver bow were slain,
Those, Cynthia's arrows stretch'd upon the plain.
So was her pride chastis'd by wrath divine,
Who match'd her own with bright Latona's line ;
But two the goddess, twelve the queen enjoy'd ;
Those boasted twelve th' avenging two destroy'd.

Steep'd in their blood, and in the dust outspread,
Nine days neglected lay expos'd the dead ;
None by to weep them, to inhume them none ;
(For Jove had turn'd the nation all to stone :)
The gods themselves at length relenting gave
Th' unhappy race the honours of a grave,
Herself a rock (for such was heaven's high will,)
Thro' deserts wild now pours a weeping rill ;
Where round the bed whence Achelöus springs,
The wat'ry fairies dance in mazy rings,
There high on Sypalus his shaggy brow,
She stands her own sad monument of wo ;
The rock for ever lasts, the tears for ever flow."

Mirage, an optical illusion which occurs in sandy deserts. The distant sands assume the appearance of water to the eye of the thirsty traveller, and he fancies that he shall be refreshed, but as he approaches the supposed waves he is cruelly undeceived. In the same manner, the poet supposes that a traveller who should seek in modern Rome for some object of which he has read in works of antiquity, would be as much deceived in imagining he had got sight of it as the traveller in the desert is deceived by the *mirage.*

The last stanza, from Lord Byron, laments the intellectual degeneracy of modern Rome, where no patriot like Brutus, no orator like Cicero, no poet like Virgil, no historian like Livy, now exists. Yet, the poet intimates that the spirit of these immortal minds yet lives, and may still revive the genius of liberty which has been stifled by the influences of despotism and superstition.

In describing the glories of the world, to disregard a place where the human mind had attained the highest perfection, and where the arts had flourished for ages, would have been an oversight not at all characteristic of the pervading intelligence which comprehended the various genius of them all. Therefore, before he descends from the mount of observation, the tempter stops awhile to point out the distinguishing genius of Athens. That city had then for two centuries been under the dominion of Rome, but her language, her monuments, her traditions, and many of her institutions still existed; and thither the best educated of the Romans resorted to complete their course of study. Milton's verses represent Athens thus:

—————————————————— Behold
Where on the Ægean shore a city stands
Built nobly, pure the air, and light the soil,
Athens the eye of Greece, mother of arts
And eloquence, native to famous wits
Or hospitable, in her sweet recess,
City or suburban, studious walks and shades;
See there the olive grove of Academe,
Plato's retirement, where the Attic bird
Trills her thick-warbled notes the summer long.
There flowery hill Hymettus with the sound
Of bees' industrious murmur oft invites
To studious musing; there Ilissus rolls
His whisp'ring stream; within the wall then view
The schools of ancient sages; his who bred
Great Alexander to subdue the world,
Lyceum there, and painted Stoa next:
There shalt thou hear and learn the secret power
Of harmony in tones and numbers hit
By voice or hand, and various-measur'd verse,
Æolian charms and Dorian lyric odes,
And his who gave them breath, but higher sung,
Blind Melesigenes thence Homer call'd,
Whose poem Phœbus challeng'd for his own.
Thence what the lofty grave tragedians taught
In chorus or iambick, teachers best
Of moral prudence, with delight receiv'd
In brief sententious precepts, while they treat
Of fate and chance, and change in human life;
High actions and high passions best describing.
Thence to the famous orators repair,
Those ancient, whose resistless eloquence

Wielded at will that fierce democratie,
Shook th' arsenal and fulmin'd over Greece,
To Macedon and Artaxerxes' throne.
    To sage philosophy next lend thine ear,
From heav'n descended to the low-rooft house
Of Socrates; see there his tenement,
Whom well inspir'd the oracle pronounc'd
Wisest of men; from whose mouth issued forth
Mellifluous streams that water'd all the schools
Of academics, old and new, with those
Sirnam'd Peripatetics, and the sect
Epicurean, and the Stoic severe.

    The poets, orators, and philosophical schools of Athens
are only mentioned here. Æschylus, Sophocles, and
Euripides were the grave tragedians—*teachers best of
moral prudence.* The challenge of Phœbus means that
Homer's poetry was declared by some to be that of Apol-
lo himself. *Æolian charms and Dorian lyric odes,* al-
ludes to different measures and dialects of Greek poetry.
He, *who bred great Alexander,* was the philosopher Aris-
totle. The chief of the thundering *orators,* was De-
mosthenes, who exhorted his countrymen, by the most
powerful eloquence, to resist Philip of Macedon; and
Socrates was so pure, humble, and powerful a moralist,
that he has sometimes been compared with the founder
of our religion.

COMUS.

    Among the ancients, Comus was the god of low plea-
sures—of those noisy and foolish frolics which are suit-
ed to night rather than to day, and which some ignorant
and intemperate people delight in. Milton's Masque
of Comus is a beautiful poem: it is founded upon the
supposed power which Comus possesses over the minds
of the pure and wise, and over the weak and sensual.
Milton presumes that when men devote themselves to the
rites of Comus, that is to excessive drinking, and, as the

Gospel says, to " riotous living," they become in reality *beasts*, though they know not that they are thus degraded, but, that if the mind is firm in good principles, it will resist every attraction of vice, and retain its innocence under the strongest temptations. Comus was written in the dramatic form, to be represented by the Earl of Bridgewater's family at Ludlow Castle.

The fable of Comus is this—A beautiful lady, accompanied by her two brothers, is journeying through the *perplexed paths* of a *drear wood*. A spirit from heaven, charged with the care of the young travellers, secretly watches over them, but the brothers for a while are separated from their sister. The lady, in the absence of her brothers, is found by Comus, but she resists all his attractions; and though she is endangered, finally escapes from his snares.

" Comus enters with a charming-rod in one hand, his glass in the other ; with him a rout of monsters, headed like sundry sorts of wild beasts, but otherwise like men and women, their apparel glistering ; they come in making a riotous and unruly noise, with torches in their hands."

The lady hears this noise, but does not see the revellers. She is introduced listening and in doubt, but encouraging herself in her own innocence, and in the gracious protection of the " Supreme Good."

The LADY *enters.*

" This way the noise was, if mine ear be true,
My best guide now ; methought it was the sound
Of riot and ill-managed merriment,
Such as the jocund flute, or gamesome pipe
Stirs up among the loose unletter'd hinds,
When from their teeming flocks, and granges full,
In wanton dance they praise the bounteous Pan,
And thank the gods amiss. I should be loath
To meet the rudeness, and swill'd insolence
Of such late wassailers ; yet O where else
Shall I inform my unacquainted feet

In the blind mazes of this tangled wood?
My brothers, when they saw me wearied out
With this long way, resolving here to lodge
Under the spreading favour of these pines,
Stept, as they said, to the next thicket side
To bring me berries, or such cooling fruit
As the kind hospitable woods provide.
They left me then, when the gray-hooded Even,
Like a sad votarist in Palmer's weed,
Rose from the hindmost wheels of Phœbus' wain,
But where they are, and why they came not back,
Is now the labour of my thoughts :   *   *   *
*   *   *   *   A thousand fantasies
Begin to throng into my memory,
Of calling shapes, and beck'ning shadows dire,
And aëry tongues, that syllable mens' names,
On sands, and shores, and desert wildernesses.
  These thoughts may startle well, but not astound
The virtuous mind, that ever walks attended
By a strong siding champion, conscience.——
O welcome pure-ey'd Faith, white-handed Hope,
Thou hovering angel girt with golden wings,
And thou unblemish'd form of chastity ;
I see ye visibly, and now believe
That he, the Supreme Good, t' whom all things ill
Are but as slavish officers of vengeance,
Would send a glist'ring guardian if need were
To keep my life and honour unassail'd.
  Was I deceiv'd, or did a sable cloud
Turn forth her silver lining on the night?
I did not err, there does a sable cloud
Turn forth her silver lining on the night,
And casts a gleam over this tufted grove.
I cannot hallow to my brothers, but
Such noise as I can make to be heard farthest
I'll venture, for my new enliv'ned spirits
Prompt me ; and they perhaps are not far off.

SONG.

Sweet Echo, sweetest nymph, that liv'st unseen
    Within thy áery shell,
   By slow Meander's margent green,
And in the violet-embroider'd vale,
    Where the love-lorn nightingale
Nightly to thee her sad song mourneth well;
Canst thou not tell me of a gentle pair
    That like thy Narcissus are?
     O if thou have
    Hid them in some flow'ry cave,
     Tell me but where,
Sweet queen of parly, daughter of the sphere,
So may'st thou be translated to the skies,
And give resounding grace to all heav'n's harmonies.

Comus *appears to the lady in the disguise of a shepherd.*

Com. Can any mortal mixture of earth's mould
Breathe such divine, enchanting ravishment?
Sure something holy lodges in that breast,
And with these raptures moves the vocal air
To testify his hidden residence:
How sweetly did they float upon the wings
Of silence, through the empty vaulted night,
At every fall smoothing the raven down
Of darkness till it smil'd! I have oft heard
My mother Circe with the Sirens three,
Amidst the flowery kirtled Naiades
Culling their potent herbs, and baleful drugs.
Who as they sung, would take the prison'd soul,
And lap it in Elysium; Scylla wept,
And chid her barking waves into attention,
And fell Charybdis murmur'd soft applause;
Yet they in pleasing slumber lull'd the sense,
And in sweet madness robb'd it of itself;
But such a sacred, and homefelt delight,
Such sober certainty of waking bliss
I never heard till now. I'll speak to her,
And she shall be my queen. Hail foreign wonder,

10*

Whom certain these rough shades did never breed,
Unless the goddess that in rural shrine
Dwell'st here with Pan, or Silvan, by blest song
Forbidding every bleak unkindly fog
To touch the prosp'rous growth of this tall wood.

Lady. Nay, gentle shepherd, ill is that praise lost
That is address'd to unattending ears;
Not any boast of skill, but extreme shift
How to regain my sever'd company,
Compell'd me to awake the courteous Echo
To give me answer from her mossy couch.

Comus. What chance, good lady, hath bereft you thus?

Lady. Dim darkness and this leafy labyrinth.

Comus. Could that divide you from near-ushering
guides?

Lady. They left me weary on a grassy turf.

Comus. By falsehood, or discourtesy, or why?

Lady. To seek i' th' valley some cool friendly spring.

Comus. And left your fair side all unguarded, Lady?

Lady. They were but twain, and purposed quick return.

Comus. Perhaps forestalling night prevented them.

Lady. How easy my misfortune is to hit!

Comus. Imports their loss, beside the present need?

Lady. No less than if I should my brothers lose.

Comus. Were they of manly prime, or youthful bloom?

Lady. As smooth as Hebe's their unrazor'd lips.

Comus. Two such I saw what time the labour'd ox
In his loose traces from the furrow came,
And the swinkt hedger at his supper sat;
I saw them under a green mantling vine
That crawls along the side of yon small hill,
Plucking ripe clusters from the tender shoots;
Their port was more than human, as they stood:
I took it for a faëry vision
Of some gay creatures of the element,
That in the colours of the rainbow live,
And play i' th' plighted clouds. I was awe-struck,
And as I pass'd, I worship'd; if those you seek,

It were a journey like the path to Heaven,
To help you find them.
  Lady. ————————— Gentle Villager,
What readiest way would bring me to that place ?
  Comus. Due west it rises from this shrubby point.
  Lady. To find out that, good Shepherd, I suppose,
In such a scant allowance of star-light,
Would overtask the best land-pilot's art,
Without the sure guess of well-practis'd feet.
  Comus. I know each lane, and every alley green,
Dingle, or bushy dell of this wild wood,
And every bosky bourn from side to side,
My daily walks and ancient neighbourhood ;
And if your stray-attendance be yet lodg'd,
Or shroud within these limits, I shall know
Ere morrow wake, or the low-roosted lark
From her thatch'd pallet rouse ; if otherwise
I can conduct you, Lady, to a low
But loyal cottage, where you may be safe
Till further quest.
  Lady. ————Shepherd, I take thy word,
And trust thy honest offer'd courtesy,
Which oft is sooner found in lowly sheds
With smoky rafters, than in tap'stry halls
And courts of princes, where it first was nam'd,
And yet is most pretended : in a place
Less warranted than this, or less secure,
I can not be, that I should fear to change it.
Eye me, blest Providence, and square my trial
To my proportion'd strength. Shepherd, lead on."

  Milton has been accused as being deficient in respect
to the female character. He speaks of Eve, in regard
to Adam, as " not equal," and seems to consider her as
not altogether worthy to discourse with the angel who
came from Heaven to Paradise. But nothing can sur-
pass the delicacy and elevation of sentiment with which
he represents the Lady in Comus, nor does he seem to

consider her as a solitary instance of the excellence and loveliness peculiar to her sex.

The celestial Spirit who attends the brothers and their sister, distinguishes between those low-minded beings, all whose thoughts are limited to this world, and that superior order,

> " ———that by due steps aspire
> To lay their just hands on that golden key
> That opes the palace of Eternity :——
> *To such my errand is*"——

says he. And the Lady's brothers, when they have left her, are relieved of their natural apprehensions for her safety, by the conviction of her exalted purity. One of them says——

> " My sister is not so defenceless left
> As you imagine ; she has a hidden strength
> Which you remember not.
> *   *   *   *   *   *   *
> So dear to Heav'n is saintly chastity,
> That when a soul is found sincerely so,
> A thousand liveried Angels lacky her,
> Driving far off each thing of sin and guilt,
> And in clear dream and solemn vision,
> Tell her of things that no gross ear can hear,
> Till oft converse with heav'nly habitants
> Begin to cast a beam on th' outward shape,
> The unpolluted temple of the mind,
> And turn it by degrees to the soul's essence,
> Till all be made immortal."

Circe——the mother of Comus, was an enchantress who inhabited an island of the Mediterranean, and who, like her son, transformed her associates to brutes.

The Syrens three——were females who inhabited a small island near Sicily. They charmed mariners by their delightful voices, and made them delay their voyage.

Scylla wept.——Scylla was a female who was transformed to a monster by the arts of Circe, and was fixed to the strait of Messina. A whirlpool on the coast opposite to Scylla was *Charybdis.*

Naiades. Young and beautiful virgins who presided over rivers and fountains.

Echo, sweetest nymph.——Echo is the return of sound—but the mythology supposes that Echo is the voice of a female, who, as a punishment for loquacity, is invisible, and only permitted to repeat the words of others. *Narcissus* was a beautiful youth whom Echo loved.

Meander—was a river of Asia Minor, remarkable for its winding course.

Pan and Sylvan—were wood gods.

Hebe—a youthful goddess, very beautiful. Canova's statue of Hebe is among the most admired works of that artist.

DRYDEN.

This eminent poet was born in 1631, and died in 1700. His poetry is not of a character to interest the young, but the passages inserted among these specimens serve to illustrate the manners of a past age, and therefore properly belong to a collection of poetry which is intended not merely to contain *verses*, but also to exhibit facts that are connected with the poetry of the English language.

TOURNAMENTS.

Chivalry went out of use because the laws in Europe were improved by the increasing knowledge and good sense of the people. When the order of government and the authority of the laws were generally understood and acknowledged in England, the rights of all people were no longer defended by the strife of arms, but were settled by courts of justice, and all ranks of the nation learned to respect each other. The English barons first disputed the arbitrary power of the kings, and the people learned from their example to consider themselves *men ;* and all classes in society, because they knew better, left off preying upon their weaker neighbours. The English nobility, when fighting began to be less needed as a defence, began to take care of their estates, and at length they gave up the military service of the vassals, who continued peaceable labourers upon the grounds of the landholders. The laws and the public opinion no longer permitted men to take up arms except in the service of the state, when the Parliament and the king should order them to do so.

The evils which had disturbed society, for the want of knowledge, and the want of laws properly administered, ceased to exist ; but the amusements and public spectacles which had been connected with Chivalry, though Chivalry no longer continued as the profession of gentlemen, still interested people. The most memorable of the exhibitions connected with Chivalry, was the Tournament, or Passage of Arms. This was a trial of strength and skill at the various exercises which the

Knights-errant and gentlemen-soldiers had practised in actual warfare. The Tournament was usually held by the desire of some prince or distinguished nobleman, and was practiced in France and England. The novel of Ivanhoe gives a delightful description of a *tournament* held at Ashby in the county of Leicester in England. It may be that this very tournament never took place, but without doubt that interesting relation is a faithful picture of such tournaments as were actually exhibited.

For the purpose of exhibiting the tournament, a smooth surface of ground of considerable extent was chosen, and an oblong square, about a quarter of a mile in length, and an eighth of a mile in breadth, was enclosed by palisades, —gates at the opposite ends of this enclosure admitted the combatants. The tents or pavilions of these Champions were ornamented with flags and pennons—these were of the particular colour which was usually worn by the Knights. " The cords of the tents were of the same colour. Before each pavilion was suspended the shield of the Knight by whom it was occupied, and beside it stood his squire, quaintly disguised as a savage or sylvan man, or in some other fantastic dress, according to the taste of his master, and the character which he was pleased to assume during the game. From the entrance into the lists, a gently sloping passage led up to the platform on which the tents were pitched, and the whole was guarded by men-at-arms."

The whole enclosed space was called the Lists. To regulate the proceedings, and to preserve order, trumpeters, heralds, and armed men were disposed in suitable places within the lists. *To enter the lists,* is a figurative expression still used to signify entering into competition with others in a difficult undertaking.

The Champions were the Challengers—those who defied others to contend with them for the mastery in certain exercises. At the extremity of the lists, opposite to that occupied by the Champions, was a space reserved for such " Knights as might be disposed to enter the lists with the challengers, behind which were placed tents containing refreshments of every kind for their accommodation, with armourers, farriers, and other attendants in readiness to give their services wherever they might be necessary.

" The exterior of the lists was in part occupied by temporary galleries spread with tapestry and carpets, and accommodated with cushions for the convenience of those ladies and nobles who attended the tournament. A narrow space, betwixt these galleries and the lists, gave accommodation for yeomanry and spectators of a better degree than the mere vulgar, and might be compared to the pit of a theatre. The promiscuous multitude arranged themselves upon large banks of turf prepared for the purpose, which, aided by the natural elevation of the ground, enabled them to look over the galleries and obtain a fair view into the lists. Besides the accommodation which these situations afforded, many hundreds perched themselves on the branches of the trees which surrounded the meadow, and even the steeple of the neighbouring church was crowded with spectators."
" Neither duty nor infirmity could keep youth or age from such exhibitions."

A gallery, more distinguished and adorned than the others, was, on these occasions, fitted up for the presiding prince and his retinue ; and opposite to it was another gallery for the accommodation of the most noble and beautiful ladies. From among these the conquering Knight was expected to choose the *fairest*, whose office it was to crown the hero of the day with her own hand—and this lady, after she had been thus distinguished, was considered as the Queen of Love and Beauty. These were

"Such sights as poets dream
On summer eve by haunted stream."

It was assemblies collected upon such brilliant occasions, concerning which Milton wrote, that,

"——— throngs of Knights and barons bold
In weeds of peace high triumphs hold,
And store of ladies with bright eyes
Rain influence, and judge the prize
Of wit or arms, while both contend
To win her grace whom all commend."

Tournaments have been compared to the Olympic games of ancient Greece, but the circumstance of admitting the ladies, and that of clothing the combatants with art and elegance, made the Tournament a far more beautiful spectacle than the contests of Greece.

The design of the combatants at the tournaments was for one of the antagonists to disable the other, either by throwing him from his horse or breaking his lance. The skill which was mutually displayed in managing the horse, and in maintaining a long contest with grace and activity, made these exhibitions very interesting ; and, as it always happened, that for some reason or other, one of the antagonists would, at the commencement of the trial, be preferred to the other, the hopes and fears of his admirers formed great part of the pleasure derived from the exhibition.

The Challengers proposed to others who would come, the Defiance, which means, that they declared their personal dignity and skill in arms superior to any adversary's, unless it should be found upon trial that those who dared to encounter were able to vanquish them.

The number of challengers mentioned in Ivanhoe was five ; the challengers were not to refuse to encounter any that should propose themselves. Any knight who should come might select his antagonist by touching his shield with his lance. If the touch was made with the blunt end of the lance, that intimated that the combat was to be conducted without a designed attack upon the life of either combatant ; but if the shield was touched with the sharp end, it intimated that the Knights were to fight as in actual battle.

"When the Knights present had accomplished their

vow, by each of them breaking five lances, the Prince who should preside at the tournament was to declare the victor in the first day's tourney, who should receive, as prize, a war-horse of exquisite beauty and matchless strength; and in addition to this reward of valour, it was announced he should have the peculiar honour of naming the Queen of Love and Beauty, by whom the prize should be given on the ensuing day.

"It was also announced that on the second day, there should be a general tournament, in which all the Knights present, who were desirous to win praise, might take part; and being divided into two bands of equal numbers, might fight it out manfully, until the signal was given by the Prince to cease the combat. The elected Queen of Love and Beauty was then to crown the Knight whom the Prince should adjudge to have borne himself best in this second day, with a coronet composed of thin gold plate, cut into the shape of a laurel crown. On this second day the knightly games ceased. But on that which followed, feats of archery, of bull-baiting, and other popular amusements, were to be practised for the more immediate amusement of the populace.

"The lists presented a most splendid spectacle. The sloping galleries were crowded with all that was noble, great, wealthy, and beautiful in the country: and the contrast of the various dresses of these dignified spectators, rendered the view as gay as it was rich, while the interior and lower space, filled with the substantial burgesses and yeomen of merry England, formed, in their more plain attire, a dark fringe, or border, around this circle of brilliant embroidery, relieving, and, at the same time, setting off its splendour."

Before the commencement of the tournament the laws which regulated it were proclaimed by a Herald, and order was preserved by men-at-arms, or marshals, who carried battle axes in their hands, and sometimes struck the disorderly with the pommel of their swords.

"The heralds ceased their proclamation with their

usual cry of 'Largesse, largesse, gallant Knights;' and gold and silver pieces were showered on them from the galleries, it being a high point of chivalry to exhibit liberality towards those who were accounted the brightest ornaments of their age.   The bounty of the spectators was acknowledged by the customary shouts of 'Love of Ladies—Death of Champions—Honour to the Generous —Glory to the Brave!'   To which the more humble spectators added their acclamations, and a numerous band of trumpeters the flourish of their martial instruments.   When these sounds had ceased, the heralds withdrew from the lists in gay and glittering procession, and none remained within them save the mashals of the field, who, armed cap-a-pee, sat on horseback, motionless as statues, at the opposite ends of the lists.   Meantime, the enclosed space at the northern extremity of the lists, large as it was, was completely crowded with Knights desirous to prove their skill against the challengers, and, when viewed from the galleries, presented the appearance of a sea of waving plumage, intermixed with glittering helmets, and tall lances, to the extremities of which were, in many cases, attached small pennons of about a span's-breadth, which, fluttering in the air as the breeze caught them, joined with the restless motion of the feathers to add liveliness to the scene.

"At length the barriers were opened, and five Knights, chosen by lot, advanced slowly into the area; a single champion riding in front, and the other four following in pairs."

The foregoing description is borrowed from Ivanhoe: it leaves the tournament at its commencement, but it tells the uninformed what a tournament was.—All that was proclaimed was done.—The strife followed,— some were defeated and some were victorious—some retired from the field covered with blood and wounds, mortified and disgraced; others went off in due time, followed by looks of admiration and acclamations of praise. The crown of that day was the renown of all their days,

and the name of the Knight was not afterwards mention-
ed without that of the field of his glory.   But

> " The Knights are dust,
> And their good swords are rust,"

and all that they did lives only in the page of the poet.
" Their *escutcheons* have long mouldered from the walls
of their castles.   Their castles themselves are but green
mounds and shattered ruins—the place that once knew
them knows them no more—nay, many a race since
theirs has died out and been forgotten in the very land
which they occupied, with all the authority of feudal pro-
prietors and feudal lords.   What then would it avail the
reader to know their names, or the evanescent symbols of
their martial rank!"

Theirs was not true glory.   There is another glory,
the most durable and the most estimable—it is that
which follows great services rendered to mankind by
great goodness and great genius.   That navigator who
gave one half of the world to the other half—that poet
whom Milton calls, " Dear son of memory, great heir of
fame"—those defenders of religion who feared not prin-
cipalities and powers, but counted their lives cheap, so
that they showed the truth and established it; and that
peaceful legislator who gave his name to the wild woods,
and laid the foundation of a state, according to the rules
of the gospel, have all benefited mankind, and inherit
true fame.—One by his immortal pen has sweetened and
gladdened life, and the others by their divers labours,
have relieved men from burthens grievous to be borne.
—They have taken off fetters from the human under-
standing, have given a wider sphere to human intelligence,
and a better direction to human conduct.

As was very natural, the ancient warriors held their
horses in high esteem : they even fancied that this most
beautiful of animals entered into their feelings, and par-
took of their glory or their grief.   The rider would

> "——————————————bestride
> The noble steed as if he felt himself

In his own proper seat.—Look how he leans
To cherish him ; and how the gallant horse
Curves up his stately neck, and bends his head,
As if again to court that gentle touch,
And answer to the voice that praises him."

And upon the spot where his lord might afterwards have been slain or conquered, this faithful animal would sometimes be found,

"——————————his silver mane
Sprinkled with blood, which hung on every hair
Aspersed like dew drops—trembling there he stood
From the toil of battle, and at times sent forth
His tremulous-voice, far echoing wide and shrill,
A frequent anxious cry, with which he seemed
To call the master whom he loved so well,
And who had thus again forsaken him."

These verses of Mr. Southey's describe Orelio, the war-horse of Roderick, the last Gothic king of Spain.

Attachment and admiration for the horse appear to be almost universal. The Hebrew poet, whoever he was, who composed the book of Job, has given a sublime description of the war-horse :

"Hast thou given the horse strength? hast thou clothed his neck with thunder? Canst thou make him afraid as a grasshopper? the glory of his nostrils is terrible. He paweth in the valley, and rejoiceth in his strength : he goeth on to meet the armed men. He mocketh at fear, and is not affrighted ; neither turneth he back from the sword. The quiver rattleth against him, the glittering spear and the shield. He swalloweth the ground with fierceness and rage : neither believeth he tha it is the sound of the trumpet. He saith among the trumpets, Ha, ha ; and he smelleth the battle afar off, the thunder of the captains, and the shouting."

11*

EXTRACT FROM PALAMON AND ARCITE.

"In Athens all was pleasure, mirth and play,
All proper to the spring, and sprightly May.
    Now scarce the dawning day began to spring,
As at a signal given, the streets with clamours ring :
At once the crowd arose ; confus'd and high
E'en from the heav'n was heard a shouting cry.
The neighing of the gen'rous horse was heard,
For battle by the busy groom prepar'd ;
Rustling of harness ; rattling of the shield ;
Clatt'ring of armour, furbish'd for the field.
Crowds, to the castle, mounted up the street,
Batt'ring the pavement with their coursers' feet :
The greedy sight might, there, devour the gold
Of glitt'ring arms, too dazzling to behold :
And polish'd steel that cast the view aside,
And *crested morions*, with their plumy pride.
Knights, with a long retinue of their squires,
In gaudy liv'ries march, and quaint attires.
One lac'd the helm, another held the lance :
A third the shining buckler did advance.
The courser paw'd the ground with restless feet,
And, snorting, foam'd, and champ'd the golden bit.
The smiths and armourers on *palfreys* ride,
Files in their hands, and hammers at their side,
And nails for loosen'd spears, and thongs for shields pro-
        vide.
The *yeomen* guard the streets in seemly bands ;
And clowns come crowding on with cudgels in their
        hands.
    The trumpets, next the gate, in order, plac'd,
Attend the sign to sound the martial blast ;
The palace-yard is fill'd with floating tides.
    *   *   *   *   *   *   *   *
The throng is in the midst : the common crew
Shut out, the hall admits the better few ;
In knots they stand, or in a rank they walk,
Serious in aspect, earnest in their talk :

Factious, and fav'ring this, or t' other side,
As their strong fancy, or weak reason guide :
Their wagers back their wishes ; numbers hold
With the fair-freckled king, and beard of gold :
So vig'rous are his eyes, such rays they cast,
So prominent his eagle's beak is plac'd.
But most their looks on the black monarch bend,
His rising muscles, and his strength commend :
His double-biting axe and *beamy spear*,
Each asking a gigantic force to rear.
All spoke as partial favour mov'd his mind :
And, safe themselves, at others' cost divin'd.
   Wak'd by the cries, th' Athenian chief arose,
The knightly forms of combat to dispose ;
And passing through th' obsequious guards, he sate
Conspicuous on a throne, sublime in state ;
There, for the two contending knights he sent :
Arm'd *cap-a-pee*, with rev'rence low they bent ;
He smil'd on both, and with superior look
Alike their offer'd adoration took.
The people press on every side, to see
Their awful prince, and hear his high decree.
Then signing to the heralds with his hand,
They gave his orders from their lofty stand.
Silence is thrice enjoin'd ; then thus, aloud,
The king-at-arms bespeaks the knights, and listening
    crowd :—
' Our sovereign lord has ponder'd in his mind
The means to spare the blood of gentle kind ;
The keener edge of battle to rebate, '
The troops for honour fighting, not for hate.
He wills, not death should terminate the strife ;
And wounds, should wounds ensue, be short of life :
But issues, ere the fight, his dread command,
That slings afar, and poniards hand to hand,
Be banish'd from the field ; that none shall dare
With shortened swords to stab in closer war ;
But in fair combat fight with manly strength,
Nor push with biting point, but strike at length.

The *tourney* is allow'd but one career,
Of the tough ash, with the sharp-grinded spear ;
But knights unhors'd may rise from off the plain,
And fight on foot, their honour to regain ;
Nor, if at mischief taken, on the ground
Be slain, but pris'ners to the pillar bound,
At either barrier plac'd ; nor (captives made)
Be freed, or arm'd anew the fight invade.
The chief of either side, bereft of life,
Or yielded to his foe, concludes the strife.
Thus dooms the lord : now valiant knights, and young
Fight each his fill, with swords and maces long.'
    The herald ends : the vaulted firmament
With loud acclaims and vast applause is rent :
' Heaven guard a prince so gracious and so good,
So just, and yet so provident of blood !'
This was the general cry.   The trumpets sound ;
And warlike symphony is heard around.
The marching troops through Athens take their way,
The great earl-marshal orders their array.
The fair, from high, the passing pomp behold ;
A rain of flow'rs is from the windows roll'd.
The casements are with golden tissue spread,
And horses' hoofs, for earth, on silken tap'stry tread ;
The king goes midmost, and the rivals ride
In equal rank, and close his either side.
Next after these, there rode the royal wife,
With Emily, *the cause and the reward of strife.*
The following cavalcade, by three and three,
Proceed by titles marshal'd in degree.
Thus through the southern gate they take their way,
And at the list arriv'd ere prime of day.
There, parting from the king, the chiefs divide,
And, wheeling East and West, before their many ride.
Th' Athenian monarch mounts his throne on high,
And, after him, the queen, and Emily :
Next these, the kindred of the crown are grac'd
With nearer seats, and lords by ladies plac'd.

Scarce were they seated, when with clamours loud
In rush'd at once a rude promiscuous crowd.
Now chang'd the jarring noise to whispers low,
As winds forsaking seas more softly blow ;
When at the western gate, on which the car
Is plac'd aloft, that bears the God of War,
Proud Arcite entering arm'd, before his train,
Stops at the barrier, and divides the plain.
Red was his banner, and display'd abroad
The bloody colours of his patron god.*
   At the self moment enters Palamon
The gate of Venus and the rising-sun ;
Wav'd by the wanton winds, his banner flies,
All maiden white, and shares the people's eyes.
From East to West, look all the world around,
Two troops so match'd were never to be found.
   Thus rang'd, the herald for the last proclaims
A silence, while they answer'd to their names :
The tale was just, and then the gates were clos'd ;
And chief to chief, and troop to troop oppos'd.
The heralds last retir'd, and loudly cry'd,
' The fortune of the field be fairly try'd.'
   At this, the challenger, with fierce defy,
His trumpet sounds, the challeng'd makes reply :
With clangor rings the field, resounds the vaulted sky.
Their visors clos'd, their lances in the rest,
Or at the helmet pointed, or the crest ;
They vanish from the barrier, speed the race,
And, spurring, see decrease the middle space.
   Full oft the rivals met ; and neither spar'd
His utmost force ; and each forgot to ward.
Both were by turns unhors'd ; the jealous blows
Fall thick and heavy, when on foot they close.
So deep their faulchions bite, that every stroke
Pierc'd to the quick; and equal wounds they gave and
   took.
   So when a tiger sucks the bullock's blood,

* Mars.

The swains come arm'd between, and both to distance
    drive.
   At length, as fate foredoom'd, and all things tend
By course of time to their appointed end ;
The strong Emetrius came in Arcite's aid,
And Palamon with odds was overlaid,
Unyielded as he was, and to the pillar bound.
   The royal judge, on his tribunal plac'd,
Who had beheld the fight from first to last,
Bade, ' Cease the war ;' pronouncing, from on high,
' Arcite of Thebes had won the beauteous Emily.'
The sound of trumpets to the voice reply'd,
And round the royal lists the heralds cry'd,
' Arcite of Thebes has won the beauteous bride.'
   The people rend the skies with vast applause ;
All own the chief, when fortune owns the cause."

———

The preceding verses nearly agree with the description of a tournament, taken from Ivanhoe. Dryden's scene of the tournament is Athens. Whether such a spectacle was ever exhibited there, is doubtful ; but the earlier English poets did not regard *local probability*, which, according to the present practice of writers of prose or poetic fable, is become indispensable. A few of the expressions used in this description may not be readily understood.

Crested morions, with their plumy pride.—The morion was the cap worn by the Knights, adorned with a plume, and expressing in its appearance something of the dignity of the wearer.

Their squires in gaudy liveries march.—Livery is a dress appropriated to a particular order of persons. In modern times, the dress of men-servants appertaining to a gentleman's family coach, is called *livery*, and is usually only a red, blue, or yellow edging to the cape and cuffs of the man's coat.

Palfreys, travelling horses, of mettle and appearance inferior to the war-horse.

Yeomen, soldiers employed as guards and attendants. The rank of the subordinate persons engaged in the private warfare of the middle ages is very clearly displayed in the first Canto of Scotts' Lay :

" Nine and twenty *Knights* of fame
   Hung their shields in Branksome hall ;
Nine and twenty *squires* of name
   Brought them their steeds from bower to stall ;
   Nine and twenty *Yeoman* tall
   Waited duteous on them all.
—————————————————*Numbers* hold
With the *fair freckled King,* &c.
But *most* their looks on the *black monarch* bend.

These lines express the *party feeling* with which the heroes of the tournaments was regarded. It has been remarked, that at the commencement of the exercises, the spectators usually gave the preference to one or other of the combatants.

His double-biting axe and beamy spear,
Each asking a gigantic force to rear.

The beamy spear, expresses the high polish of the spear's point, which reflected the *beams* or rays of light in every direction. The weight of these arms required a *gigantic force* to lift them. It appears that the active and self denying habits of the Knights gave them extraordinary strength.

Armed *cap-a-pee*—from head to foot.

King-at-Arms.—An officer employed in ancient pageants to announce the pleasure of the presiding prince in respect to the order of the ceremonies. The king-at-arms here declares it is the sovereign's will that dangerous weapons *be banished from the field,* and that the strife shall spare the lives of those engaged in it. The combatants seldom had sufficient forbearance to observe this prohibition ; and at length, in consequence of the numbers killed in them, the Popes suppressed tournaments altogether.

The tourney, the trial of horsemanship. The dismounted Knight was not allowed to repeat the *tourney*, but might *fight on foot, his honour to regain.*

————*The western gate, on which the car*
Is plac'd aloft, that bears the god of war.

The *gates* which Dryden here describes are adorned with sculpture. Over the *western gate* is the car of Mars and its terrible master; the eastern gate—that of *the rising sun*—was embellished by the beautiful figure of Venus.

BOADICEA.

Boadicea was queen of the Iceni, a tribe of native Britons. When the Romans invaded Britain, they did not at once achieve the conquest of that Island. A. D. 60, Boadicea, among other of the native princes, resisted the Roman arms, but fighting at the head of her subjects, she fell into the hands of the enemy. The Romans beat her, and treated her with the most cruel indignities, so that at last in her despair she put an end to her existence. Cowper's verses which follow, describe her, some time before her defeat, resorting for direction in her holy purpose of preserving her people from their invaders, to a Druid, one of the priests of her religion; and though the venerable man could not promise her the deliverance she sought, he predicted for her consolation the downfal of the Roman, and the exaltation of the British power.

"When the British warrior queen,
  Bleeding from the Roman rods,
Sought with an indignant mien,
  Counsel of her country's gods.

Sage beneath the spreading oak
  Sat the Druid, hoary chief;
Ev'ry burning word he spoke
  Full of rage, and full of grief.

Princess! if our aged eyes
  Weep upon thy matchless wrongs,

'Tis because resentment ties
  All the terrors of our tongues.

Rome shall perish—write that word
  In the blood that she has spilt ;
Perish, hopeless and abhorr'd,
  Deep in ruins as in guilt.

Rome, for empire far renown'd,
  Tramples on a thousand states ;
Soon her pride shall kiss the ground—
  Hark ! the Gaul is at her gates !

Other Romans shall arise,
  Heedless of a soldier's name ;
Sounds, not *arms*, shall win the prize,
  Harmony the path to fame.

Then the progeny that springs
  From the forests of *our* land,
Arm'd with thunder, clad with wings,
  Shall a wider world command.

Regions Cæsar never knew
  Thy posterity shall sway ;
Where his eagles never flew,
  None invincible as they.

Such the bard's prophetic words,
  Pregnant with celestial fire,
Bending as he swept the chords
  Of his sweet but awful lyre.

She, with all a monarch's pride,
  Felt them in her bosom glow :
Rush'd to battle, fought, and died :
  Dying hurl'd them at the foe.

Ruffians, pitiless as proud,
  Heav'n awards the vengeance due ;
Empire is on us bestow'd,
  Shame and ruin wait for you.

12

Sounds, not arms, shall win the prize—
Harmony the path to fame.

Modern Italy exhibits none of the martial spirit, or political wisdom of ancient Rome; but in place of the elevated sentiments and great actions recorded of the former inhabitants of Italy, its children of our days are distinguished, as much as for any thing, by their excellence in music. This species of excellence, being attended with absolute deficiency in the spirit of liberty, of improvement, and the sentiment of national dignity, is considered by the poet as a mark of degeneracy.

Regions Cæsar never knew
Thy posterity shall sway.

This passage intimates the establishment of the British empire in America.—The empire of the laws, language, and literature of Britain, established in a new world, and under an independent government among the remote descendants of the ancient Britons.

THE DRUIDS.

The Druids were priests among the Britons, and were exterminated by the Romans. "The religion of the Britons was one of the most considerable parts of their government; and the Druids, who were the guardians of it, possessed great authority among them. No species of superstition was ever more terrible than theirs; besides the severe penalties which they were permitted to inflict in this world, they inculcated the doctrine of transmigration of souls, and thus extended their authority as far as the fears of their votaries. They sacrificed human victims, which they burned in large wicker idols, made so capacious as to contain a multitude of persons at once, who were thus consumed together. To these rites, tending to impress ignorance with awe, they added the austerity of their manners, and the simplicity of their lives. They lived in woods, caves, and hollow trees; acorns and berries constituted their general food, and their usual beverage was water. By these arts they were not only respected, but almost adored by the people."

The sacrifice of human victims implies a horrible religious faith, but it does not appear to be wholly inconsistent with fine qualities of mind and heart. The sacrifice of Jephtha's daughter, mentioned in the Hebrew scriptures, and that of Iphigenia by the Greeks, were induced by false notions of God. To give him the dearest of our possessions, may seem to ignorant men the most acceptable service, and those who were capable of such acts, often entertained sentiments of true devotion and humanity. The Druids worshipped in the open air; and there still remain in England, circles of stones laid upon the surface of the ground, which, it is supposed, enclosed their sanctuaries. The oak was their favourite tree, and the misletoe, a parasitic plant, or one which grows upon trees, was used in their rites, and respected as a symbol of their faith. Some of the English poets regard the character of the Druids as that of simple-hearted and uncorrupted men, fond of contemplating the works of God.

"In yonder grave a *Druid* lies,"

says the poet Collins, of Thomson, the author of the Seasons—meaning by this expression to suggest the idea of Thomson's well-known character—that of a man who saw in God the "parent of good," and who considered the "universal frame" of creation as the dwelling place of infinite loveliness and beneficence.

Mr. Mason, a clergyman of the church of England, and an intimate friend of the poet Gray, wrote a drama called Caractacus. Caractacus was the last of the British princes who resisted the Romans, but in the reign of the Emperor Claudius, he was made their prisoner, and carried to Rome. About the same time the Romans, though they generally permitted all their conquered subjects to enjoy their accustomed religion, abolished the worship of the Druids. The practice of the Druids of offering human sacrifices, made it right that their rites should be annihilated.

In Caractacus, Mr. Mason describes that unfortunate king as taking refuge in the sacred groves of the Druids, and being forced thence by the Roman soldiers.   Mona, an island in the Irish sea, was the principal sanctuary of the Druids.

OPENING SCENE OF CARACTACUS.

Aulus Didius, a Roman officer with Romans.

Scene, Mona.

Au. Did. This is the secret centre of the isle:
Here, Romans, pause, and let the eye of wonder
Gaze on the solemn scene ; behold yon oak,
How stern he frowns, and with his broad brown arms
Chills the pale plain beneath him: mark yon altar,
The dark stream brawling round its rugged base,
These cliffs, these yawning caverns, this wide circus, ·
Skirted with unhewn stone: they awe my soul,
As if the very genius of the place
Himself appear'd, and with terrific tread
Stalk'd through his drear domain.   And yet, my friends,
(If shapes like his be but the fancy's coinage)
Surely there is a hidden power, that reigns
'Mid the lone majesty of untam'd nature,
Controlling sober reason ; tell me else,
Why do these haunts of barb'rous superstition
O'ercome me thus? I scorn them, yet they awe me.

Enter VELLINUS *and* ELIDURUS.

Ye pledges dear of Cartismandua's faith,
Approach! and to mine uninstructed ear
Explain this scene of horror.
  Elid.   Daring Roman,
Know that thou stand'st on consecrated ground :
These mighty piles of magic-planted rock,
Thus rang'd in mystic order, mark the place
Where but at times of holiest festival
The Druid leads his train.
  Aul. Did.   Where dwells the seer ?
  Vel. In yonder shaggy cave ; on which the moon

Now sheds a side-long gleam.   His brotherhood
Possess the neighb'ring cliffs.

   Aul. Did.   Yet up the hill
Mine eye descries a distant range of caves,
Delv'd in the ridges of the craggy steep ;
And this way still another.

   Eld.   On the left
Beside the sages skill'd in nature's lore :
The changeful universe, its numbers, powers,
Studious they measure, save when meditation
Gives place to holy rites : then in the grove
Each hath his rank and function.   Yonder grots
Are tenanted by Bards, who nightly thence,
Rob'd in their flowing vests of innocent white,
Descend, with harps that glitter to the moon,
Hymning immortal strains.   The spirits of air,
Of earth, of water, nay of heav'n itself,
Do listen to their lay ; and oft, 'tis said,
In visible shapes dance they a magic round
To the high minstrelsy.——Now, if thine eye
Be sated with the view, haste to thy ships,
And ply thine oars ; for, if the Druids learn
This bold intrusion, thou wilt find it hard
To foil their fury.

   Aul. Did.   Prince, I did not moor
My light-arm'd shallops on this dangerous strand
To soothe a fruitless curiosity ;
I come in quest of proud Caractacus ;
Who, when our veterans put his troops to flight,
Found refuge here.

   Elid.   If here the monarch rests,
Presumptuous chief! thou might'st as well essay
To pluck him from yon stars : Earth's ample range
Contains no surer refuge : underneath
The soil we tread, a hundred secret paths,
Scoop'd through the living rock in winding maze,
Lead to as many caverns, dark, and deep :
In which the hoary sages act their rites
Mysterious, rites of such strange potency,

As, done in open day, would dim the sun,
Though thron'd in noontide brightness.   In such dens
He may for life lie hid.

Vellinus and Elidurus were sons of a British Princess, Cartismandua, who had been subdued by the Romans; she had delivered her sons to the Romans as *hostages*—that is, as security, that she would fulfil her promises of continued submission to the conquerors.   The Roman officer to whom the British youths are intrusted, promises them their liberty on condition that they will discover to him the retreat of the Druids; and, corrupted by this tempting offer, they introduce the stranger into their secret haunts, in which Caractacus and his daughter Evelina had taken refuge.

CAPTURE OF CARACTACUS.

Aulus Didius bursts into the sanctuary of the Druids, with Vellinus, Elidurus, and soldiers.

Druid, Evelina, Bard, and *Caractacus.*

Aul. Did.   Ye bloody priests,
Behold we burst on your infernal rites,
And bid you pause.   Instant restore our soldiers,
Nor hope that superstition's ruthless step
Shall wade in Roman gore.   Ye savage men,
Did not our laws give licence to all faiths,
We would o'erturn your altars, headlong heave
These shapeless symbols of your barbarous gods,
And let the golden sun into your caves.
Druid. Servant of Cæsar, has thine impious tongue
Spent the black venom of its blasphemy?
It has.   Then take our curses on thine head,
E'en his fell curses, who doth reign in Mona,
Vicegerent of those gods thy pride insults.
Aul. Did. Bold priest, I scorn thy curses, and thyself.
Soldiers, go search the caves, and free the prisoners.
Take heed, ye seize Caractacus alive.

Arrest yon youth; load him with heaviest irons,
He shall to Cæsar answer for his crime.

Elid. I stand prepar'd to triumph in my crime.

Aul Did. 'Tis well, proud boy—Look to the beaute-
ous maid, [*To the soldiers.*
That tranc'd in grief, bends o'er yon bleeding corse—
Respect her sorrows.

Evel.   Hence, ye barbarous men,
Ye shall not take him welt'ring thus in blood,
To show at Rome, what British virtue was.
Avaunt! the breathless body that ye touch
Was once Arviragus!

Aul. Did.   Fear us not, princess,
We reverence the dead.

Druid.   Would too to Heav'n,
Ye reverenc'd the gods but ev'n enough
Not to debase with slavery's cruel chain
Whom they created free.

Aul. Did.   The Romans fight
Not to enslave, but humanize the world.

Druid. Go to, we will not parley with thee, Roman .
Instant pronounce our doom.

Aul. Did.   Hear it, and thank us.
This once our clemency shall spare your groves,
If at our call ye yield the British king:
Yet learn, when next ye aid the foes of Cæsar,
That each old oak, whose solemn gloom ye boast,
Shall bow beneath our axes.

Druid.   Be they blasted,
Whene'er their shade forgets to shelter virtue!

Bard. Mourn, Mona, mourn. Caractacus is captive!
And dost thou smile, false Roman? Do not think
He fell an easy prey. Know, ere he yielded,
Thy bravest veterans bled. He too, thy spy,
The base Brigantian prince, hath seal'd his fraud
With death. Bursting thro' arm'd ranks, that hemm'd
The catiff round, the brave Caractacus
Seiz'd his false throat; and as he gave him death
Indignant thunder'd, "Thus is my last stroke

The stroke of justice." Numbers then opprest him.
I saw the slave, that cowardly behind
Pinion'd his arms; I saw the sacred sword
Writh'd from his grasp : I saw, what now ye see,
Inglorious sight! those barbarous bonds upon him.
   Car. Romans, methinks the malice of your tyrant
Might furnish heavier chains.   Old as I am,
And wither'd as you see these war-worn limbs,
Trust me, they shall support the weightiest load
Injustice dares impose————
               Proud crested soldier, [*To Didius.*
Who seem'st the master-mover in this business,
Say, dost thou read less terror on my brow,
Than when thou met'st me in the fields of war
Heading my nations? No, my free-born soul
Has scorn still left to sparkle through these eyes,
And frown defiance on thee.————Is it thus!
                [*Seeing his son's body.*
Then I'm indeed a captive.   Mighty gods!
My soul, my soul submits : patient it bears
The pond'rous load of grief ye heap upon it.
Yes, it will grovel in this shatter'd breast,
And be the sad tame thing it ought to be,
Coopt in a servile body.
   Aul. Did.   Droop not, king.
When Claudius, the great master of the world,
Shall hear the noble story of thy valour,
His pity————
   Car.   Can a Roman pity, soldier!
And if he can, gods! must a Briton bear it?
Arviragus, my bold, my breathless boy,
Thou hast escap'd such pity; thou art free.
Here in high Mona shall thy noble limbs
Rest in a noble grave; posterity
Shall to thy tomb with annual reverence bring
Sepulchral stones, and pile them to the clouds;
Whilst mine————
   Aul. Did. The morn doth hasten our departure.

Prepare thee, king, to go: a fav'ring gale
Now swells our sails.
    Car.   Inhuman, that thou art!
Dost thou deny a moment for a father
To shed a few warm tears o'er his dead son?
I tell thee, chief, this act might claim a life,
To do it duly; even a longer life,
Than sorrow ever suffer'd.   Cruel man!
And thou deniest me moments.   Be it so.
I know you Romans weep not for your children;
Ye triumph o'er your tears, and think it valour;
I triumph in my tears.————————
————————————Arise, my daughter.————
Weep'st thou, my girl? I prithee hoard thy tears
For the sad meeting of thy captive mother:
For we have much to tell her, much to say
Of these good men who nurtur'd us in Mona;
Much of the fraud and malice, that pursued us;
Much of her son, who pour'd his precious blood
To save his sire and sister: think'st thou, maid,
Her gentleness can hear the tale, and live?
And yet she must.————————
But I'll be mute.   Adieu! ye holy men;
Yet one look more—Now lead us hence for ever.

WARTON.

Born 1728—*Died* 1790.

Dr. Thomas Warton is best known as a poetical anti-quary. He wrote a " History of English Poetry," and by his researches and criticisms turned the attention of English readers in his time from the mere perusal of co-temporary poets to the neglected authors of the fifteenth, sixteenth, and seventeenth centuries. Dr. Warton is not memorable for inventive talent, but he was well acquaint-ed with the earlier British writers, he admired the ancient architecture of his country, and he loved the legends of old romance. " His Crusade, and the Grave of Arthur," says Mr. Campbell, " have a genuine air of martial and minstrel enthusiasm. Those pieces exhibit, to the best advantage, the most striking feature of his poetical character, which was a fondness for the recol-lections of chivalry, and a minute intimacy of imagina-tion with its gorgeous residences, and imposing specta-cles. The spirit of chivalry, he may indeed be said to have revived in the poetry of modern times." But a genius above the reach of Warton's, was destined, in a few years after him, to soar beyond the track in which he first essayed his flights. Those who read the Grave of Arthur, must, in order to enhance their estimation of it, remember that it was written before the Lay of the Last Minstrel ;—but, short as it is, and in all respects inferior to the poetry of Scott, it is interesting as the precursor of a style of poetic composition, which, though ancient in its subjects, is altogether new in its present attractiveness and popularity.

PRINCE ARTHUR.

About the beginning of the sixth century, the Romans, who had been masters of Britain during four hundred years, withdrew from that island, and left the government and defence of the country to its native inhabitants. The northern parts of the island belonged to the Scots and Picts, and these barbarous tribes, soon after the departure of the Romans, invaded and ravaged the more southern territory.

The British were divided into small independent tribes, each governed by its own prince : and these petty sovereigns, in their common danger, had not sufficient wisdom to unite in the common defence ; though, in seasons of imminent danger, they, like the ancient Romans, appointed a Dictator invested with supreme power over the collective forces of the nation. The British Dictator was called the Pendragon. He, however, could not prevent discordant counsels and civil warfare among the inferior chiefs, so that the Saxons, who had come over from Germany as helpers of the Britons, easily subjugated them. According to some historians, though in modern times there are others who deny the existence of such a hero, Arthur, the son of Uther, succeeded his father as Pendragon about the year 517. His history, as generally received, whether it be true or false, is the following.

Arthur, prince of the Silures, in conjunction with other chiefs, his countrymen, resisted the Saxons ; but, though his prowess has been celebrated by poets and romance-writers, he was not successful against the Saxons. Mordred, a powerful British chief, went over to the enemy, and was victorious against Arthur in the battle of Camlan. Arthur, notwithstanding he was once defeated, renewed the war, and many feats of valour are imputed to him ; but, he is said to have been mortally wounded in an engagement with Mordred, and to have died, and been buried at Avalon. The place of his interment is however unknown, and Dr. Warton has founded a pretty poem upon this disputed fact. It is proper here to state, that among the fictions related of Prince Arthur is this, that he created a military order called the Knights of the Round Table. Of his, and their achievements, many marvellous stories are related.

Dr. Warton describes a festival of Henry II. king of England, as he was about embarking for Ireland. Ireland previous to the year 1172 had been divided into five independent kingdoms.   Two kings of Ireland, Dermod and Roderick O'Connor, had a desperate war, and the former came over to England to solicit the interference of Henry II. in his behalf, and Henry availed himself of this strife to include Ireland in his dominions.   He first obtained the gift of that island in a *bull from the Pope,* who in that age claimed the right to dispose of kingdoms; and when Henry went over to Ireland with the Pope's bull, and an army to enforce it, the country was partially surrendered to him.

Henry's army was, as appears by the poem, attended by a company of bards, who entertained the king with their songs.   Just before the embarkation for Ireland, one of the bards is represented as celebrating Prince Arthur, and declaring that the hero had been carried away by the enchanter Merlin, and was destined to reappear at a future time in Britain; but another of the tuneful brethren asserts that no enchanter bore him off the field of battle, and demands of the king to repair to his tomb, and, by some religious services in honour of him, pay homage to his departed glory.

" It was," says Mr. Gray, " the common belief of the Welsh nation, that king Arthur was still alive in Fairyland, and would return and reign again over Britain."

THE GRAVE OF PRINCE ARTHUR.

Stately the feast, and high the cheer:
Girt with many an armed peer,
And canopied with golden pall,
Amid Cilgarran's castle hall,
Sublime in formidable state,
And warlike splendour, Henry sate;
Prepar'd to stain the briny flood
Of Shannon's lakes with rebel blood.
  Illumining the vaulted roof,
A thousand torches flamed aloof:
From massy cups, with golden gleam
Sparkled the red metheglin's stream:

To grace the gorgeous festival,
Along the lofty window'd hall,
The storied tapestry was hung :
With minstrelsy the rafters rung
Of harps, that with reflected light
From the proud gallery glitter'd bright:
While gifted bards, a rival throng,
To crown the banquet's solemn close,
Themes of British glory chose ;
And to the strings of various chime
Attemper'd thus the fabling rhyme.
   " O'er Cornwall's cliffs the tempest roar'd,
High the screaming sea-mew soar'd ;
On Tintaggel's topmost tower
Darksome fell the sleety shower ;
Round the rough castle shrilly sung
The whirling blast, and wildly flung
On each tall rampart's thundering side
The surges of the tumbling tide :
When Arthur rang'd his red-cross ranks
On conscious Camlan's crimson'd banks :
By Mordred's faithless guile decreed
Beneath a Saxon spear to bleed !
Yet in vain a paynim foe
Arm'd with fate the mighty blow ;
For when he fell, an elfin queen,
All in secret, and unseen,
O'er the fainting hero threw
Her mantle of ambrosial blue ;
And bade her spirits bear him far,
In Merlin's agate-axled car,
To her green isle's enamell'd steep,
Far in the bosom of the deep.
O'er his wounds she sprinkled dew
From flowers that in Arabia grew :
On a rich enchanted bed
She pillow'd his majestic head;
O'er his brow, with whispers bland,
Thrice she wav'd an opiate wand ;
13

And to soft music's airy sound,
Her magic curtains clos'd around.
There, renew'd the vital spring,
Again he reigns a mighty king ;
And many a fair and fragrant clime,
Blooming in immortal prime,
By gales of Eden ever fann'd,
Owns the monarch's high command :
Thence to Britain shall return,
(If right prophetic rolls I learn)
Borne on victory's spreading plume,
His ancient sceptre to resume ;
Once more, in old heroic pride,
His barbed courser to bestride ;
His knightly table to restore,
And brave the tournaments of yore."
   They ceas'd : when on the tuneful stage
Advanc'd a bard of aspect sage ;
His silver tresses, thin besprent,
To age a graceful reverence lent ;
His beard all white as spangles frore
That clothe Plinlimmon's forests hoar,
Down to his harp descending flow'd ;
With Time's faint rose his features glow'd ;
His eyes diffus'd a softened fire,
And thus he wak'd the warbling wire.
   " Listen, Henry, to my read !
Not from fairy realms I lead
Bright-rob'd Tradition, to relate
In forged colours Arthur's fate ;
Though much of old romantic lore
On the high theme I keep in store :
But boastful Fiction should be dumb,
Where Truth the strain might best become.
If thine ear may still be won
With songs of Uther's glorious son,
Henry, I a tale unfold,
Never yet in rhyme enroll'd,

Nor sung nor harp'd in hall or bower;
Which in my youth's full early flower,
A minstrel, sprung of Cornish line,
Who spoke of kings from old Locrine,
Taught me to chant, one vernal dawn,
Deep in a cliff-encircled lawn.
" When Arthur bow'd his haughty crest,
No princess, veil'd in azure vest,
Snatch'd him, by Merlin's potent spell,
In groves of golden bliss to dwell;
Where crown'd with wreaths of misletoe,
Slaughter'd kings in glory go:
But when he fell, with winged speed,
His champions, on a milk-white steed,
From the battle's hurricane,
Bore him to Joseph's towered fane,
In the fair vale of Avalon:
There, with chanted orison,
And the long blaze of tapers clear,
The stoled fathers met the bier;
Through the dim aisles, in order dread
Of martial wo, the chief they led,
And deep entomb'd in holy ground,
Before the altar's solemn bound.
Around no dusky banners wave,
No mouldering trophies mark the grave:
Away the ruthless Dane has torn
Each trace that Time's slow touch had worn;
And long, o'er the neglected stone,
Oblivion's veil its shade has thrown:
The faded tomb, with honour due,
'Tis thine, O Henry, to renew!
Thither, when Conquest has restor'd
Yon recreant isle, and sheath'd the sword,
When peace with palm has crown'd thy brows,
Haste thee to pay thy pilgrim vows.
There observant of my lore,
The pavement's hallow'd depth explore;

And thrice a fathom underneath
Dive into the vaults of death.
There shall thine eye, with wild amaze,
On his gigantic stature gaze;
There shalt thou find the monarch laid,
All in warrior-weeds array'd;
Wearing in death his helmet-crown,
And weapons huge of old renown.
Martial prince, 'tis thine to save
From dark oblivion Arthur's grave!
So may thy ships securely stem
The western frith: thy diadem
Shine victorious in the van,
Nor heed the slings of Ulster's clan:
Thy Norman pikemen win their way
Up the dun rocks of Harald's bay:
And from the steeps of rough Kildare
Thy prancing hoofs the falcon scare:
So may thy bow's unerring yew
Its shafts in Roderick's heart imbrue.[27]
   Amid the pealing symphony
The spiced goblets mantled high;
With passions new the song impress'd
The listening king's impatient breast:
Flash the keen lightnings from his eyes;
He scorns awhile his bold emprise;
E'en now he seems, with eager pace,
The consecrated floor to trace,
And ope, from its tremendous gloom,
The treasure of the wondrous tomb:
E'en now he burns in thought to rear,
From its dark bed, the ponderous spear,
Rough with the gore of Pictish kings:
E'en now fond hope his fancy wings,
To poise the monarch's massy blade,
Of magic-temper'd metal made;
And drag to day the dinted shield
That felt the storm of Camlan's field.

O'er the sepulchre profound
E'en now, with arching sculpture crown'd,
He plans the chantry's choral shrine,
The daily dirge, and rites divine.

The treasure of the wondrous tomb, &c.—Henry longed to possess the *spear, sword* and *shield* of Arthur, from a superstitious belief that these relics of a hero would aid him in his warlike enterprises. This superstition was not peculiar to Henry; it seems to be common among religious princes of the Catholic faith. A similar circumstance is recorded of King Don Alphonso, the last Spanish king of that name. He sent to the tomb of the Cid, a renowned hero of Spain, for the cross which that warrior was accustomed to wear when he went to battle, and had it made into one for himself, "because of the faith which he had, that *through it*, (by means of some mysterious operation of it) he should obtain the victory."

His barbed courser, &c. The horses used in European wars before the discovery of gunpowder, were sometimes defended by a harness of mail.—*Barbed courser* signifies a horse thus *caparisoned*, or arrayed.

MRS. HEMANS.

This lady is among the most eminent of living writers. She resides in Wales, but her poetry is exceedingly admired in this country. Piety, various knowledge, elegant taste, and great sweetness and power of expression, with fervent and tender affections, are the characteristics of Mrs. Hemans' poetic genius.

BURIAL OF WILLIAM THE CONQUEROR.

Mrs. Hemans has taken the subject of these verses from Sismondi's *Historie des Francais*, a book not accessible to me, but the verses are in themselves so clear and picturesque, that they need little illustration.

William, the conqueror of England, was a French prince, a Duke of Normandy, and he had no humane feeling for his subjects in any part of his dominions. In England he depopulated a considerable tract of country, and caused it to remain uncultivated as a hunting ground. This was thenceforward called the New Forest. William had as little respect for the rights of his Norman as for his British subjects, when they interfered with his pleasure. He was thrown from his horse, and died in consequence, in his 64th year. He was interred at Caen, in Normandy. The circumstances of his interment are finely told by Mrs. Hemans:

    " Lowly upon his bier
        The royal conqueror lay,
    Baron and chief stood near
        Silent in war-array.

    Down the long minster's aisle,
        Crowds mutely gazing stream'd,
    Altar and tomb, the while,
        Through mists of insence gleam'd :

    And by the torch's blaze
        The stately priest had said
    High words of power and praise,
        To the glory of the dead.

They lower'd him, with the sound
　Of requiems, to repose,
When from the throngs around
　A solemn voice arose:

'Forbear, forbear!' it cried,
　'In the holiest name forbear!
He hath conquer'd regions wide,
　But he shall not slumber *there.*

'By the violated hearth
　Which made way for yon proud shrine,
By the harvests which this earth
　Hath borne to me and mine;

'By the home ev'n here o'erthrown,
　On my children's native spot,—
Hence! with his dark renown
　Cumber our birth-place not!

'Will my sire's unransom'd field
　O'er which your censers wave,
To the buried spoiler yield
　Soft slumber in the grave?

'The tree before him fell
　Which we cherish'd many a year,
But its deep root yet shall swell
　And heave against his bier.

'The land that I have till'd,
　Hath yet its brooding breast
With my home's white ashes fill'd—
　And it shall not give him rest.

'Here each proud column's bed
　Hath been wet by weeping eyes,—
Hence! and bestow your dead
　Where no wrong against him cries!'

Shame glow'd on each dark face
  Of those proud and steel-girt men;
And they bought with gold a place
  For their leader's dust e'en then.

A little earth for him
  Whose banner flew so far!
And a peasant's tale could dim
  The name, a nation's star!

One deep voice thus arose
  From a heart which wrongs had riven—
Oh! who shall number those
  That were but heard in Heaven?"

This scene is very impressive.—While the body of
William lies in one of those splendid and spacious
churches called *minsters* or cathedrals, and vast numbers
crowd into the aisles to witness the funeral ceremony—
while censers pour forth their fragrance, and lamps their
streaming light upon barons and steel-girt men, assem-
bled around their dead lord—and the *requiem*, or solemn
hymn for the dead, resounds from the vaulted roofs—
as the monarch is lowered into his last bed, an injured
peasant demands, in behalf of others who have suffered
like oppressions with himself, that the spoiler shall not
slumber there; and in consequence of this daring and
awful remonstrance, the king's attendants are obliged to
purchase a grave for him in another place.

William of Normandy, among other acts of arbitrary
power which he committed in England, depopulated a
considerable tract of country, destroyed the villages, with
the churches and enclosures, and changed a cultivated
region to a wilderness, that it might serve thereafter for
a hunting ground.   This tract is called the New Forest.
Mr. Pope, early in the eighteenth century, in his poem
of Windsor Forest, describes the beauty and prosperity
of that part of England in the reign of Queen Anne, and

contrasts that happy state, with the wretchedness of
Britain under her former tyrants.

"Not thus the land appear'd in ages past,
A dreary desert, and a gloomy waste,
To savage beasts and savage laws a prey,
And kings more furious and severe than they;
Who claim'd the skies, dispeopled air and floods,
The lonely lords of empty wilds and woods:
Cities laid waste, they storm'd the dens and caves
(For wiser brutes were backward to the slaves.)
What could be free, when lawless beasts obey'd,
And ev'n the elements a tyrant sway'd?
In vain kind seasons swell'd the teeming grain,
Soft showers distill'd, and suns grew warm in vain;
The swain with tears his frustrate labour yields,
And famish'd dies amidst his ripen'd fields.
What wonder then, a beast or subject slain
Were equal crimes in a despotic reign?
Both, doom'd alike, for sportive tyrants bled;
But, that the subject starv'd, the beast was fed.
  Proud Nimrod first the bloody chase began,
A mighty hunter, and his prey was man:
Our haughty Norman boasts that barbarous name,
And makes his trembling slaves the royal game.
The fields are ravish'd from th' industrious swains,
From men their cities, and from gods their fanes:
The levell'd towns with weeds lie cover'd o'er;
The hollow winds through naked temples roar;
Round broken columns clasping ivy twin'd;
O'er heaps of ruins stalk the stately hind:
The fox obscene to gaping tombs retires,
And savage howlings fill the sacred quires.
Aw'd by his nobles, by his commons curst,
Th' Oppressor rul'd tyrannic where he durst;
Stretch'd o'er the poor and church his iron rod,
And serv'd alike his vassals and his God.
    Whom e'en the Saxon spar'd, and bloody Dane,
The wanton victims of his sport remain.

But see, the man who spacious regions gave
A waste for beasts, *himself deny'd a grave!*
Stretch'd on the lawn his second hope survey,
At once the chaser, and at once the prey:
Lo! Rufus tugging at the deadly dart,
Bleeds in the forest like a wounded hart.
Succeeding monarchs heard the subjects' cries,
Nor saw displeas'd the peaceful cottage rise.
Then gathering flocks on unknown mountains fed,
O'er sandy wilds were yellow harvests spread;
The forests wonder'd at th' unusual grain,
And secret transport touch'd the conscious swain.
Fair Liberty, Britannia's goddess, rears
Her cheerful head, and leads the golden years."

A beast or subject slain were equal crimes. This al-
ludes to the circumstance, that William's subjects were
forbidden to kill wild animals which should be found in
the New Forest; and that the punishment which the law
inflicted upon him who took the life of a man, was no
greater than that, to which he who should kill a hare or a
rabbit, was liable.

Stretch'd on the lawn his second hope survey, &c. The
sons of William I. were peculiarly unfortunate. William
Rufus, who succeeded his father, was accidentally killed
in the New Forest; and Robert, the eldest son, was de-
prived of the Duchy of Normandy by his brother Henry
I. This cruel brother afterwards caused Robert's eyes
to be put out, and kept him a prisoner at Cardiff castle
in Wales twenty years.

THE CRUSADES.

The crusades were religious wars. After his death,
the Romans were masters of Jerusalem, and of the
whole country which had been the scene of the life and
labours of Jesus. Near the middle of the fourth cen-
tury, the Roman Empire became partially Christian, and
Helena, the mother of Constantine, took upon herself to

identify the very spot at Jerusalem "where the Lord lay," and also to erect churches and other monuments on the places consecrated by his living actions. After the erection of these edifices, and the establishment of convents in the Holy Land, as Palestine began to be called, religious persons from different and distant countries of Europe thought it a duty to make journeys thither, in order to visit the shrines or sacred buildings, which had been raised in honour of Christ. These pious travellers were called *Pilgrims,* and their journey was a *Pilgrimage.*

The pilgrims chiefly begged their way through the countries over which they travelled, and were regarded with universal respect by all Christians. They usually dressed in a plain garb, carried a *scrip,* or bag for their food, and sustained themselves upon a staff surmounted by a cross, and had fastened to the front of their hats a scallop shell. When they returned from the Holy Land they frequently brought with them a branch of *palm,* a tree of that country, whence they were called *Palmers.*

Spenser describes a Palmer thus:

"A silly man in simple weeds forewórn,
And soiled with dust of the long dried way;
His sandals were with toilsome travel torn,
And face all tanned with scorching sunny ray,
As he had travelled many a summer's day
Through burning sands of Araby and Inde ;
And in his hand a Jacob's staff, to stay
His weary limbs upon ; and eke behind
His scrip did hang, in which his needments he did bind."
                       Faery Queen, Book I. Canto 6.

Persons who wished to conceal their real name and business, when they engaged in some dangerous undertaking, would assume a Palmer's habit, because in that disguise they were sure of being admitted any where, and of being well treated among Christians. In the seventh century, the Saracens, followers of Mahomet, took Palestine and occupied the land. Abhorrence of Christians is among the principles of their religion; and the Saracens took every opportunity, by the abuse of its zealous professors, the Pilgrims, to show their contempt for the religion of Christ. These deluded men suffered all manner of indignities from the Mahommedans, but at length princes, nobles, and all classes of fanatics in Europe, thought it their duty to leave their homes, and their nearer obligations, in order to punish the *Infidels*, for their cruelties to the Pilgrims, and to tear from their sacrilegious hands the holy places.

Vast armies were fitted out by different princes, and from A. D. 1097 to A. D. 1248, about one hundred and fifty years, four different Crusades were undertaken. More than two millions of men, from England and southern Europe, are supposed to have marched into Asia upon these expeditions, and the greater number lost their lives. These wars were called Crusades, from the circumstance that a figure of the cross was a badge of these warriors—it was painted upon their banners, engraved on their shields, and embroidered in their garments.

RICHARD CŒUR DE LION.

The most distinguished of those saints-errant who led the Crusades, was Richard I. King of England, called Cœur de Lion, or the *lion-hearted*, because of his fearless and warlike disposition. Richard embarked in the third of these expeditions, A. D. 1190: Dr. Warton has celebrated his voyage to the Holy Land in the subjoined ode. It is an animated and interesting picture.

THE CRUSADE.

Bound for holy Palestine,
Nimbly we brush'd the level brine,
All in azure steel array'd:
O'er the wave our weapons play'd,
And made the dancing billows glow;
High upon the trophied prow,
Many a warrior-minstrel swung
His sounding harp, and boldly sung:

"Syrian virgins, wail and weep,
English Richard ploughs the deep!
Tremble, watchmen, as ye spy,
From distant towers, with anxious eye,
The radiant range of shield and lance
Down Damascus' hills advance:
From Sion's turrets as afar
Ye ken the march of Europe's war!
Saladin, thou paynim king,
From Albion's isle revenge we bring!
On Acon's spiry citadel,
Though to the gale thy banners swell,
Pictur'd with the silver moon;
England shall end thy glory soon!
In vain, to break our firm array,
Thy brazen drums hoarse discord bray:
Those sounds our rising fury fan:
English Richard in the van,
On to victory we go,
A vaunting infidel the foe."
     Blondel led the tuneful band,
And swept the wire with glowing hand.
Cyprus, from her rocky mound,
And Crete, with piny verdure crown'd,
Far along the smiling main
Echo'd the prophetic strain.
     Soon we kiss'd the sacred earth
That gave a murder'd Saviour birth;
Then, with ardour fresh endu'd,
Thus the solemn song renew'd:
" Lo, the toilsome voyage past,
Heav'n's favour'd hills appear at last!
Object of our holy vow,
We tread the Tyrian valleys now.
From Carmel's almon-shaded steep
We feel the cheering fragrance creep:
O'er Engaddi's shrubs of balm
Waves the date-empurpled palm.

14

See Lebanon's aspiring head,
Wide his immortal umbrage spread!
Hail, Calvary, thou mountain hoar,
Wet with our Redeemer's gore!
Ye trampled tombs, ye fanes forlorn,
Ye stones, by tears of pilgrims worn;
Your ravish'd honours to restore,
Fearless we climb your hostile shore!
And thou, the sepulchre of God!
By mocking pagans rudely trod,
Bereft of every awful rite,
And quench'd thy lamps that beam'd so bright;
For thee, from Britain's distant coast,
Lo, Richard leads his faithful host!
Aloft in his heroic hand,
Blazing, like the beacon's brand,
O'er the far-affrighted fields,
Resistless Kaliburn he wields.
　　Proud Saracen, pollute no more
The shrines by martyrs built of yore!
From each wild mountain's trackless crown
In vain thy gloomy castles frown:
Thy battering engines, huge and high,
In vain our steel-clad steeds defy;
And, rolling in terrific state,
On giant-wheels harsh thunders grate.
When eve has hush'd the buzzing camp,
Amid the moonlight vapours damp,
Thy necromantic forms, in vain,
Haunt us on the tented plain:
We bid these spectre-shapes avaunt,
Ashtaroth, and Termagaunt!
With many a demon, pale of hue,
Doom'd to drink the bitter dew
That drops from Macon's sooty tree,
Mid the dread grove of ebony.
Nor magic charms, nor fiends of hell,
The Christian's holy courage quell.

"Salem, in ancient majesty
Arise, and lift thee to the sky!
Soon on thy battlements divine
Shall wave the badge of Constantine.
Ye Barons, to the sun unfold
Our Cross with crimson wove and gold!"

All in azure steel arrayed. This alludes to the *armour*, which consisted sometimes of what is called *chain* mail, and sometimes of *scale* mail—the former was the *hauberk*, a garment composed of interlaced rings of metal, which covered the person—the latter was formed of scales of steel, attached to some flexible substance fitted to the body. The steel armour sometimes exhibited a blue tint.

The trophied prow. *Prow*, the head of a ship—that part which advances first in the water. It is usually ornamented with some carved figure, intended to represent the dignity of the nation to which the ship belongs, or some circumstance of the enterprize in which it is engaged. Trophies are emblems of military prowess. Richard was a king—a man of great hardihood, enthusiasm, and national pride—his vessels were, doubtless, embellished by figures which indicated his sense of the glory of Britain, and the importance of the adventure before him.

Many a warrior minstrel, &c. The ancient minstrels were poets who composed extempore verses, and sung them to the music of the harp, which they played themselves. The minstrels were common attendants of princes and nobles of the middle ages, and were maintained by them—they usually commanded great respect and attention wherever they went. The minstrels in Warton's ode, bid the Syrian virgins dread English Richard, and the watchmen on the walls of Jerusalem to tremble, as the ranks of his soldiers with their shining shields and lances shall descend from the city of Damascus. They also threaten Saladin, the Saracen prince, that his glories shall soon be terminated, and that his triumphant banners, adorned by the badge of his Mussulman faith—*the silver moon*, or figure of the crescent—shall fall before the British conqueror.

> ————————*the sepulchre of God!*
> *By mocking Pagans rudely trod,*
> *Bereft of every awful rite,*
> *And quench'd thy lamps that beam'd so bright.*

The Saracens, when they got possession of the Holy City, abolished the religious ceremonies which the Latin Christians had instituted, and extinguished the lamps which the Empress Helena had ordered to be kept continually burning.

The minstrel goes on to sing that the fortifications of the Saracens have no terrors for the English—that neither their *battering-rams*, nor any of the engines used in war before the discovery of gunpowder, nor the *sorceries* and *charms*, the *phantoms* and *evil spirits*, conjured up to harm the Christians, could diminish their confidence in the God of their trust. He then apostrophizes "Salem," (Jerusalem,) and would encourage this *daughter of Sion*, as this city is sometimes figuratively called, that she should again be restored to the Lord's heritage, and that the *badge of Constantine* should soon wave on her battlements, as a token that the Christians had rescued her from the Infidel. This "badge of Constantine," was the sign of the Cross. Constantine caused the Cross to be painted on the standards borne by his armies.

Blondel led the tuneful band, &c. Richard cultivated poetry. Some of the Provençal Poets, called Troubadours, had been invited from France to England before Richard's time, and had continued to be patronized in England. While Richard was absent in the holy wars, which was almost ten years, his brother John endeavoured to ingratiate himself with the English nation, and when Richard learned this, he set out on his return to England, but while he was in Palestine, some disaffection had arisen between him and the monarchs allied with him—these were the king of France and the emperor of Germany—and being shipwrecked in his voyage home, he was taken by the emperor, and made a prisoner in Germany. After more than a year a ransom was paid for him, and he was permitted to go to England. A fable concerning Blondel is so often alluded to, that it may be useful to relate it in this place.

After Richard's imprisonment in Germany, "a whole year elapsed before the English knew where their monarch was confined. Blondel de Nesle, Richard's favourite French minstrel, resolved to find out his lord; and after travelling many days without success, at last came to a castle where Richard was detained. Here he found that the castle belonged to the Duke of Austria, and that a king was there imprisoned. Suspecting that the prisoner was his master, he found means to place himself directly before the window of the chamber where the king was kept; and in this situation began to sing a French chanson which Richard and Blondel had formerly written together. When the king heard the song he knew it was Blondel who sung it; and when Blondel paused after the first half of the song, the king began the other half and completed it. Blondel then returned to England, acquainted the people with his discovery, and Richard was in due time liberated."

JOANNA BAILLIE.

This distinguished woman is still living. She is the niece of John Hunter, an eminent anatomist, not long dead, and the sister of Dr. Baillie, late physician to the King of England, one of the most celebrated medical practitioners of his time ; but her consanguinity to these men of genius reflects no more honour upon her, than their relationship to her does upon them. If there is any honourable pride in family connexions, it is in the self-complacency which we derive from the fact that one of the same race with ourselves has shed lustre upon all of our blood, by the splendour of acknowledged talent.

Miss Baillie is chiefly known as a dramatic author. Her plays are not well adapted to the public taste of this age, but abounding in highly poetic passages, they are admired by readers of the finest taste. Sir Walter Scott, Lord Byron, and many others of the most gifted minds, have loved to celebrate Joanna Baillie. Sir Walter Scott says, Shakspeare's

——— —————————"harp had silent hung,
By silver Avon's holy shore,
Till twice a hundred years roll'd o'er,
When she, the bold Enchantress, came,
With fearless hand and heart on flame,
From the pale willow snatched the treasure,
And swept it with a kindred measure,
Till Avon's swans, while rung the grove
With Monfort's hate and Basil's love,
Awakening at the inspired strain,
Dreamed their own Shakspeare lived again."

Basil and Montfort are heroes of Miss Baillie's tragedies.

On the death of Edward IV. King of England, their uncle Richard, duke of Gloucester, was made protector of the young king and his brother. Richard first imprisoned the princes, and afterwards caused them to be assassinated. Miss Baillie has made the confinement of these princes a subject of poetry, and the subjoined extracts from one of her dramas are peculiarly affecting.

PRINCE EDWARD *alone in prison.*

" Doth the bright sun from the high arch of heav'n,
In all his beauteous robes of flecker'd clouds,
And ruddy vapours, and deep glowing flames
And softly varied shades, look gloriously?
Do the green woods dance to the wind? the lakes
Cast up their sparkling waters to the light?
Do the sweet hamlets in their busby dells
Send winding up to heav'n their curling smoke
On the soft morning air?
Do the flocks bleat, and the wild creatures bound
In antic happiness? and mazy birds
Wing the mid air in lightly skimming bands?
Aye, all this is; men do behold all this;
The poorest man.   E'en in this lonely vault,
My dark and narrow world, oft I do hear
The crowing of the cock so near my walls,
And sadly think how small a space divides me
From all this fair creation.
   From the wide spreading bounds of beauteous nature
I am alone shut out; I am forgotten.
Peace, peace! He who regards the poorest worm,
Still cares for me.—Perhaps, small as these walls,
A bound unseen divides my dreary state
From a more beauteous world; that world of souls;
Fear'd and desir'd by all; a vail unseen
Which soon shall be withdrawn.
The air feels chill; methinks it should be night,
I'll lay me down; perchance kind sleep will come,
And open to my view an inward world
Of garnish'd fantasies, from which nor walls,
Nor bars, nor tyrant's pow'r can shut me out."

PRINCE EDWARD *and his* KEEPER.

   Ed. What brings thee now? it surely cannot be
The time of food: my prison hours are wont
To fly more heavily.

Keep. It is not food : I bring wherewith, my lord,
To stop a rent in these old walls, that oft
Hath griev'd me, when I've thought of you o' nights ;
Thro' it the cold wind visits you.

    Ed. And let it enter ! it shall not be stopp'd.
Who visits me besides the winds of heaven ?
Who mourns with me but the sad-sighing wind ?
Who bringeth to mine ear the mimic'd tones
Of voices once belov'd and sounds long past
But the light-wing'd and many voiced wind ?
Who fans the prisoner's lean and fever'd cheek
As kindly as the monarch's wreathed brows
But the free piteous wind?
I will not have it stopp'd.

    Keep. My lord, the winter now creeps on apace :
Hoar frost this morning on our shelter'd fields
Lay thick, and glanc'd to the up-risen sun,
Which scarce had power to melt it.

    Ed. Glanc'd to the up-risen sun ! Ay, such fair morns,
When ev'ry bush doth put its glory on,
Like a gemm'd bride ! your rustics now
And early hinds, will set their clouted feet
Thro' silver webs, so bright and finely wrought
As royal dames ne'er fashion'd, yet plod on
Their careless way, unheeding.
Alas, how many glorious things there be
To look upon ! Wear not the forests, now,
Their latest coat of richly varied dyes ?

    Keep. Yes, my good lord, the cold chill year advances,
Therefore I pray you, let me close that wall.

    Ed. I tell thee no, man ; if the north air bites,
Bring me a cloak.   Where is thy dog to day!

    Keep. Indeed I wonder that he came not with me
As he is wont.

    Ed. Bring him, I pray thee, when thou com'st again.
He wags his tail and looks up to my face
With the assured kindliness of one
Who has not injured me.

SIR WALTER SCOTT.

It has been said it is a happy circumstance for us of the nineteenth century, that we live in the age of the author of Waverly. At the time this remark was made, the author of Waverly was unknown. For more than ten years the press at Edinburgh sent forth a succession of novels, which entertained the whole reading world. Waverly was the first of these charming books, and the author studiously concealed himself from the curiosity of the public. The author of Waverly was rightly suspected to be Walter Scott. About the year 1805, the Lay of the Last Minstrel was published. This poem was acknowledged to be the production of Mr. Scott. He is a native of Scotland, curious in the antiquities of that country, and has long been known for his researches into Scottish poetry, for his talent of general criticism, and his poetic invention.

After the publication of the Lay, Scott wrote Marmion, and several other metrical romances of extraordinary beauty. The novels before mentioned bear many resemblances to the poems, and on these resemblances was founded the presumption that the *poet* was also the *novelist*. All conjecture upon this subject has been put at rest, by the declaration of Sir Walter Scott that he is in truth the author of Waverly.

This great poet has with much propriety been compared with Shakspeare. "Shakspeare," says Mr. Campbell, "lived in an age within the verge of chivalry, an age overflowing with chivalrous and romantic reading; he was led by his vocation to have daily recourse to that kind of reading; he dwelt on the spot which gave him constant access to it, and was in habitual intercourse with men of genius."

Sir Walter Scott has lived *now* that the "age of chivalry is gone;" but his country overflows with *romantic reading* and *traditions*, and his genius seems to have taken its inspirations and the subjects of invention chiefly from these sources—from the states of society, the character and sentiments of men of various ranks, as they are recorded to have existed under the influences of the *feudal* state, and the times immediately succeeding ; like Shakspeare, he has the talent *each change of many-coloured life to draw*, to move laughter and to excite tears.   The parallelism between these great men, however, applies rather to the attributes of their genius than to their fortune in life.   Mediocrity of fortune, and a moderate estimate of his talents, was all the outward meed awarded to Shakspeare by his contemporaries.

Homer says of poets, they are regarded as *divine* beings, " far as the sun displays his vital fire."—— But few poets have the happiness to *live* in the " blaze of their fame" as Scott has done.   Wherever English is read, there the poems and the novels of the immortal Northern Minstrel are known ; and from every region where they are known, the tribute of praise and admiration is offered to him.   On the accession of George IV. the present king of England, (1820) one of the first acts of his reign was to bestow on Mr. Scott the rank of baronet, and he has since been known as Sir Walter Scott.   The pecuniary profit derived to him from his works has been great, and the distinguished minds of his time have looked up to him as the first of living men.

The Lay of the Last Minstrel consists of a tale in verse, supposed to be recited by a wandering minstrel who took refuge in the castle of Anne, Dutchess of Buccleuch and Monmouth, representative of the ancient lords of Buccleuch, and widow of the unfortunate James, Duke of Monmouth, who was beheaded in 1685.

The minstrel recites to the Dutchess, and her ladies, a story of her ancestors.

THE LAST MINSTREL.

" The way was long, the wind was cold,
The minstrel was infirm and old ;
His withered cheek, and tresses gray,
Seemed to have known a better day ;

The harp, his sole remaining joy,
Was carried by an orphan boy.
The last of all the bards was he,
Who sung of border chivalry.
For, well-a-day! their date was fled,
His tuneful brethren all were dead;
And he, neglected and oppressed,
Wished to be with them and at rest.
No more, on prancing palfrey borne,
He caroll'd light as lark at morn;
No longer courted and caress'd,
High plac'd in hall, a welcome guest,
He pour'd to lord and lady gay,
The unpremeditated lay:
Old times were chang'd, old manners gone;
A stranger fill'd the Stuart's throne;
The bigots of the iron time
Had call'd his harmless art a crime.
A wandering Harper, scorn'd and poor,
He begg'd his bread from door to door;
And tun'd, to please a peasant's ear,
The harp, a king had lov'd to hear.

He pass'd where Newark's stately tower
Looks out from Yarrow's birchen bower:
The minstrel gaz'd with wishful eye—
No humbler resting-place was nigh.
With hesitating step at last,
The embattl'd portal-arch he pass'd,
Whose pondrous grate and massy bar
Had oft roll'd back the tide of war,
But never clos'd the iron door
Against the desolate and poor.
The Dutchess mark'd his weary pace,
His timid mein, and reverend face,
And bade her page the menials tell,
That they should tend the old man well:
For she had known adversity,
Though born in such a high degree;

In pride of power, in beauty's bloom,
Had wept o'er Monmouth's bloody tomb!
  When kindness had his wants supplied,
And the old man was gratified,
Began to rise his minstrel pride:
And he began to talk anon,
Of good Earl Francis, dead and gone,
And of Earl Walter, rest him God!
A braver ne'er to battle rode:
And how full many a tale he knew,
Of the old warriors of Buccleuch;
And, would the noble Dutchess deign
To listen to an old man's strain,
Though stiff his hand, his voice though weak,
He thought even yet, the sooth to speak,
That, if she lov'd the harp to hear,
He could make music to her ear.
  The humble boon was soon obtain'd;
The aged Minstrel audience gain'd.
But when he reach'd the room of state,
Where she, with all her ladies, sate,
Perchance he wish'd his boon denied:
For when to tune his harp he tried,
His trembling hand had lost the ease,
Which marks security to please;
And scenes, long past, of joy and pain,
Came wildering o'er his aged brain—
He tried to tune his harp in vain.
The pitying Dutchess prais'd its chime,
And gave him heart, and gave him time,
Till every string's according glee
Was blended into harmony.
And then, he said, he would full fain
He could recall an ancient strain,
He never thought to sing again.
It was not framed for village churls,
But for high dames and mighty earls;
He had play'd it to king Charles the Good,
When he kept court in Holyrood;

And much he wish'd, yet fear'd, to try
The long-forgotten melody.
　Amid the strings his fingers stray'd,
And an uncertain warbling made,
And oft he shook his hoary head.
But when he caught the measure wild,
The old man rais'd his face, and smil'd;
And lighten'd up his faded eye,
With all a poet's ecstasy!
In varying cadence, soft or strong,
He swept the sounding chords along:
The present scene, the future lot,
His toils, his wants, were all forgot:
Cold diffidence, and age's frost,
In the full tide of song were lost;
Each blank, in faithless memory void,
The poet's glowing thought supplied;
And, while his harp responsive rung,
'Twas thus the Latest Minstrel sung."

Of good Earl Francis, &c.　Francis Scott, Earl of
Buccleuch, father of the Dutchess.
And of Earl Walter, &c.　Walter, Earl of Buccleuch,
grandfather to the Dutchess, and a celebrated warrior.

　"Hush'd is the harp—the Minstrel gone.
And did he wander forth alone?
Alone, in indigence and age,
To linger out his pilgrimage?
No:—close beneath proud Newark's tower,
Arose the Minstrel's lowly bower;
A simple hut; but there was seen
The little garden hedged with green,
The cheerful hearth, and lattice clean.
There shelter'd wanderers, by the blaze,
Oft heard the tale of other days;
For much he loved to ope his door,
And give the aid he begg'd before.
15

So pass'd the winter's day ; but still,
When summer smil'd on sweet Bowhill,
And July's eve, with balmy breath,
Wav'd the blue-bells on Newark heath ;
When throstles sung in Hare-head shaw,
And corn was green on Carterhaugh,
And flourish'd, broad, Blacandro's oak,
The aged Harper's soul awoke !
Then would he sing achievements high,
And circumstance of chivalry,
Till the rapt traveller would stay,
Forgetful of the closing day ;
And noble youths, the strain to hear,
Forsook the hunting of the deer ;
And Yarrow, as he roll'd along,
Bore burden to the Minstrel's song."

IMPROVISATORI.

From the beginning of the seventeenth century, minstrelsy went out of practice in Britain, but in Italy the recitation of extemporary poetry still constitutes a popular amusement.

About sixty years ago Mr. Benjamin West, a native of America, went to Rome to study the art of painting. His biographer, Mr. Galt, relates the manner in which this celebrated artist was once entertained by an Improvisatore, one of the extemporaneous Italian poets.

"One night, soon after his arrival in Rome, Mr. Gavin Hamilton, the painter. to whom he had been introduced by Mr. Robinson, took him to a coffee-house, the usual resort of the British travellers. While they were sitting at one of the tables, a venerable old man, with a guitar suspended from his shoulder, entered the room, and coming immediately to their table, Mr. Hamilton addressed him by the name of Homer. He was the most celebrated improvisatore in all Italy, and the richness of expression, and nobleness of conception which he displayed in his effusions, had obtained for him that distinguished name.

"Those who once heard his poetry, never ceased to lament that it was lost in the same moment, affirming that it often was so regular and dignified, as to equal the finest compositions of Tasso and Ariosto. It will, perhaps, afford some gratification to the admirers of native genius to learn, that this old man, though led by the fine frenzy of his imagination to prefer a wild and wandering life to the offer of a settled independence, which had been made him in his youth, enjoyed in his old age, by the liberality of several Englishmen, who had raised a subscription for the purpose, a small pension, sufficient to keep him comfortable, in his own way, when he became incapable of amusing the public.

"After some conversation, Homer requested Mr. Hamilton to give him a subject for a poem. In the meantime, a number of Italians had gathered round them to look at West, who they had heard was an American, and whom, like cardinal Albani,* they imagined to be an Indian. Some of them, on hearing Homer's request, observed, that he had exhausted his vein, and had already said and sung every subject over and over. Mr. Hamilton, however, remarked that he thought he could propose something new to the bard, and pointing to Mr. West, said, that he was an American come to study the fine arts in Rome ; and that such an event furnished a new and magnificent theme.

"Homer took possession of the thought with the ardour of inspiration. He immediately unslung his guitar, and began to draw his fingers rapidly over the strings, swinging his body from side to side, and striking fine and impressive chords. When he had thus brought his motions and his feelings into unison with the instrument, he began an extemporaneous ode in a manner so dignified, so pathetic, and so enthusiastic, that Mr. West was scarcely less interested by his appearance than those who enjoyed the subject and melody of his numbers.

* A Spanish Cardinal, who presumed that American signified Indian.

"He sung the darkness which for so many ages veiled
America from the eyes of science. He described the
fulness of time, when the purposes for which it had been
raised from the deep were to be manifested. He painted
the seraph of knowledge descending from heaven, and
directing Columbus to undertake the discovery; and he
related the leading incidents of the voyage. He invoked
the fancy of the auditors to contemplate the wild magni-
ficence of mountain, lake, and wood, in the new world;
and he raised, as it were, in vivid perspective, the Indians
in the chase, and at their horrible sacrifices. 'But,' he
continued, 'the beneficent spirit of improvement is ever
on the wing, and, like the ray from the throne of God, it
has descended on this youth, and the hope which ushered
in its new miracle, like the star that guided the magi to
Bethlehem, has led him to Rome.

"'Methinks I behold in him an instrument chosen by
heaven, to raise in America the taste for those arts which
elevate the nature of man—an assurance that his coun-
try will afford a refuge to science and knowledge, when
in the old age of Europe they shall have forsaken her
shores. But all things of heavenly origin, like the glori-
ous sun, move westward; and truth and art have their
periods of shining, and of night. Rejoice then, O vene-
rable Rome, in thy divine destiny; for though darkness
overshadow thy seats, and though thy mitred head must
descend into the dust, as deep as the earth that now co-
vers thy ancient helmet and imperial diadem, thy spirit,
immortal and undecayed, already reaches towards a new
world, where, like the soul of man in paradise, it will be
perfected in virtue and beauty more and more.'

"The highest efforts of the greatest actors, even of
Garrick himself delivering the poetry of Shakspeare,
never produced a more immediate and inspiring effect
than this rapid burst of genius. When the applause had
abated, Mr. West being the stranger, and the party ad-
dressed, according to the common practice, made the
bard a present. Mr. Hamilton explained the subject of
the ode: though with the weakness of a verbal transla-
tion, and the imperfection of an indistinct echo, it was

so connected with the appearance which the author made in the recital, that the incident was never obliterated from Mr. West's recollection."

THE CHILD OF BRANKSOME.

Among the inmates of castles and the attendants of the Knights, were the Dwarfs—little deformed persons who made sport for the idle, and who were sometimes favourites of young and beautiful ladies. The old romances describe dwarfs as possessing supernatural powers. In the Lay of the Last Minstrel, a mischievous Dwarf is introduced, who had the power to deceive others, by making objects appear to be different from themselves —so as to make a rider and his horse seem to be a load of hay—a child to be a dog, &c. This dwarf of Sir Walter Scott's enters the castle of Buccleuch, and entices from it a little boy, the heir of Branksome. He leads the child into the woods, and leaves him; here the boy is scented by a blood-hound, and taken by one of the retainers of Lord Dacre, an Englishman, who was an enemy of the Scotts, the boy's father's *Clan*. *Clan* signifies, a large number of tenants who acknowledge one lord, who live upon his estate, and who, in former times, fought their lord's battles with his neighbours—the application of this word is chiefly to the Scots. The spirit of this little Scott is a fine specimen of the manners of the young chiefs of the Scottish clans, who were trained from their infancy to protect their father's dependents, and to regard his enemies without fear.

" As passed the Dwarf the outer court,
He spied the fair young child at sport :
He thought to train him to the wood ;
For, at a word, be it understood,
He was always for ill, and never for good.
Seemed to the boy, some comrade gay
Led him forth to the woods to play ;
On the drawbridge the warders stout
Saw a *terrier* and *lurcher* passing out.

15*

He led the boy o'er bank and fell,
   Until they came to a woodland brook;
The running stream dissolved the spell,
   And his old elvish shape he took,
Could he have had his pleasure vilde,
He had crippled the joints of the noble child :
Or, with his fingers long and lean,
Had strangled him in fiendish spleen :
But his *awful mother* he had in dread,
And also his power was limited ;
So he but scowled on the startled child,
And darted through the forest wild ;
The woodland brook he bounding crossed,
And laughed, and shouted, ' Lost! lost! lost !

Full sore amazed at the wonderous change,
   And frightened, as a child might be,
At the wild yell, and visage strange,
   And the dark words of gramarye,
The child, amidst the forest bower,
Stood rooted like a lilye flower ;
   And when at length, with trembling pace,
     He sought to find where Branksome lay,
   He feared to see that grisly face
     Glare from some thicket on his way.
Thus, starting oft, he journeyed on,
And deeper in the wood is gone,—
For aye the more he sought his way,
The further still he went astray,
Until he heard the mountains round
Ring to the baying of a hound.

And hark! and hark! the deep-mouthed bark
   Comes nigher still, and nigher ;
Bursts on the path a dark blood-hound,
His tawny muzzle tracked the ground,
   As his red eye shot fire.
Soon as the wildered child saw he,
He flew at him right furiouslie.

I ween you would have seen with joy
The bearing of the gallant boy,
When, worthy of his noble sire,
His wet cheek glowed 'twixt fear and ire!
He faced the blood-hound manfully;
And held his little bat on high;
So fierce he struck, the dog, afraid,
At cautious distance hoarsely bayed,
   But still in act to spring;
When dashed an archer through the glade,
And when he saw the hound was stayed,
   He drew his tough bow-string;
But a rough voice cried, ' Shoot not, hoy !
Ho! shoot not Edward—'tis a boy !'

The speaker issued from the wood,
And checked his fellow's surly mood,
   And quelled the ban-dog's ire.
He would not do the fair child harm,
But held him with his powerful arm,
That he might neither fight nor flee;
For when the red cross spied he,
The boy strove long and violently.
' Now, by St. George,' the archer cries,
' Edward, methinks we have a prize !
This boy's fair face and courage free,
Shows he is come of high degree.'—

' Yes, I am come of high degree,
   For I am the heir of bold Buccleuch;
And, if thou dost not set me free,
   False southron, thou shalt dearly rue !
For Walter of Harden shall come with speed,
And William of Deloraine, good at need,
And every Scot from Eske to Tweed;
And if thou dost not let me go,
Despite thy arrows, and thy bow,
I'll have thee hanged to feed the crow !'

' Gramercy, for thy good will, fair boy !
My mind was never set so high ;
But if thou art chief of such a clan,
And art the son of such a man,
And ever comest to thy command,
   Our wardens had need to keep good order :
My bow of yew to a hazel wand,
   Thou'lt make them work upon the Border.
Meantime, be pleased to come with me,
For good Lord Dacre shalt thou see ;
I think our work is well begun,
When we have taken thy father's son.' "

His old elvish shape he took. Those who describe the
power of witches and dwarfs, pretend that they cannot
cross a brook in their assumed form. The dwarf had
appeared to the deceived boy to be a companion of his
own age. When he took his own shape, and darted
away, yelling as he disappeared, the child was frightened
—but the real danger from the blood-hound does not ter-
rify him.

His awful mother he had in dread. The dwarf was
afraid of the child's mother. She was more skilled in
necromancy, or *gramarye,* than he was.

THE GALLIARD'S WHITE HORSE.

Under the feudal system, the vassals were considered
as cattle. A man was not valued at so much as a war-
horse. At length, however, the vassals began to feel
their importance, and they did not always comply with
the demands of their Lord, who might, if he would, pu-
nish them for their disobedience, or sell them with the
lands they cultivated, or give them another master. The
tenants under this system were superior to mere labour-
ers, they held lands *in fief*—as the grant, under certain
conditions, of their lord. These were called *feudatories,*
and their property was called a *fief.*

When a man received his fief, he became the *liegeman* of the *liege*, or lord; and when he acknowledged the relation subsisting between himself and the lord, the liegeman offered the lord *homage*.——He then knelt before him, and placing his hands upon the lord's knees, said, " Sire, I become your liegeman for such a fief, and I promise to guard and defend you against all people." The lord answered, " I receive you; and your lands I will defend as my own:" and he then kissed his tenant as a pledge of faith.

An instance of the spirit of resistance to feudal power, and its consequences, is told by Sir Walter Scott :

" Earl Morton was lord of that valley* fair,
The Beattisons were his vassals there.
The Earl was gentle, and mild of mood,
The vassals were warlike, and fierce, and rude ;
High of heart, and haughty of word,
Little they recked of a tame liege lord.
The Earl to fair Eskdale came,
Homage and Seignory to claim :
Of Gilbert the Galliard, a *heriot*† he sought,
Saying, ' Give thy best steed as a vassal ought.'
' Dear to me is my bonny white steed,
Oft has he helped me at a pinch of need ;
Lord and Earl though thou be, I trow,
I can rein Bucksfoot better than thou.'
    Word on word gave fuel to fire,
Till so highly blazed the Beattisons' ire,
But that the Earl the flight had ta'en,
The vassals there their lord had slain.
Sore he plied both whip and spur,
As he urged his steed through Eskdale muir ;
And it fell down a weary weight,
Just on the threshold of Branksome gate.

* Eskdale.
† The feudal superior, in certain cases was entitled to the best horse of the vassal, in name of Heriot, or Hereseld.

The Earl was a wrathful man to see,
Full fain avenged would he be.
In haste to Branksome's lord he spoke,
Saying, 'Take these traitors to thy yoke;
For a cast of hawks and a purse of gold.
All Eskdale I'll see thee to have and hold:
Beshrew thy heart, of the Beattisons' clan
If thou leavest on Eske a landed man;
But spare Woodkerrick's lands alone,
For he lent me his horse to escape upon.'—
  A glad man then was Branksome bold,
Down he flung him the purse of gold;
To Eskdale soon he spurred amain,
And with him five hundred riders has ta'en.
He left his merrymen in the midst of the hill;
And bade them hold them close and still;
And alone he wended to the plain.
To meet with the Galliard and all his train.
To Gilbert the Galliard thus he said:—
' Know thou me for thy liege lord and head;
Deal not with me as with Morton tame,
For Scotts play best at the roughest game.
Give me in peace my heriot due,
Thy bonny white steed, or thou shalt rue.
If my horn I three times wind,
Eskdale shall long have the sound in mind.'

Loudly the Beattison laughed in scorn;—
' Little care we for thy winded horn.
Ne'er shall it be the Galliard's lot,
To yield his steed to a haughty Scott.
Wend thou to Branksome back on foot,
With rusty spur and miry boot.'
He blew his bugle so loud and hoarse,
That the dun deer started at far Craikcross;
He blew again so loud and clear,
Through the gray mountain mist there did lances
    appear;

And the third blast rang with such a din,
That the echoes answered from Pentoun-linn ;.
And all his riders came lightly in.
Then you had seen a gallant shock,
When saddles were emptied and lances broke !
For each scornful word the Galliard had said,
A Beattison on the field was laid.
His own good sword the chieftain drew,
And he bored the Galliard through and through ;
Where the Beattisons' blood mixed with the rill,
The Galliard's Haugh, men call it still.
The Scotts have scattered the Beattison clan,
In Eskdale they left but one landed man.
The valley of Eske, from the mouth to the source,
Was lost and won for that bonny white horse."

BORDER WARS.

The history of the *border wars* of Scotland is highly in-
teresting. Scotland is only divided from England by an
artificial boundary, but the two regions were once go-
verned by different kings and laws, and the people thought
they had different and clashing interests. Those who
lived on the *border*, or contiguous territories of the two
dominions, paid little regard to any laws.—They took
justice into their own hands, or rather they defied justice,
and devastated each other's property as much as they
could, and they kept up for ages the hostilities which
some needy robber had begun.

In the third canto of The Lady of the Lake—The
Gathering—Sir Walter Scott represents, in a very vivid
manner, the spirit and alacrity with which the clansmen
assembled themselves at the call of their chiefs. When
they were suddenly summoned to his defence, or that of
his allies, a signal was carried through the tract of coun-
try which they inhabited, and with almost incredible speed
they assembled themselves at the " trysting place," or as
we say from the French, at the *Rendezvous*. The Fu-
neral and the Wedding were alike suspended at this

summons, and the mourner and the bride were forgotten in the claim of a Scottish chief.

 " Fast as the fatal symbol flies,
 In arms the huts and hamlets rise ;
 From winding glen, from upland brown,
 They poured each hardy tenant down.
 Nor slacked the messenger his pace ;
 He showed the sign, he named the place,
 And, pressing forward like the wind,
 Left clamour and surprise behind.
 The fisherman forsook the strand,
 The swarthy smith took dirk and brand ;
 With changed cheer, the mower blithe
 Left in the half-cut swathe his scythe ;
 The herds without a keeper strayed,
 The plough was in mid-furrow staid,
 The falc'ner tossed his hawk away,
 The hunter left the stag at bay ;
 Prompt at the signal of alarms,
 Each son of Alpine rushed to arms ;
 From the gray sire, whose trembling hand
 Could hardly buckle on his brand,
 To the raw boy, whose shaft and bow
 Were yet scarce terror to the crow.
 Each valley, each sequestered glen,
 Mustered its little horde of men,
 That met as torrents from the height
 In Highland dale their streams unite,
 Still gathering, as they pour along,
 A voice more loud, a tide more strong,
 Till at the rendezvous they stood·
 By hundreds prompt for blows and blood ;
 Each trained to arms since life began,
 Owning no tie but to his clan,
 No oath, but by his Chieftain's hand,
 No law, but Rhoderick Dhu's command."

 The predatory habits of these clans originated in their rapacity and indolence, and were carried on by the spirit of retaliation. The chiefs, however, possessed some high qualities in conjunction with the passions which produced such shocking results. Ellen, in The Lady of the Lake, describes this combination of revolting and praise-worthy traits. She speaks of Roderick Dhu, the chief of Clan Alpine:

" I grant him liberal, to fling
Among his clan the wealth they bring,
When back by lake and glen they wind,
And in the Lowland leave behind,
Where once some pleasant hamlet stood,
A mass of ashes slaked with blood.
The band, that for my father fought,
I honour, as his daughter ought;
But can I clasp it reeking red,
From peasants slaughtered in their shed?
No! wildly while his virtues gleam
They make his passions darker seem,
And flash along his spirit high,
Like lightning o'er the midnight sky."

THE ALARM.

The story of Sir Walter Scott's Minstrel is one of the warfare of the Scotts, (the family of the Dukes of Buccleuch,) with *southern force and guile*.——

"When Scrope, and Howard, and Percy's powers
Threatened Branksome's lordly towers."

Branksome was the castle of the Buccleuch family, and the English names are those of English noblemen from " Warkworth, and Naworth, and merry Carlisle," who were open enemies of the Scotts of Buccleuch. The action of the poem is dated about 1550.

In anticipation of an attack from the southern powers, the Scotts *mustered the clans*, their neighbours and allies. The alarm is exhibited with wonderful animation.

" ————————the evening fell,
'Twas near the time of curfew bell;
16

The air was mild, the wind was calm,
The stream was smooth, the dew was balm,
E'en the rude watchman, on the tower,
Enjoyed and blessed the lovely hour.
Far more fair Margaret loved and blessed
The hour of silence and of rest.
On the high turret sitting lone,
She waked at times the lute's soft tone;
Touched a wild note, and all between
Thought of the bower of hawthorns green.
Her golden hair streamed free from band,
Her fair cheek rested on her hand,
Her blue eye sought the west afar,
For lovers love the western star.

Is yon the star, o'er Penchryst Pen,
That rises slowly to her ken,
And, spreading broad its wavering light,
Shakes its loose tresses on the night?
Is yon red glare the western star?—
O, 'tis the beacon blaze of war!
Scarce could she draw her tightened breath,
For well she knew the fire of death!

The warder viewed it blazing strong,
And blew his war-note loud and long,
Till, at the high and haughty sound,
Rock, wood, and river, rang around.
The blast alarmed the festal hall,
And startled forth the warriors all;
Far downward, in the castle-yard,
Full many a torch and cresset glared;
And helms and plumes confusedly tossed,
Were in the blaze half-seen, half-lost;
And spears in wild disorder shook,
Like reeds beside a frozen brook.

The Seneschal, whose silver hair
Was reddened by the torches' glare,
Stood in the midst, with gesture proud,

And issued forth his mandates loud,
'On Penchryst glows a *bale* of fire
And three are kindling on Priesthaughswire ;
   Ride out, ride out,
   The foe to scout !
Mount, *mount, for Branksome*, every man !
Thou, Todrig, warn the Johnstone clan,
   That ever are true and stout.
Ye need not send to Liddlesdale ;
For, when they see the blazing bale,
Elliots and Armstrongs never fail.——
Ride, Alton, ride for death and life !
And warn the warden of the strife.
Young Gilbert, let our beacon blaze,
Our kin, and clan, and friends, to raise.'

Fair Margaret, from the turret head,
Heard, far below, the coursers' tread,
   While loud the harness rung,
As to their seats with clamour dread,
   The ready horsemen sprung ;
And trampling hoofs, and iron coats,
And leaders' voices mingled notes,
   And out ! and out !
   In hasty route,
  The horsemen galloped forth ;
Dispersing to the south to scout,
   And east, and west, and north,
To view their coming enemies,
To warn their vassals, and allies.

The ready page, with hurried hand,
Awaked the *need-fire's* slumbering brand,
   And ruddy blushed the heaven :
For a sheet of flame, from the turret high,
Waved like a bloodflag on the sky,
   All flaring and uneven ;
And soon a score of fires, I ween,
From height, and hill, and cliff, were seen ;

Each with warlike tidings fraught ;
Each from each the signal caught ;
Each after each they glanced to sight,
As stars arise upon the night.
They gleamed on many a dusky *tarn*,
Haunted by the lonely *carn* ;
On many a *cairn's* gray pyramid,
Where urns of mighty chiefs lie hid ;
Till high Dunedin the blazes saw,
From Soltra and Dumpender Law ;
And Lothian heard the regent's order,
That all should *bowne* them from the Border.

The livelong night in Branksome rang
　The ceaseless sound of steel :
The castle bell, with backward clang,
　Sent forth the larum peal ;
Was frequent heard the heavy jar,
Where massy stone and iron bar
Were piled on echoing keep and tower,
To whelm the foe with deadly shower ;
Was frequent heard the changing guard,
And watchword from the sleepless ward ;
While, wearied by the endless din,
Blood-hound and ban-dog yelled within.

The noble dame, amid the broil,
Shared the gray Seneschal's high toil,
And spoke of danger with a smile ;
Cheered the young knights, and council sage
Held with the chiefs of riper age.
No tidings of the foe were brought,
Nor of his numbers knew they aught,
Nor in what time the truce he sought.
　Some said that there were thousands ten ;
And others weened that it was nought
　But Leven clans, or Tynedale men,
Who came to gather in *black mail* ;
And Liddesdale, with small avail,
　Might drive them lightly back agen.

> So passed the anxious night away,
> And welcome was the peep of day."

The castle of the Scotts was, at the time expressed in the verses, in possession of the widow of its late lord. The *fair Margaret* is the Lady's daughter.

Is yon red glare the western star? No. It is a war signal. On some distant and elevated spot, the Scotts kept *a post of observation*—a place where some of their clan were stationed to observe if any armed force marched towards the castle. As soon as the watch discovered movements among the enemy, he gave notice of it by lighting a fire, which was seen at another high place, where another watch was stationed. The second watch lighted a *bale fire*, which another saw; and thus, by a succession of signs, the endangered family got information of their danger, and prepared themselves for defence. This mode of giving information, was in ancient times in use among the Greeks and Asiatics. In Agamemnon, a tragedy of Eschylus, the circumstance of the taking of Troy is represented to have been thus transmitted to Peloponnesus.

The time of curfew bell—about eight o'clock at night.

Warder—a watchman who gave notice of danger to the inmates of a castle.

Seneschal—an officer who regulated ceremonies, and gave orders upon emergencies.

Bale—beacon-faggot.

Mount for Branksome was the gathering word of the Scotts.

Need-fire—beacon.

Tarn—a mountain lake.

Earn—the Scottish eagle.

Cairn—a pile of stones.

Bowne—make ready.

The regent's order. A regent is a person appointed to act for a king in his infancy, his absence from his kingdom, and during his illness.

Who came to gather in black mail. The Scotts did not certainly know who was approaching their domain, it

16*

might be some lawless men of the country who were coming to carry off cattle, and such things as they could find, yet who might be prevented from doing this violence by money distributed among them. This *bribe* for refraining from robbery was called *black-mail.*

This disorderly and perilous state of society exists no longer. The region once disturbed in this manner, is now in security and prosperity. This change is sweetly described in the poem from which the preceding verses are extracted :

> " Sweet Teviot! on thy silver tide
>   The glaring bale-fires blaze no more ;
> No longer steel-clad warriors ride
>   Along thy wild and willowed shore ;
> Where'er thou wind'st by dale or hill
> All, all is peaceful, all is still,
>   As if thy waves, since time was born,
> Since first they rolled their way to Tweed,
> Had only heard the shepherd's reed,
>   Nor startled at the bugle-horn.
>
> Unlike the tide of human time,
>   Which, though it change in ceaseless flow,
> Retains each grief, retains each crime,
>   Its earliest course was doomed to know ;
> And darker as it downward bears,
> Is stained with past and present tears."

LORD SURREY.

Henry Howard, Earl of Surrey, was the son of a Duke of Norfork, an English nobleman. Lord Surrey was born in England about the year 1516. He was educated in the fashion of that age for young persons of his elevated rank. According to an old writer of the time, " they began early with languages and manners ; from *ten* to *twelve* were taught music and dancing, and to *speak of gentleness ;*' (to converse like gentlemen) then

scoured the fields as sportsmen ; at sixteen were prac-
tised in mock battles—*jousting*, and breaking and riding
the war-horse ; and at *seventeen* or *eighteen* were reck-
oned fit to enter the world, and be entrusted with the du-
ties of men.''

Lord Surrey was highly accomplished, and a writer of
poetry. His poetry in now only read by those students
who take pleasure in reviving what is old and obsolete,
and in tracing the past progress of English literature.
Surrey spent his short life chiefly in the court of Henry
VIII, or in the military service in France. His genius
and accomplishments made him enemies.—The unset-
tled state of laws, and the despotism of the royal autho-
rity at that period in England, made it easy for cruel and
unprincipled men in high stations to ruin those they hated,
and to such men, Lord Surrey fell a victim.

The circumstances of Surrey's death, are not very pre-
cisely known, but he was falsely accused of *treason*, (a
project against the government of his country.) and in
the 31st year of his age was sentenced to death, and
publicly beheaded. The king. being near his end, and
enfeebled in mind, gave his sanction to this vile measure.

"Thus was cut off, gallant and guiltless, the most ac-
complished man of his age.''

————————lovely to the last :
Extinguished, not decayed.

This melancholy fact affords a clear inference of the
value of a wise civil government, founded in the rights
of all men.—A young person who should now read the
frivolous pretences which brought Lord Surrey to the
block, ought to feel his heart glow with gratitude to pro-
vidence, that he lives under political institutions, which
forbid the shedding of blood except for the worst
crimes ; and he ought to make himself worthy of that
personal safety and liberty which when they bestow the
privileges of a good citizen, require of him all the duties
of one.

Surrey's character and fate are so interesting that

many fictions have been composed upon his history. One of these is, that he loved a beautiful English lady named Geraldine—that he travelled in Italy and Germany, and in order to obtain some intelligence of the lady Geraldine while he was on the continent of Europe, that he repaired to a certain *necromancer* for information. The reputed name of that *fortune-teller*, as we call such impostors, was Cornelius Agrippa. According to this fable, Agrippa showed Lord Surrey the figure of his absent lady in a mirror.—She was seen by him reclining on a couch and reading one of his sonnets. To complete this story it was further asserted, that Lord Surrey was just married to Geraldine when he was torn from her, and put to death.

Towards the end of Sir Walter Scott's Lay of the Last Minstrel, a marriage feast is described.—The time in which the circumstances related in the poem are supposed to happen, is soon after the death of Surrey. One of the entertainments at feasts, then in fashion, was the musical recitation of poetry, in honor of *beautiful ladies* and *true knights*. At the marriage feast alluded to, Fitztraver, a favourite Minstrel of Lord Surrey, is supposed to be present, and to relate the fabled vision of his unhappy master.

SURREY'S VISION.

As ended Albert's simple lay,
   Arose a bard of loftier port ;
For sonnet, rhyme, and roundelay,
   Renowned in haughty Henry's court :
There hung thy harp, unrivalled long,
Fitztraver of the silver song !
   The gentle Surrey loved his lyre—
     Who has not heard of Surrey's fame ?
His was the hero's soul of fire,
     And his the bard's immortal name,
And his was love, exalted high
By all the glow of chivalry.

They sought together, climes afar,
   And oft, within some olive grove,

When evening came, with twinkling star,
  They sung of Surrey's absent love.
His step the Italian peasant staid,
  And deemed, that spirits from on high,
Round where some hermit saint was laid,
  Were breathing heavenly melody ;
So sweet did harp and voice combine,
To praise the name of Geraldine.

Firztraver ! O what tongue may say
  The pangs thy faithful bosom knew,
When Surrey, of the deathless lay,
  Ungrateful Tudor's sentence slew ?

'Twas All-soul's eve, and Surrey's heart beat high ;
  He heard the midnight-bell with anxious start,
Which told the mystic hour, approaching nigh,
  When wise Cornelius promised, by his art,
To show to him the ladye of his heart,
  Albeit betwixt them roared the ocean grim ;
Yet so the sage had hight to play his part,
  That he should see her form in life and limb,
And mark, if still she loved, and still she thought of
      him.

Dark was the vaulted room of gramarye,
  To which the wizard led the gallant Knight
Save that before a mirror, huge and high,
  A hallowed taper shed a glimmering light
On mystic implements of magic might ;
  On cross, and character, and talisman,
And almagest, and altar,—nothing bright ;
  For fitful was the lustre, pale and wan,
As watch-light by the bed of some departing man.

But soon within that mirror huge and high,
  Was seen a self-emitted light to gleam ;
And forms upon its breast the earl 'gan spy,
  Cloudy and indistinct as feverish dream ;
Till, slow arranging, and defined, they seem
  To form a lordly, and a lofty room,

Part lighted by a lamp with silver beam,
  Placed by a couch of Agra's silken loom,
And part by moonshine pale, and part was hid in
  gloom.

Fair all the pageant—but how passing fair
  The slender form, which lay on couch of Ind
O'er her white bosom strayed her hazel hair,
  Pale her dear cheek, as if for love she pined;
All in her night-robe loose she lay reclined,
  And, pensive, read from tablet eburnine
Some strain that seemed her inmost soul to find :——
  That favoured strain was Surrey's raptured line,
That fair and lovely form the Ladye Geraldine.

———

Magic is a false art—a pretension of cunning men
who live among the ignorant to impose upon the latter,
but some men, wise in other respects, have believed in
this deception.   The *magicians* of Egypt are mentioned
in the Bible.   In some countries, persons called *magi-
cians* have been really learned, and others, less informed,
have believed them to be endowed with the knowledge
of future events, and able to change their own appear-
ance, or to transform one substance into another, as *lead*
to *gold, &c.* To have such abilities, would be to possess
supernatural powers—powers greater than other men—
No such ability has been conferred upon men.
  Room of Gramarye.   Gramarye means *magic.*   The
talisman and *almagest*, were certain instruments which
the magicians pretended to employ, when they practised
their art.   The *almagest* was a book of astrology.

———

CONSTANCE DE BEVERLY.

" The Catholic religion," says Madame de Staël, " has
taken up the inheritance of Paganism every where." She
means that ceremonies, images and institutions, in use
among the Pagans of Rome, were adopted by Christians
of that country, and of that form of religion which origina-

ted there. The statues of Jupiter and Apollo had their heads displaced that they might receive those of St. Paul and Peter, and religious orders of the exploded faith were remodeled under the new. One instance of this may be found by comparing the order of the Vestal virgins of ancient Rome, with those of the convents for Christian females.

In Rome the people worshipped the goddess Vesta, or Fire,—originally, perhaps, because that element is so happily diffused through all nature, that it is the active agent which produces almost all the sensible changes in every thing, is one of the essential principles of life, and the indispensable power which ministers in the operation of all arts, and to the enjoyment of all comforts.

The servants of Vesta were young females from noble families ; they were neither given nor persuaded to this ministry, but taken. The Pontifex Maximus, the chief priest among the Romans, when he saw a young girl who pleased him, took her by the hand, and declaring that she was appointed a vestal virgin, devoted her to the education ordained for this order, and her parents acquiesced with readiness, believing that they gave up their child to a *holy vocation.*

The vestal virgins were few in number, their principal duty was to keep alive the sacred fire, which was kindled from the rays of the sun. The elder educated the younger ones, and they all spent their time in performing ceremonies now forgotten, but to which ignorance and superstition then attached a false importance. So much were the priestesses of Vesta honoured, that when they went abroad the magistrates of Rome gave place to them. But if they dared to break their vows they were buried alive.

. The frightful punishment of burying alive has not been confined to the vestals of ancient Rome. Convents are houses of religious retirement, where women, and sometimes men, agree to spend their lives in the services of the Roman Catholic faith.

The nuns, the female inhabitants of convents, often

lead useful, benevolent, and happy lives, but they formerly adhered to very severe regulations. The governess, or mistress of a convent, sometimes called the Abbess, and sometimes the Prioress, was made a judge in cases of crimes committed by the nuns; and the laws of these establishments ordered, if a nun eloped from a convent with the connivance of any man she loved, that when she should afterwards be seized, she should, like the faithless vestals of Rome, be buried, warm with life, in a premature grave.

A most affecting representation of such a cruel sacrifice, is found in the second Canto of Sir Walter Scott's Marmion. Constance de Beverly, the professed sister of Fontevraud, was enticed from her convent by Lord Marmion. Some time after this, the wealth of the Lady Clare tempted Marmion to forsake Constance, and to seek Clara for his bride. Clara was engaged to marry young De Wilton, but Marmion contrived to bring some disgrace upon De Wilton, and to engage his master, the king of England, to command that Clara should accept Marmion as her husband. Clara fled from these importunities to the convent of Whitby, and while she was in that asylum, Constance, resolving that none other than herself should marry Lord Marmion, conspired with a treacherous monk to poison Clara.

This guilty design was discovered, and its plotters were punished according to the laws of that age. The offence of Constance was double, and rendered her liable to the death she afterwards suffered. An "ancient Man," the Abbot of Saint Cuthbert, the Abbess of Saint Hilda, and the Prioress of Tynemouth, sat in judgment upon these unhappy criminals, in a deep vault far beneath the surface of the earth.

> " Before them stood a guilty pair;
> But though an equal fate they share,
> Yet one alone deserves our care.
> Her sex a page's dress belied;
> The cloak and doublet loosely tied,
> Obscured her charms but could not hide.

Her cap down o'er her face she drew ;
    And on her doublet breast
She tried to hide the badge of blue,
    Lord Marmion's falcon crest.
But at the Prioress' command,
A monk undid the silken band
    That tied her tresses fair,
And raised the bonnet from her head,
And down her slender form they spread
    In ringlets rich and rare,
Constance de Beverly they know
Sister professed of Fontevraud,*
Whom the church numbered with the dead
For broken vows and convent fled.

When thus her face was given to view,
(Although so pallid was her hue,
It did a ghastly contrast bear
To those bright ringlets glistering fair,)
Her look composed, and steady eye,
Bespoke a matchless constancy ;
And there she stood, so calm and pale
But, that her breathing did not fail,
And motion slight of eye and head,
And of her bosom, warranted
That neither life nor pulse she lacks,
You might have thought a form of wax,
Wrought to the very sense was there,
So still she was, so pale, so fair.

Her comrade was a sordid soul—
  *   *   *   *   *   *
This wretch was clad in frock and cowl,
And shamed not loud to moan and howl,
His body on the floor to dash,
And crouch like hound beneath the lash :
While his mute partner standing near,
Waited her doom without a tear.

* Pronounced Frontevro.
17

Yet well the luckless wretch might shriek,
Well might her paleness terror speak!
For there were seen in that dark wall,
Two niches narrow. deep, and tall.
Who enters at such grisly door,
Shall ne'er, I ween, find exit more.
In each a slender meal was laid
Of roots, of water, and of bread.
By each in Benedictine dress
Two haggard monks stood motionless;
Who, holding high a blazing torch,
Showed the grim entrance of the porch :
Reflecting back the smoky beam,
The dark red walls and arches gleam.
Hewn stones and cement were displayed,
And building tools in order laid.

     *   *   *   *   *   *   *

And now that blind old abbot rose,
   To speak the chapter's doom
On those the walls were to enclose
   Alive, within the tomb ;
But stopped, because that woful maid,
Gathering her powers, to speak essayed;
Twice she essayed, and twice in vain,
Her accents might no utterance gain;
Nought but imperfect murmurs slip
From her convulsed and quivering lip :

     *   *   : *   *   *   *   *

At length an effort sent apart
The blood that curdled to her heart,
   And light came to her eye,
And colour dawned upon her cheek
A hectic and a fluttered streak
Like that left on the Cheviot peak,
   By autumn's stormy sky ;

And when her silence broke at length,
Still as she spoke she gathered strength,
   And armed herself to bear.——
It was a fearful sight to see
Such high resolve and constancy,
   In form so soft and fair.

"I speak not to implore your grace,
Well knew I for one minute's space
   Successless might I sue:
Nor do I speak your prayers to gain;
For if a death of lingering pain,
To cleanse my sins be penance vain,
   Vain are your masses too.——
I listened to a traitor's tale,
I left the convent and the veil,
For three long years I bowed my pride
A horse-boy in his train to ride.

  *   *   *   *   *   *   *

He saw young Clara's face more fair,
And knew her of broad lands the heir,
Forgot his vows, his faith forswore,
And Constance was beloved no more.——
'Tis an old tale and often told;
   But did my fate and wish agree,
Ne'er had been read, in story old
Of maiden true, betrayed for gold,
   That loved or was avenged like me.

  *   *   *   *   *   *   *

This catiff monk, for gold, did swear
He would to Whitby's shrine repair,
And by his drugs, my rival fair
   Saint in heaven should be.
But ill the dastard kept his oath,
Whose cowardice has undone us both.

  *   *   *   *   *   *   *

Now men of death work forth your will,
For I can suffer and be still;

And come he slow or come he fast,
It is but death who comes at last.

Yet dread me from my living tomb,
Ye *vassal slaves of bloody Rome,*
If Marmion's late remorse should wake
Full soon such vengeance would he take
That you should wish the fiery Dane
Had rather been your guest again.
Behind a darker hour ascends !
The *altars quake, the crosier bends,*
The ire of a despotic king
Rides forth upon destruction's wing ;
Then shall these vaults so large and deep
Burst open to the sea-wind's sweep ;
Some traveller then shall find my bones,
Whitening amid disjointed stones,
And, ignorant of priests' cruelty,
Marvel such relics here should be."

Fixed was her look and stern her air ;
Back from her shoulders streamed her hair ;
The locks that wont her brow to shade,
Stood up erectly from her head ;
Her figure seemed to rise more high
Her voice, despair's wild energy
Had given a tone of prophecy.
Appalled the astonished *conclave* sate ;
With stupid eyes, the men of fate
Gazed on the light inspired form ;
And listened for the avenging storm ;
The judges felt the victim's dread,
No hand was moved, no word was said.
Till thus the Abbot's doom was given;
Raising his sightless balls to heaven :—
" Sister, let thy sorrows cease ;
Sinful brother, part in peace !"
        From that dire dungeon, place of doom,
    Of execution too, and tomb,
        Paced forth the judges three ;

Sorrow it were, and shame, to tell
The butcher-work that there befel,
When they had glided from the cell
   Of sin and misery.

An hundred winding steps convey
That conclave to the upper day ;
But, ere they breathed the fresher air,
They heard the shriekings of despair,
   And many a stifled groan :
With speed their upward way they take,
(Such speed as age and fear can make,)
And crossed themselves for terror's sake,
   As hurrying tottering on.
Even in the vesper's heavenly tone,
They seemed to hear a dying groan,
And bade the passing knell to toll
For welfare of a parting soul.
Slow o'er the midnight wave it swung,
Northumbrian rocks in answer rung ;
To Warkworth cell the echoes rolled,
His beads the wakeful hermit told ;
The Bamborough peasant raised his head,
But slept ere half a prayer he said ;
So far was heard the mighty knell,
The stag sprung up on Cheviot Fell,
Spread his broad nostril to the wind,
Listed before, aside, behind ;
Then couched him down beside the hind,
And quaked among the mountain fern,
To hear that sound so dull and stern.

ILLUSTRATIONS.

Two haggard monks in this awful and melancholy pic-
ture are arrayed in "Benedictine dress." The different
orders of monks first originated in some religious men
who retired from all business and collected about them
others disposed like themselves. These persons lived

and associated together, possessed the same property, and followed nearly the same occupations.   Those who joined their society, one after another, and followed them, generation after generation, took the name of the first founder of the society.   This person was afterwards called a Saint.   Saint Benedict, Saint Francis, Saint Dominick, were distinguished Fathers of the religious orders in the Catholic Church.   The words Benedictine, Franciscan, and Dominican, signify persons severally attached to the *orders* or institutions of these priests.

Among different orders of the Catholic priesthood, the Jesuits—the order of Jesus—is the most extraordinary. The history of the Jesuits and of their founder, Ignatius Loyola, is highly interesting to those who are sufficiently matured and experienced to understand the effects produced by a great genius in designing great things, and the still greater results which numbers of men acting with untiring energy and united wills, can accomplish.

Constance first threatens her judges with the vengeance of Marmion, when " late remorse" should revive his affection for her ; and her voice, taking the "tone of prophecy," foretold that yet a " darker hour" than his provoked spirit could hasten, awaited them in " the ire of a despotic King." This despotic King was Henry the VIII.

When the Romans possessed Britain they doubtless brought the intelligence of Christianity with them, and Christian converts must have been made in Britain, but how much this Christianity prevailed is not now known. The Saxon masters of Britain, who succeeded the Romans, brought with them the tyranny of ignorance and of physical power ; and Christianity was so little regarded after the time of the Saxon domination, that the Popes of Rome considered Britain among the waste places of Heathenism, and sent thither one of the first Christian missions upon record.

About the year 596 Pope Gregory I. sent St. Augustine, or Austin, with forty monks, to instruct the people of

Britain in the Christian religion. England and Wales were divided into different principalities at that time. Ethelred, king of Kent, was among the first proselytes of Augustine, and became an important aid to his purposes. Augustine was a spiritual governor as well as teacher, and he baptized converts, and established churches and ministers from Kent to Northumberland; he also penetrated into Wales, where he found a form of Christianity more simple than the Romish faith. It had been learned in the second century after Christ from the Romans, and was still cherished.

Augustine was destitute of humility, and expected to be acknowledged by all the inhabitants of Britain, as head of the English church under the Pope. The Welsh, not comprehending the authority of the Pope and Saint Austin, thought fit to reject it, and the saint denounced vengeance upon them. A King of Northumberland took upon himself the accomplishment of this prophecy, and without affording them time for defence, slaughtered about twelve hundred of the Welsh Christians. Fear, as well as confidence, served to establish the Catholic religion, and after the sixth century it was acknowledged in Britain, by the Kings and the people.

From this time large grants and gifts enriched and multiplied monasteries or religious houses, and they continued to increase in power and wealth for nearly a thousand years. The increase of their power, however, received several checks. Reformers at different times lifted up their voices. Wickliffe and Lord Cobham declared for religious liberty, King Henry II. and Edward III. restrained ecclesiastical power, and the scriptures were translated.

At the beginning of the sixteenth century, Pope Leo X. was engaged in building that wonder of modern architecture, St. Peter's church at Rome, and in order to obtain money for the accomplishment of that expensive undertaking, he gave a commission to certain Catholic priests to sell Indulgences, and send the profits to him at

Rome.   These Indulgences were privileges to commit actions forbidden by the laws and the Gospel, without liability to punishment in this world, or another.   The impossibility that any human sovereign could discharge his fellow men from the laws of his Maker, made multitudes of almost all Catholic countries distrust the authority of the Pope who affected to do this, and. made the religious establishments less venerable in all the countries which afterwards became Protestant.

Henry VIII. adhered to the ceremonies of Popery all his life, but he was a most powerful enemy to the Pope's authority in Britain.   Henry caused himself to be declared by the *parliament*, the Protector and independent head of the church of England.   In virtues of this authority, Henry caused a visitation to be made to all the convents, and a report of their condition to be published.   This account, perhaps with too little regard to truth, gave a most detestable character to the monasteries, so that the public mind was easily reconciled to their suppression.   Not long after the visitation, three hundred and seventy-six houses were suppressed, and the lands and other property attached to them were *confiscated*, or applied by the King to public uses,

The new appropriation of the wealth of the Church did not stop here, for the number of religious houses of different kinds that were suppressed has been estimated to be six hundred and forty-three convents, and more than two thousand small establishments for worship, education, and charity.   It is impossible that much distress should not have attended such a sweeping remedy of real or supposed abuses, and well might Constance give that lively personification of the monarch's anger which led to these illustrations.

The altars quake, the crosier bend.   The altars which Catholic superstition has erected shall be shaken.   The *crosier* is a staff surmounted by a cross.   It was carried by Catholic bishops as a symbol of ecclesiastical power—those who bore it might dread the time when it should be bent in subjection to the reformed religion.

LADY OF THE LAKE.

This beautiful tale is a more universal favourite than any by Sir Walter Scott. It is exquisitely descriptive, and so peculiarly fascinating, that a person who takes it up for the first time is seldom known to leave it till the whole is read. The first Canto of the Lady of the Lake describes a *chase*. Hunting is a necessary occupation to men in the savage state, and in civilized countries the opulent men of leisure love to excite their spirits by the sports of the field. To hunt the boar, the stag, and the fox, besides many other animals, is considered by some active and adventurous persons, in many civilized countries, as among the most animating pleasures of life.

The Chase in the Lady of the Lake describes a hunt of the King of Scotland, which ended in the loss of the game, and the death of King James's fine horse. After the loss of his horse, the King expects to sleep in the open air; but the state of the country made it dangerous, and he wandered for a short time in quest of a safe place, when he came full in view of Loch Katrine, a beautifully wooded lake embosomed in profound solitude. In the lake lie several islands—one of them is the retreat of an outlaw, Rhoderick Dhu, and also the asylum of Lord Douglas and his daughter Ellen. Lord Douglas was under the displeasure of the King, and had taken refuge with his kinsman. In hope to summon some *straggler of his train*, the King sounds his bugle: it was heard by Ellen Douglas, who was navigating her *fairy frigate* on the lake,—and believing she replied to her father or to Malcolm Græme, a welcome visitor to her retreat, she answers the stranger, who soon explains his circumstances. Ellen, in the generous confidence and hospitality of that age, takes him into the shallop. He rows to the island, and is made welcome to the rustic habitation of Dame Margaret, the lady of Clan Alpine, and the mother of Rhoderick. The Douglas and the chieftain are both absent, and the stranger Knight announces himself in the assumed character of James Fitz-James, (*Fitz-James,*

son of James.) The next morning the Knight leaves the
island under safe conduct.

THE CHASE.

" The stag at eve had drunk his fill,
When danced the moon on Monan's rill,
And deep his midnight lair had made
In lone Glenartney's hazel shade ;
But, when the sun his beacon red
Had kindled on Benvoirlich's head,
The deep-mouthed blood-hound's heavy bay
Resounded up the rocky way,
And faint, from farther distance borne,
Were heard the clanging hoof and horn.

As chief who hears his warder call,
'To arms ! the foemen storm the wall,"—
The antlered monarch of the waste
Sprung from his heathery couch in haste.
But, ere his fleet career he took,
The dew-drops from his flanks he shook :
Like crested leader proud and high,
Tossed his beamed frontlet to the sky :
A moment gazed adown the dale,
A moment snuffed the tainted gale,
A moment listened to the cry,
That thickened as the chase drew nigh ;
Then, as the headmost foes appeared,
With one brave bound the copse he cleared,
And, stretching forward free and far,
Sought the wild heaths of Uam-Var.

Yelled on the view the opening pack,
Rock, glen and cavern paid them back ;
To many a mingled sound at once
The awakened mountain gave response.
An hundred dogs bayed deep and strong,
Clattered an hundred steeds along,
Their peal the merry horns rung out,
An hundred voices joined the shout :

With hark and whoop and wild halloo
No rest Benvoirlich's echo knew.
Far from the tumult fled the roe,
Close in the covert cowered the doe,
The falcon, from her earn on high,
Cast on the rout a wondering eye,
Till far beyond her piercing ken
The hurricane had swept the glen.
Faint, and more faint, its failing din
Returned from cavern, cliff and linn,
And silence settled wide and still,
On the lone wood and mighty hill.

Less loud the sounds of sylvan war
Disturbed the heights of Uam-Var,
And roused the cavern, where 'tis told
A giant made his den of old:
For ere that steep ascent was won,
High in his path-way hung the sun,
And many a gallant, stayed per-force,
Was fain to breathe his faltering horse:
And of the trackers of the deer,
Scarce half the lessening pack was near;
So shrewdly on the mountain side,
Had the bold burst their mettle tried.

The noble stag was pausing now
Upon the mountain's southern brow,
Where broad extended far beneath,
The varied realms of fair Monteith.
With anxious eye he wandered o'er
Mountain and meadow, moss and moor,
And pondered refuge from his toil,
By far Lochard or Aberfoyle.
But nearer was the copse-wood grey,
That waved and wept on Loch Achray,
And mingled with the pine trees blue,
On the bold cliffs of Ben-venue.
Fresh vigor with the hope returned,
With flying foot the heath he spurned,

Held westward with unwearied race,
And left behind the panting chase.

'Twere long to tell what steeds gave o'er,
As swept the hunt through Cambus-more;
What reins were tightened in despair,
When rose Benledi's ridge in air;
Who flagged upon Bochastle's heath,
Who shunned to stem the flooded Teith.——
For twice, that day, from shore to shore,
The gallant stag swam stoutly o'er.
Few were the stragglers, following far,
That reached the lake of Vennachar:
And when the Brigg of Turk was won,
The headmost horseman rode alone.

Alone, but with unbated zeal,
That horseman plied the scourge and steel:
For, jaded now, and spent with toil,
Embossed with foam, and dark with soil,
While every gasp with sobs he drew,
The labouring stag strained full in view.
Two dogs of black Saint Hubert's breed,
Unmatched for courage, breath and speed,
Fast on his flying traces came,
And all but won that desperate game;
For, scarce a spear's length from his haunch,
Vindictive toiled the blood-hounds stanch;
Nor nearer might the dogs attain,
Nor farther might the quarry strain.
Thus up the margin of the lake,
Between the precipice and brake,
O'er stock and rock their race they take.

The hunter marked that mountain high,
The lone lake's western boundary,
And deemed the stag must turn to bay,
Where that huge rampart barred the way;
Already glorying in the prize,
Measured his antlers with his eyes;

For the death-wound and death halloo,
Mustered his breath, his whinyard drew;
But, thundering as he came prepared,
With ready arm and weapon bared,
The wily quarry shunned the shock,
And turned him from the opposing rock;
Then, dashing down a darksome glen,
Soon lost to hound and hunter's ken,
In the deep Trosach's wildest nook
His solitary refuge took.
There while, close couched, the thicket shed
Cold dews and wild flowers on his head,
He heard the baffled dogs in vain
Rave through the hollow pass amain,
Chiding the rocks that yelled again.

Close on the hounds the hunter came,
To cheer them on the vanished game;
But stumbling in the rugged dell,
The gallant horse exhausted fell.
The impatient rider strove in vain
To rouse him with the spur and rein,
For the good steed, his labours o'er,
Stretched his stiff limbs, to rise no more;
Then touched with pity and remorse,
He sorrowed o'er the expiring horse.
'I little thought when first thy rein
I slacked upon the banks of Seine,
That highland eagle e'er should feed
On thy fleet limbs, my gallant steed!
Wo worth the chase, wo worth the day,
That cost thy life, my gallant grey!'"

———

ELLEN DOUGLAS.

"But scarce again his horn he wound,
When lo! forth starting at the sound,
From underneath an aged oak,
That slanted from the islet rock,
A damsel, guider of its way,

18

A little skiff shot to the bay,
That round the promontory steep,
Led its deep line in graceful sweep,
Eddying in almost viewless wave,
The weeping willow twig to lave,
And kiss with whispering sound and slow,
The beach of pebbles bright as snow.
The boat had touched this silver strand,
Just as the hunter left his stand,
And stood concealed amid the brake,
To view this Lady of the lake.
The maiden paused, as if again
She thought to catch the distant strain,
With head upraised, and look intent,
And eye and ear attentive bent,
And locks flung back, and lips apart
Like monument of Grecian art.
In listening mood she seemed to stand,
The guardian Naiad of the strand.

And ne'er did Grecian chisel trace
A Nymph, a Naiad, or a Grace,
Of finer form, or lovelier face !
What though the sun with ardent frown,
Had slightly tinged her cheek with brown,—
The sportive toil, which, short and light,
Had dyed her glowing hue so bright,
Served too in hastier swell to show,
Short glimpses of a breast of snow ;
What though no rule of courtly grace
To measured mood had trained her pace,—
A foot more light, a step more true,
Ne'er from the heath-flower dashed the dew ;
E'en the slight hare-bell raised its head,
Elastic from her airy tread :
What though upon her speech there hung
The accents of the mountain tongue,—
Those silver sounds so soft, so dear
The listener held his breath to hear.

A chieftain's daughter seemed the maid ;
Her satin snood, her silken plaid,
Her golden brooch, such birth betray'd.
And seldom was a snood amid
Such wild luxuriant ringlets hid,
Whose glossy black to shame might bring
The plumage of the raven's wing ;
And seldom o'er a breast so fair
Mantled a plaid with modest care,
And never brooch the folds combined
Above a heart more good and kind.
Her kindness and her worth to spy,
You need but gaze on Ellen's eye ;
Not Katrine, in her mirror blue,
Gives back the shaggy banks more true,
Than every free-born glance confessed
The guileless movements of her breast ;
Whether joy danced in her dark eye,
Or wo or pity claimed a sigh,
Or filial love was glowing there,
Or meek devotion poured a prayer,
Or tale of injury called forth
The indignant spirit of the north.
One only passion unrevealed,
With maiden pride the maid concealed,
Yet not less purely felt the flame ;—
O need I tell that passion's name ?

Impatient of the silent horn,
Now on the gale her voice was borne :—
' Father!' she cried ; the rocks around
Loved to prolong the gentle sound.
A while she paus'd, no answer came,
' Malcolm, was thine the blast ?' the name
Less resolutely uttered fell,
The echoes could not catch the swell.
' A stranger I,' the huntsman said,
Advancing from the hazel shade.

The maid alarmed, with hasty oar,
Pushed her light shallop from the shore,
And when a space was gained between,
Closer she drew her bosom's screen ;
(So forth the startled swan would swing,
So turn to prune his ruffled wing.
Then safe, though fluttered and amazed,
She paused, and on the stranger gazed.
Not his form, nor his the eye,
That youthful maidens wont to fly.

On his bold visage middle-age
Had slightly pressed its signet sage,
Yet had not quenched the open truth,
And fiery vehemence of youth ;
Forward and frolic glee was there,
The will to do, the soul to dare,
The sparkling glance soon blown to fire,
Of hasty love, or headlong ire.
His limbs were cast in manly mould,
For hardy sports, or contest bold ;
And though in peaceful garb arrayed,
And weaponless, except his blade,
His stately mien as well implied
A high-born heart, a martial pride,
As if a baron's crest he wore,
And sheathed in armour trod the shore.
Slighting the petty need he showed,
He told of his benighted road ;
His ready speech flowed fair and free,
In phrase of gentlest courtesy ;
Yet seemed that tone and gesture bland,
Less used to sue than to command.

A while the maid the stranger eyed,
And, reassured at last replied,
That highland halls were open still
To wildered wanderers of the hill.
" Nor think you unexpected come
To yon lone isle, our desert home ;
Before the heath had lost the dew,

This morn a couch was pulled for you ;
On yonder mountain's purple head
Have ptarmigan and heath-cock bled,
And our broad nets have swept the mere,
To furnish forth your evening cheer."
" Now, by the rood, my lovely maid,
Your courtesy has erred," he said ;
" No right have I to claim, misplaced,
The welcome of expected guest.
A wanderer here, by fortune tost,
My way, my friends, my courser lost,
I ne'er before, believe me, fair,
Have ever drawn your mountain air,
Till on this lake's romantic strand,
I found a fay in fairy land."

" I well believe," the maid replied,
As her light skiff approached the side,
" I well believe that ne'er before
Your foot has trod Loch-Katrine shore ;
But yet, as far as yesternight,
Old Allan-bane foretold your plight,——
A grey-haired sire, whose eye intent,
Was on the visioned future bent.
He saw your steed, a dappled grey,
Lie dead beneath the birchen way ;
Painted exact your form and mien,
Your hunting suit of Lincoln green,
That tassel'd horn so gayly gilt,
That falchion's crooked blade and hilt,
That cap with heron's plumage trim,
And yon two hounds so dark and grim.
He bade that all should ready be,
To grace a guest of fair degree ;
But light I held his prophecy,
And deemed it was my father's horn,
Whose echoes o'er the lake were borne."

The stranger smiled :——" Since to your home
A destined errant knight I come,

Announced by prophet sooth and old,
Doomed, doubtless, for achievement bold,
I'll lightly front each high emprize,
For one kind glance of those bright eyes;
Permit me, first, the task to guide
Your fairy frigate o'er the tide."
The maid, with smiles suppressed and sly,
The toil unwonted saw him try;
For seldom sure, if e'er before,
His noble hand had grasped an oar;
Yet with main strength his strokes he drew,
And o'er the lake the shallop flew;
With heads erect, and whimpering cry,
The hounds behind their passage ply.
Nor frequent does the bright oar break
The darkening mirror of the lake,
Until the rocky isle they reach,
And moor their shallop on the beach.

The stranger viewed the shore around;
'Twas all so close with copse-wood bound,
Nor track nor pathway might declare
That human foot frequented there,
Until the mountain maiden showed
A clambering unsuspected road,
That winded through the tangled screen,
And opened on a narow green.
Here, for retreat in dangerous hour,
Some chief had framed a rustic bower.

It was a lodge of ample size,
But strange of structure and device.
Due westward, fronting to the green,
A rural portico was seen,
Aloft on native pillars borne,
Of mountain fir with bark unshorn,
Where Ellen's hand had taught to twine
The ivy and Idæan vine,
The clematis, the favoured flower,
Which boasts the name of virgin-bower;

And every hardy plant could bear
Loch-Katrine's keen and searching air.
An instant in the porch she stayed,
And gayly to the stranger said,
" On heaven and on thy lady call,
And enter the enchanted hall."
" My hope, my heaven, my trust must be,
My gentle guide, in following thee."—

ROKEBY.

Rokeby is an English story ; the scene is in the north of England, and the date 1644. The most interesting characters in Rokeby are Redmond O'Neale, a young Irishman trained by the lord of Rokeby, and Matilda, the only daughter of Rokeby.

MATILDA.

" Wreathed in its dark brown rings, her hair
Half hid Matilda's forehead fair,
Half hid and half revealed to view
Her full dark eye of hazel hue.
The rose, with faint and feeble streak,
So slightly tinged the maiden's cheek,
That you had said her hue was pale,
But if she faced the summer gale,
Or spoke, or sung, or quicker moved,
Or heard the praise of those she loved,
Or when of interest was expressed
Aught that waked feeling in her breast,
The mantling blood in ready play
Rivalled the blush of rising day.
    There was a soft and pensive grace,
A cast of thought upon her face,
That suited well the forehead high,
The eye-lash dark, and downcast eye ;
The mild expression spoke a mind
In duty firm, composed, resigned ;—
'Tis that which Roman art has given,

To mark their maiden queen of heaven.
In hours of sport, that mood gave way
To Fancy's light and frolic play,
And when the dance, or tale, or song,
In harmless mirth sped time along,
Full oft her doating sire would call
His Maud the merriest of them all.
   But days of war, and civil crime,
Allowed but ill such festal time,
And her soft pensiveness of brow
Had deepened into sadness now.
And boding thoughts that she must part
With a soft vision of her heart,—
All lowered around the lovely maid,
To darken her dejection's shade."

Some years before the time of the poem of Rokeby, the Irish had rebelled against the English government in Ireland, and the Earl of Essex was employed to crush the rebellion ; but O'Neale, a descendant of the ancient Irish princes, assumed the sovereignty of the province of Ulster, and for a while was acknowledged king.   While O'Neale held out against the English, the author of the poem supposes that the Knight of Rokeby, with his confederate Mortham, was employed in the English military service in Ireland, and that falling into the power of O'Neale, they were treated with generosity and hospitality, and sent *safe and unransomed* home.   On account of the friendship thus commenced, on the reverse of his fortune, the grandson of Rokeby's preserver was sent to his protection, was afterwards trained under his roof, and in due time married to his daughter Matilda.

REDMOND O'NEALE.

" Years sped away.   On Rokeby's head
Some touch of early snow was shed ;
Calm he enjoyed, by Greta's wave,
The peace which James the peaceful gave,
While Mortham, far beyond the main,
Waged his fierce wars on Indian Spain—

It chanced upon a wintry night,
That whitened Stanemore's stormy height,
The chase was o'er, the stag was killed,
In Rokeby-hall the cups were filled,
And, by the huge stone chimney, sate
The knight, in hospitable state.
Moonless the sky, the hour was late,
When a loud summons shook the gate.
And sore for entrance and for aid
A voice of foreign accent prayed.
The porter answered to the call,
And instant rushed into the hall
A man, whose aspect and attire
Startled the circle by the fire.

His plaited hair in elf-locks spread
Around his bare and matted head ;
On leg and thigh, close stretched and trim,
His vesture showed the sinewy limb ;
In saffron dyed, a linen vest
Was frequent folded round his breast ;
A mantle long and loose he wore,
Shaggy with ice, and stained with gore.
He clasped a burthen to his heart,
And, resting on a knotted dart,
The snow from hair and beard he shook,
And round him gazed with wildered look :
Then up the hall, with staggering pace,
He hastened by the blaze to place,
Half lifeless from the bitter air,
His load, a boy of beauty rare.
To Rokeby, next, he louted low,
Then stood erect his tale to show,
With wild majestic port and tone,
Like envoy of some barbarous throne.
' Sir Richard, lord of Rokeby, hear !
Turlough O'Neale salutes thee dear ;
He graces thee, and to thy care
Young Redmond gives, his grandson fair.

He bids thee breed him as thy son,
For Turlough's days of joy are done;
And other lords have seized his land,
And faint and feeble is his hand,
And all the glory of Tyrone
Is like a morning vapour flown.
To bind the duty on thy soul,
He bids thee think on Erin's bowl!
If any wrong the young O'Neale,
He bids thee think of Erin's steel.
To Mortham first this charge was due,
But, in his absence, honours you.——
Now is my master's message by,
And Ferraught will contented die.'——

His look grew fixed, his cheek grew pale,
He sunk when he had told his tale;
For, hid beneath his mantle wide,
A mortal wound was in his side.
Vain was all aid——in terror wild,
And sorrow, screamed the orphan child.
Poor Ferraught raised his wistful eyes,
And faintly strove to soothe his cries;
All reckless of his dying pain,
He blest, and blest him o'er again!
And kissed the little hands outspread,
And kissed and crossed the infant head,
And, in his native tongue and phrase,
Prayed to each saint to watch his days;
Then all his strength together drew,
The charge to Rokeby to renew.
When half was faltered from his breast,
And half by dying signs expressed,
' Bless the O'Neale!'' he faintly said,
And thus the faithful spirit fled.

'Twas long ere soothing might prevail
Upon the child to end the tale;
And then he said, that from his home
His grandsire had been forced to roam,

Which had not been if Redmond's band
Had but had strength to draw the brand,
The brand of Lenaugh More the Red,
That hung beside the gray wolf's head.——
'Twas from his broken phrase descried,
His foster-father was his guide,
Who, in his charge, from Ulster bore
Letters, and gifts a goodly store —
But ruffians met them in the wood,
Ferraught in battle boldly stood,
Till wounded and o'erpowered at length,
And stripped of all, his failing strength
Just bore him here—and then the child
Renewed again his moaning wild.

The tear, down childhood's cheek that flows,
Is like the dew-drop on the rose ;
When next the summer breeze comes by,
And waves the bush, the flower is dry.
Won by their care, the orphan child
Soon on his new protectors smiled,
With dimpled cheek and eyes so fair,
Through his thick curls of flaxen hair.
But blithest laughed that cheek and eye,
When Rokeby's little maid was nigh ;
'Twas his, with elder brother's pride,
Matilda's tottering steps to guide ;
His native lays in Irish tongue,
To soothe her infant ear he sung,
And primrose twined with daisy fair,
To form a chaplet for her hair.
By lawn, by grove, by brooklet's strand,
The children still were hand in hand,
And good sir Richard smiling eyed
The early knot so kindly tied.

But summer months bring wilding shoot
From bud to bloom, from bloom to fruit ;
And years draw on our human span,
From child to boy, from boy to man :

"And soon in Rokeby's woods is seen
A gallant boy in hunter's green.
He loves to wake the felon boar,
In his dark haunt on Greta's shore,
And loves, against the deer so dun,
To draw the shaft, or lift the gun;
Yet more he loves, in autumn prime,
The hazel's spreading boughs to climb,
And down its clustered stores to hail,
Where young Matilda holds her veil.
And she, whose veil receives the shower,
Is altered too, and knows her power;
Assumes a mistress' pride,
Her Redmond's dangerous sports to chide,
Yet listens still to hear him tell
How the grim wild-boar fought and fell,
How at his fall the bugle rung,
Till rock and green-wood answer flung;
Then blesses her, that man can find
A pastime of such savage kind!

But Redmond knew to weave his tale
So well with praise of wood and dale,
And knew so well each point to trace,
Gives living interest to the chace,
And knew so well o'er all to throw
His spirit's wild romantic glow,
That, while she blamed, and while she feared,
She loved each venturous tale she heard.
Oft, too, when drifted snow and rain
To bower and hall their steps restrain,
Together they explored the page
Of glowing bard or gifted sage;
Oft, placed the evening fire beside,
The minstrel art alternate tried,
While gladsome harp and lively lay
Bade winter-night flit fast away;
Thus from their childhood blending still
Their sport, their study, and their skill."

HOMER.

Homer is usually styled the father of poetry. The oldest poet with whom we are acquainted, is Moses.— Moses' song, which may be found in Deuteronomy, chapter xxxii: is translated from the Hebrew, and is the most ancient specimen of poetry with which we are acquainted. The probable date of it is 1550 years before Christ—six hundred years before Homer, the Greek poet.

MOSES' SONG.

" Give ear, 'O ye heavens, and I will speak ; and hear, O earth, the words of my mouth. My doctrine shall drop as the rain, my speech shall distil as the dew, as the small rain upon the tender herb, and as the showers upon the grass : Because I will publish the name of the LORD : ascribe ye greatness unto our God. He is the Rock, his work is perfect : for all his ways are judgment : a God of truth and without iniquity, just and right is he."

" They have corrupted themselves, their spot is not the spot of his children : they are a perverse and crooked generation. Do ye thus requite the LORD, O foolish people and unwise ? is not he thy father that hath bought thee ? hath he not made thee, and established thee? Remember the days of old, consider the years of many generations : ask thy father, and he will show thee ; thy elders, and they will tell thee. When the Most High divided to the nations their inheritance, when he separated the sons of Adam, he set the bounds of the people according to the number of the children of Israel.

" For the LORD's portion is his people ; Jacob is the lot of his inheritance. He found him in a desert land, and in the waste howling wilderness ; he led him about, he instructed him, he kept him as the apple of his eye. As an eagle stirreth up her nest, fluttereth over her young, spreadeth abroad her wings, taketh them, beareth them on her wings : so the LORD alone did lead him, and there was no strange god with him."

<hr>

The *foolish people and unwise*, before whom Moses

19

celebrates the divine majesty and goodness, are the Israelites, whom, during more than forty years, this great man had governed, and whom he was now about to leave for ever.

Homer's verses were first preserved by oral tradition. Lycurgus heard them recited in Ionia, and made the people of Sparta acquainted with them; but according to Cicero, it is to Pisistratus, the Athenian, that we are indebted for the ultimate preservation of Homer's works and fame. Pisistratus caused the books of Homer to be transcribed and placed in the public library which he founded at Athens. From this copy other manuscripts were taken, and these in modern times, have been copied, multiplied, and diffused by means of the art of printing.

Scholars of the sixteenth century in England employed themselves in translations from Greek and Latin. Greek and Latin tragedies, and the poetry of Virgil, and Ovid, were thus made familiar to the English reader. When Pope was a boy, about the year 1700; he "was initiated in poetry by the perusal of Ogilby's Homer, and Sandy's Virgil." Chapman's translation of Homer is also mentioned about the same time. The date of these translations is not accurately known to me, but they were not of a character to exclude the utility and desirableness of an improved version of Homer.

Mr. Pope began an English translation of Homer's Iliad in 1712, and finished it in 1718. It was first published by subscription in six volumes, with notes illustrative of the text. "The encouragement given to this translation," says Dr. Johnson, "was such as the world has not often seen." Mr. Pope received from Lintot the bookseller for this work £5320, more than $18,000 of our American money.

"It is," said Dr. Johnson, "the noblest version of poetry which the world has ever seen; and its publication must therefore be considered as one of the great events in the annals of learning." The publication of the Iliad was completed in 1720. The Odyssey, in the translation of which Mr. Pope was assisted by two gentlemen, Fenton and Broome, was finished in 1725, and from this work the principal translator derived a large sum, so that he cannot be ranked among *poor* poets.

Pope's Homer is among the most popular books in our language. Mr. Gibbon, the historian of the Roman empire, was delighted with Pope's Homer when he was a boy, and could hardly be persuaded that the venerable Grecian could be more beautiful in his original form. Lord Byron says—"Who ever read Cowper's Homer?" and at the same time he speaks of the lively pleasure which Pope's version, with its smooth and flowing versification, had afforded him. Mr. Cowper did not thus love Pope's Homer—that elegant and upright poet did not consider it the "noblest version" which might be made of the ancient classic.

Cowper completed a translation of the Iliad and Odyssey, on the 25th of August, 1790. He was occupied in the work five years and one month. It is written in blank verse, and how faithful soever it may be to the original, it wants the attractiveness of rhyme; and nothwithstanding the judgment of some excellent scholars, that the translation of Pope is often obscure and paraphrastic, and that Cowper is more simple and more faithful to Homer, the public mind nearly agrees with Lord Byron's expression of his own taste upon this subject.

Those who sympathize with Cowper, must take some interest in a work which alleviated the sufferings of the afflicted poet. Of his completed translation he says—" Now I have only to regret that my pleasant work is ended. To the illustrious Greek I owe the smooth and easy flight of many thousand hours. He has been my companion at home and abroad, in the garden, and in the field; and no measure of success, let my labours succeed as they may, will ever compensate to me the loss of the innocent luxury that I have enjoyed as a translator of Homer."

The Iliad is the history of a war. The Odyssey is chiefly the history of an individual, and his family, and though it is connected with the Trojan war, it is a description of domestic manners, and throws much light upon the religion, the state of knowledge, and the useful and ornamental arts of that time.

The Iliad describes a series of battles between the Greeks and Trojans. The whole narrative is highly interesting. Some rigid moralists have considered the works of Homer as dangerous to the principles of the young. He, say they, makes war attractive, and exalts the false glory of military heroes. The pure virtues which Christianity recommends are forgotten by the admirer of Homer, as he feasts his imagination in the lustre of great crimes dignified by the authority of great names.

Homer represents barbarous men as they were, but he does not forget to infuse the sentiments of religion and humanity which might be found among them: and these relieve his dark pictures of violent passions, ferocious manners, and wanton waste of human life. There is something fascinating to the young in the character of the warrior, but other causes besides the reading of Homer, form the false moral taste which is charmed with military glory, such are the want of Christian education—the want of an early and deep conviction that the praise of God is better than the praise of men. A mind early impressed with the beautiful character of Jesus, will feel that benevolence, and the dignity of a soul sustained by unfaltering trust in God under all circumstances, may afford nobler displays of virtue than all the occasions that war ever produced.

————There exists
A higher than the warrior's excellence.
In war itself, war is no ultimate purpose.
The vast and sudden deeds of violence,
Adventures wild, and wonders of the moment—
These are not they, my son, that generate
The Calm, the Blissful, the enduring Mighty?
    Coleridge's translation of Wallenstien.

Some of the finest thoughts we have seen upon this subject have been lately offered to the world in Dr.

Channing's review of the life of Napoleon Bonaparte.—
"The greatness of the warrior," says Dr. Channing, "is
poor and low compared with the magnanimity of virtue.
It vanishes before the greatness of principle. The mar-
tyr to humanity, to freedom, or religion ; the unshrinking
adherent of despised and deserted truth ; who alone, un-
supported, and scorned, with no crowd to infuse into him
courage, no variety of objects to draw his thoughts from
himself, no opportunity of effort or resistance to rouse
and nourish energy, still yields himself calmly, resolutely,
with invincible philanthropy, to bear prolonged and ex-
quisite suffering, which one retracting word might re-
move : such a man is as superior to the warrior, as the
tranquil and boundless heavens above us, to the low earth
we tread beneath our feet.

"Great generals away from the camp, are commonly no
greater men than the mechanician taken from his
workshop. In conversation they are often dull. Works
of profound thinking on general and great topics they
cannot comprehend. The *conqueror of Napoleon, the
hero of Waterloo, undoubtedly possesses great military
talents ; but we have never heard of his eloquence in the
senate, or of his sagacity in the cabinet ; and we venture
to say, that he will leave the world, without adding one
new thought on the great themes, on which the genius of
philosophy and legislature has meditated for ages. We
will not go down for illustration to such men as Nelson,
a man great on the deck, but debased by gross vices, and
who never pretended to enlargement of intellect. To
institute a comparison in point of talent and genius be-
tween such men and Milton, Bacon, and Shakspeare, is
almost an insult on these illustrious names.

" Who can think of these truly great intelligences ; of
the range of their minds through heaven and earth ; of
their deep intuition into the soul ; of their new and glow-
ing combinations of thought ; of the energy with which
they grasped and subjected to their main purpose, the in-

* The Duke of Wellington.

19*

finite materials of illustration which nature and life afford. who can think of the forms of transcendent beauty and grandeur which they created, or which were rather emanations of their own minds ; of the calm wisdom and fervid impetuous imagination which they conjoined ; of the dominion which they have exerted over so many generations, and which time only extends and makes sure ; of the voice of power, in which, though dead, they still speak to nations, and awaken intellect, sensibility, and genius in both hemispheres ; who can think of such men, and not feel the immense inferiority of the most gifted warrior, whose elements of thought are physical forces and physical obstructions, and whose employment is the combination of the lowest class of objects, on which a powerful mind can be employed."

It cannot be misplaced here to express our sense of the superiority of him in whose mind these sentiments originated, to those heroes who are such enticing examples to the young. "He is," said Mr. Southey, " a man who does honour to his age and country." We feel pride and pleasure in this foreign tribute, and we feel also that the best acknowledgment we can make of such a man's worth, is practically to adopt, and zealously to inculcate his principles, that while he is celebrated abroad, his best influence may operate at home.

Hector, a Trojan prince, is perhaps the most interesting of Homer's heroes. The charm of Hector's character is principally derived from his amiable domestic affections. The parting of Hector and Andromache is in most collections of poetry, but it is not a less touching scene because it is well known.

PARTING OF HECTOR AND ANDROMACHE.

" Ere yet I mingle in the direful fray,
My wife, my infant, claim a moment's stay ;
This day (perhaps the last that sees me here)
Demands a parting word, a tender tear :
This day, some god who hates our Trojan land
May vanquish Hector by a Grecian hand.

He said, and pass'd with sad presaging heart
To seek his spouse, his soul's far dearer part ;
At home he sought her, but he sought in vain :
She, with one maid of all her menial train,
Had thence retir'd ; and with her second joy,
The young Astyanax, the hope of Troy,
Pensive she stood on Ilion's tow'ry height,
Beheld the war, and sicken'd at the sight ;
There her sad eyes in vain her lord explore,
Or weep the wounds her bleeding country bore.
 But he who found not whom his soul desir'd,
Whose virtue charm'd him as her beauty fir'd,
Stood in the gates, and ask'd what way she bent
Her parting step ? if to the fane she went,
Where late the mourning matrons made resort ;
Or sought her sisters in the Trojan court?
Not to the court, (reply'd the attendant train,)
Nor mix'd with matrons to Minerva's fane :
To Ilion's steepy tow'r she bent her way,
To mark the fortunes of the doubtful day.
Troy fled, she heard, before the Grecian sword ;
She heard, and trembled for her absent lord :
Distracted with surprise, she seemed to fly,
Fear on her cheek, and sorrow in her eye.
The nurse attended with her infant boy,
The young Astyanax, the hope of Troy.
 Hector, this heard, return'd without delay ;
Swift through the town he trode his former way,
Through streets of palaces, and walks of state,
And met the mourner at the Scæan gate.
With haste to meet him sprung the joyful fair,
His blameless wife, Aetion's wealthy heir ;
The nurse stood near, in whose embraces prest
His only hope hung smiling at her breast,
Whom each soft charm and early grace adorn,
Fair as the new born star that gilds the morn.
To this lov'd infant Hector gave the name
Scamandrius, from Scamander's honour'd stream ;

Astyanax, the Trojans call'd the boy,
From his great father, the defence of Troy.
Silent the warrior smil'd, and pleas'd resign'd
To tender passions all his mighty mind:
His beauteous princess cast a mournful look,
Hung on his hand, and then dejected spoke;
Her bosom labour'd with a boding sigh,
And the big tear stood trembling in her eye.

    Too daring prince! ah whither dost thou run?
Ah too forgetful of thy wife and son!
And think'st thou not how wretched we shall be,
A widow I, a helpless orphan he!
For sure such courage length of life denies,
And thou must fall, thy virtue's sacrifice.
Greece in her single heroes strove in vain;
Now hosts oppose thee, and thou must be slain!
Oh grant me, gods! ere Hector meets his doom,
All I can ask of heav'n, an early tomb!
So shall my days in one sad tenor run,
And end in sorrows, as they first begun.
No parent now remains, my griefs to share,
No father's aid, no mother's tender care.

    The fierce *Achilles wrapt our walls in fire,*
Laid Thebe waste, and slew my warlike sire!
His fate compassion in the victor bred;
Stern as he was, he yet rever'd the dead,
His radiant arms preserv'd from hostile spoil,
And laid him decent on the fun'ral pile;
Then rais'd a mountain where his bones were burn'd;
The mountain-nymphs the rural tomb adorn'd;
Jove's sylvan daughters bade their elms bestow
A barren shade, and in his honour grow.
By the same arm my sev'n brave brothers fell,
In one sad day beheld the gates of hell;
While the fat herds and snowy flocks they fed,
Amid their fields the hapless heroes bled.
My mother liv'd to bear the victor's bands,
The queen of Hippoplacia's sylvan lands:

Redeem'd too late, she scarce beheld again
Her pleasing empire, and her native plain,
When ah! oppress'd by life-consuming wo,
She fell a victim to Diana's bow.
    Yet, while my Hector still survives, I see
My father, mother, brethren, all in thee.
Alas! my parents, brothers, kindred, all,
Once more will perish, if my Hector fall.
Thy wife, thy infant, in thy danger share;
Oh prove a husband's and a father's care!
That quarter most the skilful Greeks annoy,
Where yon wild fig trees join the wall of Troy:
Thou, from this tow'r, defend th' important post;
There Agamemnon points his dreadful host,
That pass Tydides, Ajax, strive to gain,
And there the vengeful Spartan fires his train.
Thrice our bold foes the fierce attack have giv'n,
Or led by hopes, or dictated from heav'n.
Let others in the field their arms employ,
But stay my Hector here, and guard his Troy.
    The chief reply'd: That post shall be my care,
Nor that alone, but all the works of war.
How would the sons of Troy, in arms renown'd,
And Troy's proud dames, whose garments sweep the
   ground,
Attaint the lustre of my former name,
Should Hector basely quit the field of fame!
My early youth was bred to martial pains,
My soul impels me to th' embattl'd plains:
Let me be foremost to defend the throne,
And guard my father's glories, and my own.
    Yet come it will, the day decreed by fates;
(How my heart trembles while my tongue relates!)
The day when thou, imperial Troy! must bend,
And see thy warriors fall, thy glories end.
And yet no dire presage so wounds my mind,
My mother's death, the ruin of my kind,
Not Priam's hoary hairs defil'd with gore,
Not all my brothers gasping on the shore,

As thine, Andromache! thy griefs I dread;
I see thee trembling, weeping, captive led!
In Argive looms our battles to design,
And woes, of which so large a part was thine!
To bear the victor's hard commands, or bring
The weight of waters from Hyperia's spring.
There, while you groan beneath the load of life,
They cry, Behold the mighty Hector's wife!
Some haughty Greek, who lives thy tears to see,
Embitters all thy woes, by naming me.
The thoughts of glory past, and present shame,
A thousand griefs shall waken at the name;
May I lie cold before that dreadful day,
Press'd with a load of monumental clay!
Thy Hector, wrapt in everlasting sleep,
Shall neither hear thee sigh, nor see thee weep.

    Thus having spoke, th' illustrious chief of Troy
Stretch'd his fond arms to clasp the lovely boy.
The babe clung crying to his nurse's breast,
Scar'd at the dazzling helm, and nodding crest.
With secret pleasure each fond parent smil'd,
And Hector hasted to relieve his child,
The glitt'ring terrors from his brows unbound,
And plac'd the beaming helmet on the ground;
Then kiss'd the child, and lifting high in air,
Thus to the gods preferr'd a father's pray'r:

    O thou, whose glory fills th' etherial throne,
And all ye deathless pow'rs! protect my son!
Grant him, like me, to purchase just renown,
To guard the Trojans, to defend the crown,
Against his country's foes the war to wage,
And rise the Hector of the future age!
So when, triumphant from successful toils
Of heroes slain he bears the reeking spoils,
Whole hosts may hail him with deserv'd acclaim,
And say, This chief transcends his father's fame:
While pleas'd amidst the gen'ral shouts of Troy,
His mother's conscious heart o'erflows with joy.

He spoke, and, fondly gazing on her charms,
Restor'd the pleasing burden to her arms ;
Soft on her fragrant breast the babe she laid,
Hush'd to repose, and with a smile survey'd.
The trouble'd pleasure soon chastis'd by fear,
She mingled with the smile a tender tear.
The soften'd chief with kind compassion view'd,
And dry'd the falling drops, and thus pursu'd :
   Andromache ! my soul's far better part,
Why with untimely sorrows heaves thy heart ?
No hostile hand can antedate my doom,
Till fate condemns me to the silent tomb.
Fix'd is the term to all the race of earth,
And such the hard condition of our birth.
No force can then resist, no flight can save,
All sink alike, the fearful and the brave.
No more—but hasten to thy task at home,
There guide the spindle, and direct the loom :
Me glory summons to the martial scene,
The field of combat is the sphere for men,
Where heroes war, the foremost place I claim,
The first in danger, as the first in fame.
   Thus having said, the glorious chief resumes
His tow'ry helmet, black with shading plumes ;
His princess parts with a prophetic sigh,
Unwilling parts, and oft reverts her eye,
That stream'd at every look ; then moving slow,
Sought her own palace, and indulg'd her wo.
There, while her tears deplor'd the godlike man,
Through all her train the soft infection ran,
The pious maids their mingled sorrows shed,
And mourn the living Hector as the dead."

———————

Achilles was the most valiant of the Greeks, as Hec-
tor was of the Trojans. *The fierce Achilles wrapt our
walls in fire,* &c. The lines immediately following this,
describe the conduct of Achilles as the victor of Thebes
and Hippoplacia in Cilicia. Andromache was a prin-
cess of that country : she says Achilles respected her

dead father, and gave him the honour of a funeral pile, raised a heap of earth over his ashes, and permitted a grove of elms to be planted by the young women of the place around his tomb.   The brothers of Andromache, feeding their flocks, were surprised by the ferocious chief, and sent *to hell.*   This expression, in this place, only intimates sudden death.   Andromache's mother, *the queen of Hippoplacia, was* at first made a slave to the victor, but he restored her to her *sylvan lands*—too late however —*she fell a victim to Diana's bow.*   Diana was one of the powers of life and death.   This is a figurative manner of saying—*the queen died.*

I see thee trembling, weeping, captive led, &c.   Hector foresees the day in which his wife, according to the custom of that time, should, when she had become a prisoner of war, be made a slave to the conquerors of his country.

There guide the spindle, and direct the loom.   This shows the simplicity of the modes of life among princes at that time.   Andromache's brothers, like Jacob's sons, fed their flocks—The *mighty Hector's wife* employed herself in domestic manufactures.

REVENGE OF ACHILLES.

Hector killed Patroclus, the beloved friend of Achilles. Achilles felt unbounded fury at this act, and resolves upon the death of Hector.   Upon this event, which Achilles accomplishes, the implacable vengeance of his heart is shocking—he refuses funeral rites to the dead, and drags his corpse in the most outrageous manner round the monument of Patroclus.

"Then his fell soul a thought of vengeance bred,
(Unworthy of himself, and of the dead,)
The nervous ankles bor'd, his feet he bound
With thongs inserted through the double wound;
These fix'd up high behind the rolling wain,
His graceful head was trail'd along the plain.

Proud on his car th' insulting victor stood,
And bore aloft his arms distilling blood.
He smites the steeds ; the rapid chariot flies ;
The sudden clouds of circling dust arise.
Now lost is all that formidable air ;
The face divine, and long descending hair,
Purple the ground, and streak the sable sand ;
Deform'd, dishonour'd, in his native land !
Giv'n to the rage of an insulting throng !
And, in his parents' sight, now dragg'd along !"

FUNERAL OF HECTOR.

Achilles, after offering these indignities to the remains of Hector, retains the body.   Priam, king of Troy, the unfortunate father of Hector, entreats Achilles to restore the corpse, and, though he had sworn to refuse, his obdurate heart at length yields to the pleading of humanity, and he permits the afflicted Priam to pay the last honours to his son.

"Now shed Aurora round her saffron ray,
Sprung thro' the gates of light, and gave the day :
Charg'd with their mournful load. to Ilion go
The sage and king, majestically slow.
Cassandra first beholds, from Ilion's spire,
The sad procession of her hoary sire,
Then, as the pensive pomp advanc'd more near,
Her breathless brother stretch'd upon the bier ;
A show'r of tears o'erflows her beauteous eyes,
Alarming thus all Ilion with her cries.
Turn here your steps, and here your eyes employ,
Ye wretched daughters, and ye sons of Troy !
If e'er ye rush'd in crowds, with vast delight,
To hail your hero glorious from the fight ;
Now meet him dead, and let your sorrows flow !
Your common triumph, and your common wo.
In thronging crowds they issue to the plains,
Nor man, nor woman, in the walls remains,

In ev'ry face the self-same grief is shown,
And Troy sends forth one universal groan.
At Scæa's gates they meet the mourning swain,
Hang on the wheels, and grovel round the slain.
The wife and mother, frantic with despair,
Kiss his pale cheek, and rend their scatter'd hair;
Thus wildly wailing, at the gates they lay,
And there had sigh'd and sorrow'd out the day;
But godlike Priam from the chariot rose;
Forbear (he cry'd) this violence of woes;
First to the palace let the car proceed,
Then pour your boundless sorrows o'er the dead.

   The waves of people at his word divide,
Slow rolls the chariot thro' the following tide;
Ev'n to the palace the sad pomp they wait:
They weep, and place him on the bed of state.
A melancholy choir attend around,
With plantive sighs, and music's solemn sound:
Alternately they sing, alternate flow
Th' obedient tears, melodious in their wo.
While deeper sorrows groan from each full-heart,
And nature speaks at ev'ry pause of art.

   First to the corse the weeping consort flew;
Around his neck her milk-white arms she threw,
And, oh my Hector! oh my lord! she cries,
Snatch'd in thy bloom from these desiring eyes!
Thou to the dismal realms for ever gone!
And I abandon'd, desolate, alone!
An only son, once comfort of our pains,
Sad product now of hapless love remains!
Never to manly age that son shall rise,
Or with increasing graces glad my eyes:
For Ilion now (her great defender slain)
Shall sink a smoking ruin on the plain.
Who now protects her wives with guardian care?
Who saves her infants from the rage of war?
Now hostile fleets must waft those infants o'er,
(Those wives must wait them) to a foreign shore

Thou too, my son! to barb'rous climes shalt go,
The sad companion of thy mother's wo ;
Driv'n hence a slave before the victor's sword ;
Condemn'd to toil for some inhuman lord.
Or else some Greek whose father prest the plain,
Or son, or brother, by great Hector slain,
In Hector's blood his vengeance shall enjoy,
And hurl thee headlong from the tow'rs of Troy.
For thy stern father never spar'd a foe :
Thence all these tears, and all this scene of wo !
Thence many evils his sad parents bore,
His parents many, but his consort more..
Why gav'st thou not to me thy dying hand ?
And why receiv'd not I thy last command ?
Some word thou would'st have spoke, which sadly dear
My soul might keep, or utter with a tear ;
Which never, never, could be lost in air,
Fix'd in my heart, and oft repeated there !
 Thus to her weeping maids she makes her moan ;
Her weeping handmaids echo groan for groan.
 The mournful mother next sustains her part.
O thou, the best, the dearest to my heart !
Of all my race thou most by heav'n approv'd,
And by th' immortals ev'n in death belov'd !
While all my other sons in barb'rous bands,
Achilles bound, and sold to foreign lands,
This felt no chains, but went a glorious ghost
Free, and a hero to the Stygian coast,
Sentenc'd, 'tis true, by his inhuman doom,
Thy noble corse was dragg'd around the tomb,
(The tomb of him thy warlike arm had slain,)
Ungen'rous insult, impotent and vain !
Yet glow'st thou fresh with ev'ry living grace,
No mark of pain, or violence of face ;
Rosy and fair ! as Phœbus' silver bow
Dismiss'd thee gently to the shades below.
 Thus spoke the dame, and melted into tears.
Sad Helen next in pomp of grief appears :

Fast from the shining sluices of her eyes
Fall the round crystal drops, while thus she cries:
   Ah dearest friend! in whom the gods had join'd
The mildest manners with the bravest mind;
Now twice ten years (unhappy years) are o'er,
Since Paris brought me to the Trojan shore;
Yet was it ne'er my fate, from thee to find
A deed ungentle, or a word unkind:
When others curst the authress of their wo,
Thy pity check'd my sorrows in their flow:
If some proud brother ey'd me with disdain,
Or scornful sister with her sweeping train,
Thy gentle accents soften'd all my pain.
For thee I mourn; and mourn myself in thee,
The wretched source of all this misery!
The fate I caus'd for ever I bemoan;
Sad Helen has no friend now thou art gone!
Thro' Troy's wide streets abandon'd shall I roam!
In Troy deserted, as abhorr'd at home!
   So spoke the fair, with sorrow-streaming eye;
Distressful beauty melts each stander-by;
On all around th' infectious sorrow grows;
But Priam check'd the sorrow as it rose.
Perform, ye Trojans! what the rites require,
And fell the forests for a fun'ral pyre;
Twelve days, nor foes, nor secret ambush dread,
Achilles grants these honours to the dead.
   He spoke; and, at his word, the Trojan train
Their mules and oxen harness to the wain,
Pour through the gates, and fell'd from Ida's crown,
Roll'd back the gather'd forests to the town.
These toils continue nine succeeding days,
And high in air a sylvan structure raise.
But when the tenth fair morn began to shine,
Forth to the pile was borne the man divine,
And plac'd aloft: while all, with streaming eyes,
Beheld the flames and rolling smoke arise.

Soon as Aurora, daughter of the dawn,
With rosy lustre streak'd the dewy lawn ;
Again the mournful crowds surround the pyre,
And quench with wine the yet remaining fire,
The snowy bones his friends and brothers place
(With tears collected) in a golden vase ;
The golden vase in purple palls they roll'd,
Of softest texture, and inwrought with gold.
Last o'er the urn the sacred earth they spread,
And rais'd their tomb, memorial of the dead.
(Strong guards and spies, till all the rites were done,
Watch'd from the rising to the setting sun :)
All Troy then moves to Priam's court again,
A solemn, silent, melancholy train :
Assembled there, from pious toils they rest,
And sadly shar'd the last sepulchral feast.
Such honours Ilion to her hero paid,
And peaceful slept the mighty Hector's shade."

The sage and king, &c.   Priam was accompanied in
his journey to the tent of Achilles by Idæus the herald.

Hecuba, the mother of Hector, appears to take a
melancholy pleasure in the thought that Hector de-
scended *free* to the *Stygian coast*.   The Hell of the an-
cients was watered by the Styx.   The deceased lingered
on the *Stygian shore*—the banks of the Styx—"*a naked,
wandering, melancholy ghost*," till the rites of sepulture
were paid, and then the judges of the dead sentenced
him to the reward of the " deeds done in the body."

Helen was the wife of Menelaus, the Spartan king.
Paris, the brother of Hector, had enticed her to accom-
pany him to Troy.   To punish this act, the princes of
Greece had invaded Troy.   Helen's grief is very honour-
able to Hector—it describes that affectionate and gentle
nature so dear to his parents, his wife, and his domes-
tics.

SARPEDON.

Sarpedon was a king of Lycia, in Asia Minor, reputed
to be a son of Jupiter.   He, with his friend Glaucus, re-
paired to Troy, to assist Priam against the Greeks.   He
is represented by Homer to have been a man of high
honour : being about to attack the Greeks, he exhorts
Glaucus in a manner worthy of his station :—

" Nor Troy could conquer, nor the Greeks would yield,
'Till great Sarpedon tower'd amid the field ;
For mighty Jove inspir'd with martial flame
His matchless son, and urg'd him on to fame.
In arms he shines, conspicuous from afar,
And bears aloft his ample shield in air :
Within whose orb the thick bull-hides were roll'd,
Pond'rous with brass, and bound with ductile gold :
And while two pointed jav'lins arm his hands,
Majestic moves along, and heads his Lycian bands.
    Why boast we, Glaucus ! our extended reign,
Where Xanthus' streams enrich the Lycian plain,
Our num'rous herds that range the fruitful field,
And hills where vines their purple harvest yield,
Our foaming bowls with purer nectar crown'd,
Our feasts enhanc'd with music's sprightly sound ?
Why on those shores are we with joy survey'd,
Admir'd as heroes, and as gods obey'd ?
Unless great acts superior merit prove,
And vindicate the bounteous pow'rs above.
'Tis ours, the dignity they give, to grace ;
The first in valour, as the first in place.
    That when, with wond'ring eyes our martial bands
Behold our deeds transcending our commands,
Such, they may cry, deserve the sov'reign state,
Whom those that envy, dare not imitate !
Could all our care elude the gloomy grave,
Which claims no less the fearful than the brave,
For lust of fame I should not vainly dare
In fighting fields, nor urge my soul to war.

But since, alas! ignoble age must come,
Disease, and death's inexorable doom ;
The life which others pay, let us bestow,
And give to fame what we to nature owe ;
Brave though we fall, and honour'd if we live,
Or let us glory gain, or glory give !"

Why on these shores? &c.   These lines are rendered
thus in Cowper's Iliad :—

"Why gaze they all on us as we were gods
In Lycia, and why share we pleasant fields
And spacious vineyards where the Xanthus winds ?
Distinguished thus in Lycia we are called
To firmness here, and to encounter bold
The burning battle, that our fair report
Among the Lycians may be blazoned thus—
No dastards are the potentates who rule
The bright-armed Lycians ; on the fatted flock
They banquet, and they drink the richest wines,
But they are also valiant, and the fight
Wage dauntless"—

These very different modes of expression hardly sug-
gest the idea of the same passage.   In English prose the
sense of Pope's version is this—Why boast we the favours
of the gods—our prosperity and our high station ?—Why
do our subjects regard us as gods, unless our conduct is
worthy of our privileges ?—It becomes us to prove that
we deserve the divine favour, and the homage of our sub-
jects, by actions suitable to the dignity we enjoy, and the
respect we command.

In the sixteenth book of the Iliad, Sarpedon is killed
by Patroclus, a Greek :—

"The tow'ring chiefs to fiercer fight advance,
And first Sarpedon whirl'd his weighty lance,
Which o'er the warrior's shoulder took its course,
And spent in empty air its dying force.

Not so Patroclus' never-erring dart ;
Aim'd at his breast, it pierc'd the mortal part
Where the strong fibres bind the solid heart.
Then, as the mountain oak, or poplar tall,
Or pine, (fit mast for some great admiral,)
Nods to the axe, till with a groaning sound
It sinks, and spreads its honours on the ground :
Thus fell the king ; and, laid on earth supine,
Before his chariot stretch'd his form divine :
He grasp'd the dust distain'd with streaming gore,
And, pale in death, lay groaning on the shore.
    Then to the leader of the Lycian band
The dying chief addrest his last command.
Glaucus be bold ; thy task be first to dare
The glorious dangers of destructive war.
To lead my troops, to combat at their head,
Incite the living, and supply the dead.
Tell them, I charg'd them with my latest breath
Not unreveng'd to bear Sarpedon's death.
What grief, what shame must Glaucus undergo,
If these spoil'd arms adorn a Grecian foe !
Then as a friend, and as a warrior fight ;
Defend my body, conquer in my right ;
That, taught by great examples, all may try
Like thee to vanquish, or like me to die.
He ceas'd ; the fates suppress'd his lab'ring breath,
And his eyes darken'd with the shades of death.
Th' insulting victor in disdain bestrode
The prostrate prince, *and on his bosom trode.*
All impotent of aid, transfix'd with grief,
Unhappy Glaucus heard the dying chief.
First to the fight his native troops he warms,
Then loudly calls on Troy's vindictive arms.
    He spoke : each leader in his grief partook,
Troy, at the loss, through all her legions shook.
Transfix'd with deep regret, they view o'erthrown,
At once his country's pillar and their own ;
A chief who led to Troy's beleaguer'd wall
A host of heroes, and outshin'd them all.

Fir'd they rush on ; first Hector seeks the foes,
And with superior vengeance greatly glows.
  Now great Sarpedon, on the sandy shore,
His heav'nly face deform'd with dust and gore,
And struck with darts by warring heroes shed,
Lies undistinguish'd from the common dead.
His long-disputed corse the chiefs inclose,
On ev'ry side the busy combat grows :
  Then, nor before, the hardy Lycians fled,
And left their monarch with the common dead ;
Around, in heaps on heaps, a dreadful wall
Of carnage rises as the heroes fall.
(So Jove decreed !) at length the Greeks obtain
The prize contested, and despoil the slain.
The radiant arms are by Patroclus borne,
Patroclus' ships the glorious spoils adorn.
  Then thus to Phœbus, in the realms above,
Spoke from his throne the cloud-compelling Jove :
Descend, my Phœbus ! on the Phrygian plain,
And from the fight convey Sarpedon slain ;
Then bathe his body in the crystal flood,
With dust dishonour'd, and deform'd with blood :
O'er all his limbs ambrosial odours shed,
And with celestial robes adorn the dead.
Those rites discharg'd, his sacred corse bequeath
To the soft arms of silent Sleep and Death :
They to his friends the mournful charge shall bear,
His friends a tomb and pyramid shall rear;
What honours mortals after death receive,
Those unavailing honours we may give !
  Apollo bows, and from mount Ida's height,
Swift to the field precipitates his flight ;
Thence from the war the breathless hero bore,
Veil'd in a cloud to silver Simois' shore ;
There bath'd his honourable wounds, and drest
His manly members in th' immortal vest ;
And with perfumes of sweet ambrosial dews,
Restores his freshness, and his form renews.

Then Sleep and Death, two twins of winged race,
Of matchless swiftness, but of silent pace,
Receiv'd Sarpedon, at the god's command,
And in a moment reach'd the Lycian land ;
The corse amidst his weeping friends they laid,
Where endless honours wait the sacred shade."

The insulting victor trod on his prostrate foe. This
horribly revengeful spirit, gives a shocking idea of savage warfare. Christianity has taught men a more merciful mode of treating fallen enemies.

ULYSSES.

Ulysses, King of Ithaca, was the most accomplished
of the Greeks who went to the siege of Troy. He is
described by Homer to have been diffident though eloquent, not to have commanded admiration the moment he
rose to speak, but by degrees to have charmed those who
listened to him.

But when Ulysses rose, in thought profound,
His modest eyes he fix'd upon the ground,
As one unskill'd or dumb, he seem'd to stand,
Nor raised his head nor stretch'd his sceptr'd hand ;
But, when he speaks, what elocution flows !
Soft as the fleeces of descending snows,
The copious accents fall with easy art ;
Melting they fall, and sink into the heart !
Wond'ring we hear, and fix'd in deep surprise ;
Our ears refute the censure of our eyes.

On his return from Troy Ulysses fell under the displeasure of Apollo. The men under his command had
————————————dared to prey
On herds devoted to the God of Day.
That, is they had seized upon flocks reserved for the
sacrifices to Apollo. *The God vindictive,* doomed
them never to return to their country,—they were destined to perish by a series of accidents, and their com-

mander was at length to be restored to his dominions. But he was shipwrecked in Ogygia, a supposed island of the Mediterranean, and for want of a ship to convey him away was detained in the island seven years. This island was the abode of Calypso, one of the Oceanides— of ocean. She was a daughter of Atlas, one of Titans, or giants who rebelled against Jupiter. Ca- loved Ulysses, and was grieved at his departure, was effected by the *decree of Jove*, or Jupiter, who Mercury with the celestial message. In the fifth book of the Odyssey the passage may be found.

CALYPSO.

" The god who mounts the winged winds
Fast to his feet the golden pinions binds,
That high through fields of air his flight sustain
O'er the wide earth, and o'er the boundless main.
He grasps the wand that causes sleep to fly,
Or in soft slumbers seals the wakeful eye :
Then shoots from heav'n to high Pieria's steep,
And stoops incumbent on the rolling deep.
So wat'ry fowl, that seek their fishy food,
With wings expanded o'er the foaming flood,
Now sailing smooth the level surface sweep,
Now dip their pinions in the briny deep.
Thus o'er the world of waters Hermes flew,
'Till now the distant island rose in view :
Then swift ascending from the azure wave,
He took the path that winded to the cave.
Large was the grot in which the nymph he found,
(The fair hair'd nymph with ev'ry beauty crown'd)
She sat and sung ; the rocks resound her lays :
The cave was brighten'd with a rising blaze :
Cedar and frankincense, an od'rous pile,
Flam'd on the hearth, and wide perfum'd the isle ;
While she with work and song the time divides,
And thro' the loom the golden shuttle guides.
Without the grot, a various sylvan scene
Appear'd around, and groves of living green ;

Poplars and alders ever quiv'ring play'd,
And nodding cypress form'd a fragrant shade;
On whose high branches, waving with the storm,
The birds of broadest wing their mansion form,
The chough, the sea-mew, the loquacious crow,
And scream aloft, and skim the deeps below.

Depending vines the shelving cavern screen,
With purple clusters blushing thro' the green.
Four limpid fountains from the clefts distil,
And ev'ry fountain pours a sev'ral rill,
In mazy windings wandering down the hill;
Where blooming meads with vivid greens were crown'd,
And glowing violets threw odours round.
A scene, where if a God should cast his sight,
A God might gaze and wonder, with delight!
Joy touch'd the messenger of heav'n; he stay'd
Entranc'd, and all the blissful haunt survey'd.
Him ent'ring in the cave, Calypso knew;
For pow'rs celestial to each other's view
Stand still confest, though distant far they lie
To habitants of earth, or sea, or sky.

But sad Ulysses, by himself apart,
Pour'd the big sorrows of his swelling heart;
All on the lonely shore he sat to weep,
And roll'd his eyes around the restless deep;
Toward his lov'd coast he roll'd his eyes in vain,
'Till dimm'd with rising grief, they stream'd again.

Now graceful seated on her shining throne,
To Hermes thus the nymph divine begun.

God of the golden wand! on what behest
Arriv'st thou here, an unexpected guest?
Lov'd as thou art, thy free injunctions lay;
'Tis mine, with joy and duty to obey,
Till now a stranger, in a happy hour
Approach and taste the dainties of my bow'r.

Thus having spoke, the nymph the table spread,
(Ambrosial cates, with Nectar rosy-red)
Hermes the hospitable rite partook,
Divine refection! then recruited, spoke.

What mov'd this journey from my native sky,
A Goddess asks, nor can a God deny:
Hear then the truth. By mighty Jove's command,
Unwilling, have I trod this pleasing land:
For who, self-mov'd, with weary wing would sweep
Such length of ocean and unmeasur'd deep:
A world of waters! far from all the ways
Were men frequent, or sacred altars blaze?
But to Jove's will submission we must pay;
What pow'r so great, to dare to disobey?
A man, he says, a man resides with thee,
Of all his kind most worn with misery:
The Greeks (whose arms for nine long years employ'd
Their force on Ilion, in the tenth destroy'd)
At length embarking in a luckless hour,
With conquest proud, incens'd Minerva's pow'r:
Hence on the guilty race her vengeance hurl'd
With storms pursued them through the liquid world.
There all his vessels sunk beneath the wave!
There all his dear companions found a grave!
Sav'd from the jaws of death by heaven's decree,
The tempest drove him to these shores and thee.
Him, Jove now orders to his native lands
Straight to dismiss; so Destiny commands:
Impatient Fate his near return attends,
And calls him to his country, and his friends.

Ev'n to her inmost soul the Goddess shook;
Then thus her anguish and her passion broke.
Ungracious Gods! with spite and envy curst!
So till your own etherial race the worst!
And is it now my turn, ye mighty powr's!
Am I the envy of your blisful bow'rs?
A man, an outcast to the storm and wave,
It was my crime to pity, and to save;
When he who thunders rent his bark in twain,
And sunk his brave companions in the main.
Alone, abandon'd, in mid-ocean tost,
The sport of winds, and driv'n from ev'ry coast,

Hither this man of miseries I led,
Received the friendless, and the hungry fed;
Nay promis'd (vainly promis'd!) to bestow
Immortal life, exempt from age and wo.
'Tis past; and Jove decrees he shall remove;
Gods as we are, we are but slaves to Jove.
Go then he may; (he must, if he ordain,
Try all those dangers, all those deeps, again)
But never, never shall Calypso send
To toils like these, her husband and her friend.
What ships have I, what sailors to convey,
What oars to cut the long laborious way?
Yet, I'll direct the safest means to go:
That last advice is all I can bestow.

To her the pow'r, who bears the charming rod.
Dismiss the man, nor irritate the God;
Prevent the rage of him who reigns above,
For what so dreadful as the wrath of Jove?
Thus having said, he cut the cleaving sky,
And in a moment vanish'd from her eye.

The nymph, obedient to divine command,
To seek Ulysses, paced along the sand.
Him pensive on the lonely beach she found,
With streaming eyes in briny torrents drown'd,
And inly pining for his native shore;
For now the soft enchantress pleas'd no more:
He sat all desolate, and sigh'd alone,
While echoing sorrows made the mountains groan,
And roll'd his eyes o'er all the restless main,
'Till dimmed with rising grief, they stream'd again.

Here, on the musing mood the Goddess prest,
Approaching soft; and thus the chief addrest.
Unhappy man! to wasting woes a prey,
No more in sorrows languish life away;
Free as the winds I give thee now to rove.—
Go fell the timber of yon lofty grove
And form a raft, and build the rising ship,
Sublime to bear thee o'er the gloomy deep.

To store the vessel let the care be mine,
With water from the rock, and rosy wine,
And life-sustaining bread, and fair array,
And prosp'rous gales to waft thee on the way.
These if the Gods with my desires comply,
(The Gods, alas! more mighty far than I,
And better skill'd in dark events to come)
In peace shall land thee at thy native home.

The god who mounts the winged wind.—Mercury, or
Hermes, the son of Jupiter and Maia. Mercury was the
messenger of the gods. He was the god of merchants,
orators, and *thieves.* The mythology says he robbed
Neptune of his *trident;* Venus of her *girdle,*—the Cestus which made her appear so beautiful—Mars of his
sword, and Vulcan of the *anvil.*

The wand that causes sleep to fly. The Caduceus,
a rod entwined with two serpents. It was the emblem
of Mercury's *vigilance,* or watchfulness.

Ambrosial cates with Nectar rosy red. Ambrosia was
the food, and Nectar the wine of the Gods.

It is related in the Odyssey, that when Ulysses, was in
the Mediterranean, he stopped at the island of Circe: his
men were in want of food, and they went to the palace of
the enchantress to procure it, but she transformed them,
all except one, to *hogs.* He who escaped returned to
Ulysses and told him the misfortune of his companions.
Mercury appeared to Ulysses and gave him an herb
called Moly, which was to serve as a protection to him
against the arts of Circe. Ulysses then went to the goddess, and obtained the restoration of his men. It is related
that one of these men named Gryllus refused to be restored to his human shape, preferring the degraded condition of a hog, to that of a man.

Fenelon, Archbishop of Cambray in France, composed
a dialogue between Ulysses and Gryllus. Fenelon did
this for the instruction of a young prince whom he edu-

cated. This dialogue has been translated, and it may be useful and entertaining to young persons who are not princes.

ULYSSES AND GRYLLUS.

Ulysses. Are you not rejoiced, my dear Gryllus, to see me again, and to be able to recover your human form?

Gryllus. I am very glad to see you, favourite of Minerva: but for the change of form, excuse me, if you please.

Ulysses. Alas! unhappy Gryllus, do you know the condition in which you are?—You are a disgusting object; your gross body grovels on the earth, you have long pendulous ears, little eyes, hardly open, an odious grunt, a disagreeable physiognomy, and a skin covered with coarse and stiff bristles,—in short, your whole appearance is hideous. . I tell you of it; if you know it not, and you have so little sense of enjoyment in this deplorable state that you will find yourself happy to resume that of man.

Gryllus. You talk very well, but I do not wish to resume my former condition:—that of a hog is more agreeable. It is true my figure is not elegant; but this does not disturb me, since I never look in a mirror, and in my present humour I need not dread to see myself in the water, and to be reminded of my ugliness, for I prefer a muddy pool to a clear fountain.

Ulysses. Does not this filthiness excite horror in you? You live only in loathsome places, and the very odour you diffuse offends the senses of all about you.

Gryllus. What do I care, all depends upon taste. This odour which is detestable to you, is more fragrant than amber to me, and the refuse substances, which man abhors, are nectar to my appetite.

Ulysses. I blush for you. Is it possible that you have so soon forgotten the dignity and happiness of man!

Gryllus. Speak not to me of the state of man: all his calamities are real, and his blessings are only imaginary. I have a healthful body covered with a bristled coat, and I have no need of garments: you would be more happy in your unfortunate adventures if your body was covered like mine, that you might feel no anxiety how you should be clothed. I find my subsistence every where. Law-suits, and wars, and all the other embarrassments of life do not disturb me. I have no need of cook, barber, tailor or architect. Behold me free and content at little expense. Why then would you again subject me to the wants of man?

Ulysses. It is true that man experiences great wants, but the arts, which he has invented to supply his wants, become his glory, and form his happiness.

Gryllus. It is better to be exempted from all these wants than to possess the most wonderful means to remedy them. It is better to enjoy perfect health, without the science of medicine, than to be always sick—with excellent means of cure.

Ulysses. But, Gryllus, count you for nothing, eloquence, poetry, music, and the science of all arts, and all civilized nations,—figures and numbers?—Would you renounce the love of your native country and your friends, the pleasures of religious worship, the celebration of public benefits, and the honours to be obtained from public approbation?—Answer me.

Gryllus. My constitution as a hog is so happy, that it raises me above these fine things. I love better to grunt than to be eloquent as you are, who are persuasive as Minerva. I wish neither to persuade, nor to be persuaded. I am as indifferent to verse as to prose. The honour which Greece bestows are crowns to wrestlers and chariot racers: I leave them to those who love laurels as infants love playthings. I am no more disposed to bear away prizes than to envy those who are less burthened with fat than myself.

As for Music, I have lost my taste for it, and taste determines the value of every thing: let us talk no more about these matters. Return to Ithaca—*My* country is any where—the country of a hog is wherever there are acorns. Go, reign, behold Penelope once more, and punish her lovers. For me my queen is here, she reigns in my sty, and no one troubles our empire. Many kings in sumptuous palaces cannot attain to my felicity; men call them cowards and unworthy of a throne when they wish to reign like me, without disturbing mankind.

Ulysses. You forgot that you are at the mercy of men; they feed only to devour you. Men, in the rank, in which you wish not to be, will convert you into lard, sausages, and bacon.

Gryllus. Truly that is the danger of my state; but yours has also its perils. I expose myself to death by a sensual life, of which the enjoyment is real; you at the same time, are in danger of a sudden death, by an unhappy life, and in the pursuit of vain glory. Should Apollo himself sing your achievements, his praises could not cure your pains, nor prolong your days.

Ulysses. You are then so brutified as to despise wisdom which assimilates men to the Gods?

Gryllus. On the contrary, wisdom instructs me to despise men.—Since they are unjust, deceitful, ungrateful, miserable by their own folly, cruelly armed against each other, and often as much their own as the enemies of their neighbours, what is the purpose of that wisdom of which they boast? Is it not better to be without reason, than to use her to authorize crimes? Without flattering myself, I may say, that a hog is a very good kind of animal: he makes neither false money nor false contracts, he never perjures himself; he has neither avarice nor ambition, and he is without malice; he spends his life in eating, drinking, and sleeping. If men resembled our species the world would enjoy profound repose, and you would not be here. Paris would never have carried off Helen. The Greeks would not have destroyed the splendid city of Troy after a siege of ten years. You would not have wandered over sea and land, the sport of fortune; and it would not be necessary that you should make war with a crowd of usurpers to recover your own kingdom.

Ulysses. I am astonished at your stupidity, but you

must admit that the immortality reserved for man after this life elevates him infinitely above brutes ?

Gryllus. If you could convince me that man is an *immortal* being, I am not such a brute as to renounce the nature which you hold in honour.——Convince me that man has in him something more noble than his body which shall live for ever.   Because I am not convinced of this I persist in being a hog. Show me that, that which thinks in man, exists after his body is decayed and dissolved. If you will assure me that man can never die, that virtue has its reward in another life, instantly, divine son of Laertes, I will share with you all the dangers that await you ; I will gladly come out of the sty of Circe ;   I will divest myself of this sensual body, and become a man raised to the enjoyments of an immortal being.   But in no other way can I accept your offer to restore my last shape.   I love rather to be a mere animal, satisfied with the proper nature of animals, than to be a man, feeble, ignorant, frivolous, malignant, deceitful or unjust, or to be a *melancholy phantom* discontented with life, and in the dark concerning eternity.

When Gryllus declares he would rather be a brute than a *melancholy phantom,* &c. he is made to allude to the admission of Ulysses to the eternal world.   In the eleventh book of the Odyssey, Ulysses is sent to the *shades*—the abodes of departed souls—and the dead are described, not as happy, but sad and dispirited in their final lot.   This view of another life is such, that one might naturally choose to be exempted from immortality, rather than to be subject to eternal discontent.

Fenelon meant to teach by this dialogue, that the existence of brutes is the gift of a benevolent God, and that they are as happy as the means and faculties which God allots to them will permit ; that man, when he is selfish, cruel, and deceitful, when he is without benevolence, without piety, and without a true religion, is as miserable as he is degraded ; and that the religion of the heathen was so insufficient to make them happy and good, that another and more perfect religious system was necessary to reclaim men from their vices, and to satisfy their hopes. This religion, he would imply, and it may readily be perceived, is the religion of Christ, which establishes that fact most important to our satisfaction in this life, that there is another and an eternal world, in which we shall be delivered from the afflictions of this state of being, and be admitted to perfect and unending happiness.

Apollo. A heathen god—sometimes called the "god of health, and light, and arts"—properly the sun. The sun, by his genial and happy influence upon the human body, produces health, and agreeable sensations; but by the intensity of his heat in some seasons, climates, and places, he becomes apparently the effective cause of disease. Light is well known to emanate directly from the sun. It is not quite so plain how music, eloquence, and poetry are inspired by that luminary, but darkness and obscurity are *figurative* expressions for ignorance, stupidity, and the absence of all accomplishments. Without the "blessed sun" we could not perceive nor communicate any thing but sound, and music itself may derive much beauty from the cheerful ideas connected with light.

Minerva. Gryllus says of Ulysses, "you are as *persuasive as Minerva.* Minerva is sometimes called Pallas, and sometimes Athenæ: she was the tutelary genius of Athens. In that city, her temple, and the services performed in honour of her, were more splendid than any where else—the Athenians expressing by this homage their character, more intellectual and spiritual than the rest of the heathen world.

Minerva, or Wisdom, was the daughter of Jove, the supreme god of the heathens, and sprung from her father's head. This fable implies that God is the origin or beginning of Wisdom. Wisdom signifies knowledge, not only the knowledge of whatever exists, but the knowledge of what is right and best in conduct.

God's wisdom is *infinite*—extends through time and eternity, and to all beings and events, and appoints and executes all his laws. *Man's wisdom* extends to all his duties—his virtues and his knowledge. *Human wisdom* is like *divine wisdom*, but infinitely *less in degree*. It is sufficient to enable man to do right, to please God, and to make him happy.

Solomon, in the book of Proverbs, has *personified* Wisdom—that is, spoken of this moral attribute of God as of an intelligent and living being. The power and virtue which the heathen imputed to Minerva, are far less exalted than the power and virtue of that Wisdom which the king of Israel described.

Solomon makes Wisdom say, "I love them that love me; and those that seek me early shall find me. Receive my instruction and not silver; and knowledge rather than choice gold. Riches and honour are with me; yea, durable riches and righteousness. Hear instruction and be wise, and refuse it not. He that sinneth against me, wrongeth his own soul. O ye simple, understand wisdom: and, ye fools, be ye of an understanding heart. Hear: for I will speak of excellent things; and the opening of my lips shall be right things.

"The Lord possessed me in the beginning of his way, before his works of old. I was set up from everlasting, from the beginning, or ever the earth was. When there were no depths, I was brought forth; when there were no fountains abounding with water. Before the mountains were settled, before the hills was I brought forth: while as yet he had not made the earth, nor the fields, nor the highest part of the dust of the world.

"When he prepared the heaven I was there: when he set a compass upon the face of the depth: when he established the clouds above: when he strengthened the fountains of the deep: when he gave to the sea his decree, that the waters should not pass his commandment: when he appointed the foundations of the earth: then I was by him, as one brought up with him: and I was daily his delight, rejoicing always before him."

CIRCE'S PALACE.

The following description of Circe's palace, and the transformations she wrought, is taken from the tenth book of the Odyssey.

"The palace in a woody vale they found,
High rais'd of stone; a shaded space around :
Where mountain wolves and brindled lions roam,
(By magic tam'd) familiar to the dome.
With gentle blandishment our men they meet,
And wag their tails, and fawning lick their feet.
As from some feast a man-returning late,
His faithful dogs all meet him at the gate,
Rejoicing round, some morsel to receive,
(Such as the good man ever us'd to give.)
Domestic thus the grisly beasts draw near ;
They gaze with wonder, not unmix'd with fear.
Now on the threshold of the dome they stood,
And heard a voice resounding through the wood :
Plac'd at her loom within, the goddess sung ;
The vaulted roofs and solid pavement rung.
O'er the fair web the rising figures shine,
Immortal labour ! worthy hands divine.
Polites to the rest the question mov'd,
(A gallant leader, and a man I lov'd.)
What voice celestial, chanting to the loom
(Or nymph, or goddess) echoes from the room ?
Say shall we seek access ? with that they call ;
And wide unfold the portals of the hall.
The goddess rising, asks her guests to stay,
Who blindly follow where she leads the way.
Eurylochus alone of all the band,
Suspecting fraud, more prudently remain'd.
On thrones around with downy cov'rings grac'd,
With semblance fair th' unhappy men she plac'd.
Milk newly press'd, the sacred flour of wheat,
And honey fresh, and Pramnian wines the treat :
But venom'd was the bread, and mix'd the bowl,
With drugs of force to darken all the soul :

Soon in the luscious feast themselves they lost,
And drank oblivion of their native coast.
Instant her circling wand the goddess waves,
To hogs transforms 'em, and the sty receives.
No more was seen the human form divine;
Head, face, and members, bristle into swine :
Still curst with sense, their minds remain alone,
And their own voice affrights them when they groan.
Meanwhile the goddess in disdain bestows
The mast and acorn, brutal food! and stows
The fruits of cornel, as their feast around ;
Now prone and grov'ling on unsav'ry ground."

When Ulysses was absent, the princes and noblemen of the neighbouring countries went into his kingdom, lived in his palace, fed upon his flocks, and severally demanded the queen Penelope in marriage—these, in the Odyssey, are called the Suitors.

Penelope, who loved her husband, refused them all, and lived with her son Telemachus in Ithaca, always in hopes of the return of Ulysses. After twenty years from his departure for Troy, he again entered the walls of his palace in the disguise of a beggar : he was treated with kindness by the Queen and Telemachus, but with contempt and insolence by the Suitors; however he was soon recognized by an old domestic. In due time he declared himself, and with his son and their faithful adherents, killed the Suitors, and was restored to his ancient dignity.

ARGUS.

A very interesting account is given of the dog Argus, who recognized his master Ulysses, when he approached his palace, attended by Eumæus, an old servant. This sagacious dog has been celebrated for three thousand years; and his history is thus related in the Odyssey.

"Thus, near the gates conferring as they drew,
Argus, the dog his ancient master knew;
He, not unconcious of the voice, and tread,
Lifts to the sound his ear, and rears his head;
Bred by Ulysses, nourish'd at his board,
But ah! not fated long to please his lord!
To him, his swiftness and his strength were vain;
The voice of glory call'd him o'er the main.
'Till then in ev'ry sylvan chase renown'd,
With Argus, Argus, rung the woods around;
With him the youth pursu'd the goat or fawn,
Or trac'd the mazy leveret o'er the lawn.
Now left to man's ingratitude he lay,
Unhous'd, neglected in the public way;
And where on heaps the rich manure was spread,
Obscene with reptiles, took his sordid bed.
    He knew his lord; he knew, and strove to meet
In vain he strove, to crawl, and kiss his feet:
Yet (all he could) his tail, his ears, his eyes
Salute his master, and confess his joys.
Soft pity touch'd the mighty master's soul;
Adown his cheek a tear unbidden stole,
Stole unperceiv'd; he turn'd his head, and dry'd
The drop humane: then thus impassion'd cry'd:
    What noble beast in this abandon'd state
Lies here all helpless at Ulysses' gate?
His bulk and beauty speak no vulgar praise;
If, as he seems, he *was* in better days,
Some care his age deserves: or was he priz'd
For worthless beauty; therefore now despis'd!
Such dogs, and men there are, mere things of state,
And always cherish'd by their friends, the great.
    Not Argus so, (Eumæus thus enjoin'd)
But serv'd a master of a nobler kind,
Who never, never shall behold him more!
Long, long since perish'd on a distant shore!
Oh had you seen him, vig'rous, bold, and young,
Swift as a stag, and as a lion strong;

Him no fell savage on the plain withstood,
None 'scap'd him, bosom'd in the gloomy wood ;
His eye how piercing, and his scent how true,
To winde the vapour in the tainted dew !
Such, when Ulysses left his natal coast :
Now years unnerve him, and his lord is lost !
The women keep the gen'rous creature bare,
A sleek and idle race is all their care :
The master gone, the servants what restrains ?
Or dwells Humanity where Riot reigns ?
Jove fix'd it certain, that whatever day
Makes man a slave, takes half his worth away."

GREEK POETS.

It is not the province of a teacher limited to a literature purely English, to afford much knowledge of the writers of ancient Greece. But these writers have recorded the religion, the moral sentiments, the domestic manners, and the public amusements of the Greeks; and matters of fact in relation to this people. if not the elegance of their language, and the utmost refinement of their thoughts, are offered to common readers in the form of translation.

The connexion of the Greek literature with the English, is derived from this circumstance, that the greater part of our writers are classical scholars—have been instructed in the language and literature of Greece; and those who have not been thus instructed, have been informed in the spirit of the Greek literature by their intercourse with books and scholars: so that young persons who cultivate any knowledge of the literature of their own language, have need of some popular elementary information concerning the Greek.

The *translations* of Homer and the Greek dramatists are the best means which merely English students have to inform themselves of the fables. the religion, the public amusements, and the domestic life of the Greeks. Theatrical amusements are not approved by many religious persons, but, *dramatic literature*—written plays—include so much of the poetry of Greece and England, that it is difficult to exclude it from the liberal studies of any young person.

The origin and progress of the Drama among the Greeks cannot be an unsuitable illustration of a collection of poetry, of which the professed object is to connect poetry with the history of nations, and the progress of society.

ÆSCHYLUS.

" Æschylus was an Athenian of an honourable family, distinguished for the sublimity of his genius and the ardour of his martial spirit. In his youth he had read Homer with the warmest enthusiasm: and finding his great master unrivalled in the Epic, he early conceived the design of creating a new province for himself, and forming the drama; so much we may bo allowed to infer from the fable, that whilst he was yet a boy Bacchus appeared to him as he lay asleep in a vineyard, and commanded him to write tragedies. This noble design he soon executed, and before the twenty-fifth year of his age began to entertain his countrymen with representations worthy of an Athenian audience.

He had pursued these studies about ten years, when Darius invaded Greece. His generals, Datis and Artaphernes, with an army of two hundred thousand foot and ten thousand horse, were now advanced to the plains of Marathon, distant only ten miles from Athens. The danger, which threatened his country, called forth the martial spirit of our poet ; and very honourable mention is made of him, and his two brothers, Cynægirus and Amynias, for their eminent valour in that battle : to have wanted courage on such an occasion would have been a mark of the most abject baseness ; but to be distinguished in an action, where every soldier was a hero, is a proof of superior merit : in a picture representing the battle of Marathon the portrait of Æschylus was drawn : this was all the honour that Miltiades himself received from the state for his glorious conduct on that day ; he was placed at the head of the ten commanders, and drawn in the act of encouraging the soldiers and beginning the battle.

Some time after, Cynægirus was one of the four naval commanders, who with an armament of one thousand Grecians, defeated thirty thousand Persians ; but he lost his life in the action.

Ten years after the battle of Marathon, when Xerxes made that immense preparation to revenge the defeat of his father, we find the two surviving brothers exerting their courage in the sea fight off Salamis : here Amynias too, boldly laying hold of a Persian ship, had his hand lopped off with a sabre ; but Æschylus defended him, and saved his life ; and the Athenians decreed him the first honours, because he was the first to attack the commander of the Persian fleet, shattered the ship to pieces, and killed the Satrap. It is observed that the two brothers were ever after inseparable. The following year Æschylus acquired fresh glory in the battle of Platæa, where the brave Persian Mardonius was defeated and slain.

Having taken this active part in the three most memorable battles that grace the annals of Greece, and distinguished himself as a good citizen and a brave man, he returned with ardour to his former studies, and completed his design of making the drama a regular, noble, and rational entertainment. He wrote about seventy tragedies, and was in great esteem with his countrymen : but upon some disgust in the latter part of his life he retired from Athens to the court of Hiero king of Sicily, where about three years after he died, in the sixty-ninth year of his age.

The tragedy of the Furies gave great offence ; and the poet, whether for that or on some other pretence, was accused of impiety. His brother Amynias pleaded his cause : the Athenians were struck with this instance of fraternal affection, they reverenced their maimed veteran, and Æschylus was acquitted. But such a spirit was not formed to submit to the affront ; it made too deep an impression to be effaced ; and the poet quitted the city with great indignation, declaring with a noble pride that he would intrust his tragedies to posterity, certain that he should receive from thence the honour he deserved. This honour the Athenians soon paid to his noble works : by a decree of the senate, never granted to any other, they offered rewards to any man that should again exhibit his plays ; they frequently adjudged the prize to him after his decease, and acknowledged him *the Father of Tragedy.*

The Grecians, advancing in polished manners, carried into their towns a feast that sprung from the leisure of the country : their best poets took a pride in composing these religious hymns to the honour of Bacchus, and embellished them with the agreeable entertainments of music and dancing. After a length of time, the songs advancing in perfection, it was found necessary to give the singer some relief; and that the company might be amused during the pauses of the music, an actor was introduced : his part could be no other than a single speech, setting forth that he represented Hercules, or Theseus, or some other hero of antiquity, and had performed such or such an illustrious achievement ; at the next pause another personated character advanced ; at the next another ; but each unrelated and unconnected with the other.

Such was the rude state of tragedy, when Æschylus conceived the great design of forming it into a new species of poetry that should rival even the Epic in dignity. The humble arbour interwoven with vine branches gave place to scenes of astonishing grandeur ; the actor, no longer mounted on the cart of Thespis, with his face smeared over with lees of wine, or covered with a mask formed from the bark of a tree, now trod a spacious stage, magnificently habited in a robe of honour and the stately buskin ; even the mask, that eternal disgrace of the Athenian theatre, wore a new and elegant form, expressive of the character represented. But these exterior decorations were proofs only of the taste of Æschylus : his superior genius appeared in giving life to the piece, by introducing the dialogue, without which there could be no action ; and from this circumstance it is, that he is with the highest propriety called the Father of the Drama. It is commonly said that Æschylus never produced more than two speakers upon the stage at the same time ; there are proofs to the contrary, though he generally adhered to that simple plan : but the new part, which the Chorus now took, amply supplied what we should call that poverty of the stage."

Chorus. In the ancient tragedy, a number of persons sufficient probably to give animation to the appearance of the stage, joined in the representations of the drama,— these formed the Chorus. The Chorus seems to consist of persons of a character that might naturally desire to be witnesses of the action represented. Sometimes they were the old men of a city who came to behold some public transaction, at others the attendants of a great family, and at others strangers apparently collected from curiosity. Their observations served to explain what would else be obscure, and to connect what would otherwise be broken and confused in the order of incident.

SCENE FROM THE TRAGEDY OF AGAMEMNON.

A Herald announces to CLYTEMNESTRA, *the wife of* AGA-MEMNON, *the destruction of Troy.*

CLYTEMNESTRA, CHORUS, and HERALD.

Herald. Hail, thou paternal soil of Argive earth !
In the fair light of the tenth year to thee
Return'd, from the sad wreck of many hopes
This one I save ; sav'd from despair e'en this ;
For never thought I in this honour'd earth
To share in death the portion of a tomb.
Hail then, lov'd earth ; hail, thou bright sun ; and thou,
Great guardian of my country, Supreme Jove ;
Thou, Pythian king, thy shafts no longer wing'd
For our destruction ; on Scamander's banks
Enough we mourn'd thy wrath ; propitious now
Come, king Apollo, our defence. And all
Ye gods, that o'er the works of war preside,
I now invoke thee ; thee, Mercury, my avenger,
Rever'd by heralds, that from thee derive
Their high employ ; you heroes, to the war
That sent us, friendly now receive our troops,
The relics of the spear.
    Imperial walls,
Mansion of kings, ye seats rever'd ; ye gods,
That to the golden sun before these gates
Present your honour'd forms ; if e'er of old
Those eyes with favour have beheld the king,
Receive him now, after this length of time,
With glory ; for he comes, and with him brings
To you, and all, a light that cheers this gloom :
Then greet him well ; such honour is his meed,
The mighty king, that with the mace of Jove
Th' avenger, wherewith he subdues the earth,

Hath levell'd with the dust the tow'rs of Troy ;
Their altars are o'erturn'd, their sacred shrines,
And all the race destroy'd.   This iron yoke
Fix'd on the neck of Troy, victorious comes
The great Atrides, of all mortal men
Worthy of highest honours.   Paris now,
And the perfidious state, shall boast no more
His proud deeds unreveng'd ; stript of his spoils,
The debt of justice for his thefts, his rapines,
Paid amply, o'er his father's house he spreads
With two-fold loss the wide-involving ruin.

   Clyt. Joy to thee, herald of the Argive host.
   Her. For joy like this, death were a cheap exchange.
   Clyt. Strong thy affection to thy native soil.
   Her. So strong, the tear of joy starts from my eye.
   Clyt. What, hath this sweet infection reach'd e'en
     you ?
   Her. Beyond the pow'r of language have I felt it.
   Clyt. The fond desire of those, whose equal love—
 Her. This of the army say'st thou, whose warm love
Streams to this land? is this thy fond desire ?
   Clyt. Such, that I oft have breath'd the secret sigh.
   Her. Whence did the army cause this anxious sad-
     ness ?
   Clyt. Silence I long have held a healing balm.
   Her. The princes absent, had'st thou whom to fear ?
   Clyt. To use thy words, death were a wish'd ex-
     change.
   Her. Well is the conflict ended.   In the tide
Of so long time, if 'midst the easy flow
Of wish'd events some tyrannous blast assail us.
What marvel ? who, save the blest gods, can claim
Through life's whole course an unmix'd happiness ?
Should I relate our toils, our wretched plight,
Wedg'd in our narrow ill-provided cabins,
Each irksome hour was loaded with fatigues.
Yet these were slight essays to those worse hardships
We suffer'd on the shore : our lodging near
The walls of the enemy, the dews of heaven

Fell on us from above, the damps beneath
From the moist marsh annoy'd us, shrouded ill
In shaggy coverings   Or should one relate
The winter's keen blasts, which from Ida's snows
Breathe frore, that pierc'd through all their plumes the
     birds
Shiver and die ;   or th' extreme heat that scalds,
When in his mid-day caves the sea reclines,
And not a breeze disturbs his calm repose.
But why lament these sufferings ? they are past ;
Past to the dead indeed ; they lie, no more
Anxious to rise.   What then avails to count
Those, whom the wasteful war hath swept away,
And with their loss afflict the living ? rather
Bid we farewell to misery : in our scale,
Who haply of the Grecian host remain,
The good preponderates, and in counterpoise
Our loss is light ; and after all our toils
By sea and land, before you golden sun
It is our glorious privilege to boast,
" At length from vanquish'd Troy our warlike troops
Have to the gods of Greece brought home these spoils,
And in their temples, to record our conquests,
Fix'd these proud trophies."   Those, that hear this
     boast,
It well becomes to gratulate the state,
And the brave chiefs : revering Jove's high pow'r
That grac'd our conquering arms.   Thou hast my mes-
     sage.

Pythian king. Apollo was called so because he slew
the serpent Python. This is figurative : Python was
Disease or Malady, and as enemy to the human con-
stitution is called a serpent. Apollo being the god of
health, the healer or destroyer of disease, is described
as having slain a serpent.

Thy shafts no longer winged for our destruction. This
alludes to that pestilence in the Greek camp, which is
described in the first book of the Iliad. The instantaneous

operation of the pest, causes its effects to be compared to the sudden and mortal wound of an arrow from the bow. This pestilence is ascribed by Homer to Apollo, as a punishment for the affront offered to his priest Chryses.

Mercury, as the messenger of the gods, was esteemed the patron of heralds, whose character therefore was always held sacred.

SOPHOCLES.

"Sophocles, surnamed the Bee and the Attic Siren, was born at Athens, in the year 495 B. C. He gave early proofs of his talent for poetry, and aptitude for the business of government. He reached the dignity of Archon, and, in this capacity, commanded the armies of the republic of Athens, with considerable reputation. As a tragic writer, he shared the favour of the Athenian public with Euripides, his contemporary and rival. Sophocles died at the advanced age of eighty-five. Some of his biographers relate that he expired from an ecstasy of joy, produced by his having carried the prize at the Olympic Games. But his number of years may alone account for his dissolution. He is said to have composed one hundred and twenty tragedies, of which seven only remain."

ANTIGONE.

The character of Antigone, as she is represented by Sophocles, is that of the loveliest and best of women. She was the daughter of Œdipus, king of Thebes. Her father being driven from his kingdom, and having in despair torn out his eyes, his faithful and patient child follows his wanderings, and soothes his sufferings as long as he lives. When her father is no more, she is afflicted by the discord of her brothers, and the persecutions of her uncle Creon. Her affection, fortitude, and undismayed sense of duty, are worthy of a Christian heroine.

To illustrate the dialogue which follows, these notes are extracted from Francklin's Sophocles.

" Eteocles and Polynices, sons of the unfortunate
Œdipus, having an equal claim to the kingdom of Thebes,
had agreed to divide the power, and to reign year by year
alternately ; but Eteocles stepping first into the throne,
and tasting the sweets of sovereignty, broke the contract,
and maintained himself in the possession of his domi-
nions   Polynices, in revenge, raised an army of Argians,
and made an incursion on Thebes ; a battle ensued, and,
after much slaughter on both sides, the brothers agreed
to decide it by single combat ; they fought, and were
slain by each other.   After the death of the brothers, the
kingdom of Thebes devolved to their uncle Creon, whose
first act of supreme power was an edict forbidding all rites
of sepulture to Polynices, as a traitor ; and pronouncing
instant death on any who should dare to bury him.   Here
the action of the tragedy commences, the subject of
which is the piety of Antigone in opposition to the edict
of Creon, with the distresses consequent upon it.   Anti-
gone calls her sister out of the palace into the adjoining
area, to inform her of the decree which had been issued
on the preceding day, and her resolutions concerning
it.

Of all the honours paid to the dead by the ancients, the
care of their funerals was looked upon by them as most
necessary and indispensable ; as to be deprived of sepul-
ture was accounted the greatest misfortune, and the high-
est injury.   No imprecation was therefore so terrible as
that any person might ' die destitute of burial ;' it was not
to be wondered at that they were thus solicitous about the
interment of their dead, when they were strongly possess-
ed with the opinion that the souls of the deceased could
not be admitted into the Elysian shades, but were forced
to wander desolate and alone, till their bodies were com-
mitted to the earth.   Nor was it sufficient to be honoured
with the solemn performance of their funeral rites, except
their bodies were prepared for burial by their relations,
and interred in the sepulchres of their fathers."

The importance attached by the Greeks to the rites of
sepulture, is clear from that passage in Homer, in which

Achilles is described as seeing, in a vision of the night, his friend Patroclus, who had recently been killed, and who reproaches him with neglecting the last duty to his remains:

"'Tis true, 'tis certain, man, though dead, retains
Part of himself—the immortal mind remains.

* * * * * * *

This night my friend so late in battle lost
Stood at my side, a pensive, plaintive ghost.
' Sleeps my Achilles'—thus the phantom said—
' Sleeps my Achilles—his Patroclus dead ?
Living I seem'd his dearest, tenderest care,
But now forgot I wander in the air.
Let my pale corse the rites of burial know,
And give me entrance to the realms below :
Till then the spirit finds no resting place' "——

ANTIGONE and ISMENE.

Ant. O ! my dear sister, my best-belov'd Ismene,
Is there an evil, by the wrath of Jove
Reserv'd for Œdipus' unhappy race,
We have not felt already ? sorrow and shame,
And bitterness and anguish, all that's sad,
All that's distressful hath been ours, and now
This dreadful edict from the tyrant comes
To double our misfortunes ; hast thou heard
What harsh commands he hath impos'd on all,
Or art thou still to know what future ills
Our foes have yet in store to make us wretched ?
Ism. Since that unhappy day, Antigone,
When by each other's hand our brothers fell,
And Greece dismiss'd her armies, I have heard
Nought that could give or joy or grief to me.
Ant. I thought thou wert a stranger to the tidings,
And therefore call'd thee forth, that here alone
I might impart them to thee.
Ism.   O ! what are they ?
For something dreadful labours in my breast.

Ant. Know then, from Creon, our indulgent lord,
Our hapless brothers met a different fate,
To honour one, and one to infamy
He hath consign'd ; with fun'ral rites he grac'd
The body of our dear Eteocles,
Whilst Polynices' wretched carcass lies
Unburied, *unlamented*, left expos'd
A feast for hungry vultures on the plain ;
No pitying friend will dare to violate
The tyrant's harsh command, for public death
Awaits th' offender ; Creon comes himself
To tell us of it, such is our condition ;
This is the crisis, this the hour, Ismene,
That must declare thee worthy of thy birth,
Or show thee mean, base, and degenerate.
    Ism. What would'st thou have me do ? defy his power?
Contemn the laws ?
    Ant.   To act with me, or not :
Consider and resolve.
    Ism.   What daring deed
Would'st thou attempt ? what is it ? speak.
    Ant.   To join
And take the body, my Ismene.
    Ism.   Ha !
And would'st thou dare to bury it, when thus
We are forbidden ?
    Ant.   Ay, to bury HIM :
He is my brother, and thine too, Ismene ;
Therefore consent or not, I have determin'd
I'll not disgrace my birth.
    Ism.   Hath not the king
Pronounc'd it death to all ?
    Ant.   He hath no right,
No power to keep me from my own.
    Ism.   Alas !
Remember our unhappy father's fate,
And last, in one sad day, Eteocles
And Polynices by each other slain.
Left as we are, deserted and forlorn,

What from our disobedience can we hope
But misery and ruin? poor weak women,
Helpless, nor form'd by nature to contend
With powerful man; we are his subjects too;
Therefore to this, and worse than this, my sister,
We must submit: for me, in humblest prayer
Will I address me to th' infernal powers
For pardon of that crime which well they know
Sprang from necessity, and then obey;
Since to attempt that we can never hope
To execute, is folly all and madness.
   Ant. Wert thou to proffer what I do not ask,
Thy poor assistance, I would scorn it now:
Act as thou wilt; I'll bury him myself;
Let me perform but that, and death is welcome;
I'll do the pious deed, and lay me down
By my dear brother; loving and belov'd
We'll rest together: to the powers below
'Tis fit we pay obedience; longer there
We must remain, than we can breathe on earth,
There I shall dwell for ever; thou, meantime,
What the gods hold most precious may'st despise.
   Ism. I reverence the gods; but, in defiance
Of laws, and unassisted to do this,
It were most dang'rous.
   Ant.   That be thy excuse,
Whilst I prepare the fun'ral pile.
   Ism.   Alas!
I tremble for thee.
   Ant.   Tremble for thyself,
And not for me.
   Ism.   O! do not tell thy purpose,
I beg thee, do not; I shall no'er betray thee.
   Ant. I'd have it known; and I shall love thee less
For thy concealment, than, if loud to all,
Thou would'st proclaim the deed.
   Ism.   Thou hast a heart
Too daring, and ill-suited to thy fate.

23

Ant. I know my duty, and I'll pay it there
Where 'twill be best accepted.
Ism.   Could'st thou do it?
But 'tis not in thy power.
Ant.   When I know that
It will be time enough to quit my purpose.
Ism. It cannot be; 'tis folly to attempt it.
Ant. Go on, and I shall hate thee; our dead brother.
He too shall hate thee as his bitt'rest foe;
Go, leave me here to suffer for my rashness;
Whate'er befalls, it cannot be so dreadful,
As not to die with honour.
Ism.   Then farewell,
Since thou wilt have it so; and know, Ismene
Pities thy weakness, but admires thy virtue.

"*Unlamented.* This was the judgment which God de-
nounced against Jehoiakim, king of Judah: 'they shall
not lament for him, saying, ah! my brother, or ah! sis-
ter; they shall not lament for him, saying, ah! lord, or
ah! his glory; he shall be buried with the burial of an
ass,' &c. Jerem. 22, v. 18, 19. The customs and man-
ners of the Greeks were originally drawn from the east-
ern nations, which accounts for the similitude so observ-
able in Sophocles and other heathen writers with some
parts of holy writ."

EURIPIDES.

" The prodigious armament, with which Xerxes invaded
Greece, is well known: when he was advancing towards
Attica, to revenge the defeat of his father's forces at
Marathon, the Athenians, by the advice of Themistocles,
retired with their effects to Salamis, Trœzene, and Ægi-
na. Among those who took refuge at Salamis, were
Mnesarchus and Clito, the parents of Euripides, who
was born at that Island on the very day in which the
Grecians there gained that memorable victory over the

Persian fleet. His parents educated their son with great attention, and at a considerable expense. Besides the athletic exercises, in which he excelled, he was taught grammar, music, and painting. He applied himself to the study of oratory under the refined and learned Prodicus, who admitted none to his school but the sons of great and noble families; the celebrated Pericles was also formed under this excellent master. He studied philosophy with Anaxagoras, and contracted an early friendship with Socrates, who was twelve years younger than himself, and survived him almost six years; this friendship, formed on the firmest principles of virtue and wisdom, and cemented by a similarity of manners and studies, continued indissoluble. These studies form the history of his life from the eighteenth to the seventy-second year of his age, during which time he composed seventy-five tragedies, frequently retiring to his native Salamis, and there indulging his melancholy muse in a rude and gloomy cavern.

His reputation was now so illustrious, that Archelaus, king of Macedonia, invited him to his court: this monarch, to his many royal virtues, added a fondness for literature and the muses, and had drawn to him from Greece many who excelled in the polite arts, particularly those who were eminent for their learning and genius. Euripides, after much and earnest invitation, at length complied with the king's request, and went to Pella, where he was received with every mark of esteem and honour.

Archelaus knew how to value a man of modesty and wisdom, a lover of truth and virtue; but he particularly admired the disinterestedness, the amiable candour, and gentleness of manners, which distinguished Euripides, and made him worthy of the liberality, the esteem, and the affection of such a king. In this court at this time, among many other eminent men, were Agatho, an excellent tragic poet, an honest and agreeable man, a friend and admirer of Euripides; Timotheus, the famous musician; and Teuxus, the celebrated painter. In this society

Euripides lived happy, beloved, and honoured, and died lamented, in the third year after his coming to Macedonia, and the seventy-fifth year of his age. Archelaus mourned for him as for a near relation, buried him among the kings of Macedonia, and erected a magnificent monument to his memory.

The news of his death was brought to Athens as Sophocles was about to exhibit one of his tragedies; he appeared in mourning, and made his actors come on the stage without crowns: this great poet had long been the intimate friend of Euripides, he was then in the ninetieth year of his age, and died about the end of this year. The Athenians immediately sent ambassadors to Archelaus, requesting his permission to remove the bones of Euripides into his own country; this the king and the Macedonians firmly refused; as they could not obtain his ashes, they raised a cenotaph to their poet, in the way hat led from the city to the Piræus."

IPHIGENIA.

This interesting female was the daughter of Agamemnon, king of Mycenæ, and leader of the expedition to Troy. When the whole Greek armament had assembled at Aulis, and were ready to depart, they were detained by contrary winds. To procure a safe departure, a horrible alternative is proposed to Agamemnon. He thus states it himself.

" Collected and embodied, here we sit
Inactive, and from Aulis wish to sail
In vain.   The prophet Calchas, 'midst the gloom
That darken'd on our minds, at length pronounc'd
That Iphigenia, my virgin daughter,
I to Diana, goddess of this land,
Must sacrifice : this victim giv'n the winds
Shall swell our sails, and Troy beneath our arms
Be humbled in the dust ; but if denied,
These things are not to be."

Agamemnon feels himself compelled to make this cruel sacrifice. He acquaints his gentle child, and her love of life for a while contends against this dreadful necessity, but at length she yields.

AGAMEMNON, IPHIGENIA, and CLYTEMNESTRA.

Iph. Had I, my father, the persuasive voice
Of Orpheus, and his skill to charm the rocks
To follow me, and soothe whome'er I please
With winning words, I would make trial of it:
But I have nothing to present thee now
Save tears, my only eloquence ; and those
I can present thee.   On thy knees I hang,
A suppliant.————
Ah ! kill me not in youth's fresh prime.
Sweet is the light of heaven : compel me not
What is beneath to view   I was the first
To call thee father, me thou first didst call
Thy child : I was the first that on thy knees
Fondly caress'd thee, and from thee receiv'd
The fond caress. This was thy speech to me——
Shall I, my child, e'er see thee in some house
Of splendour, happy in thy husband, live
And flourish, as becomes my dignity ?
My speech to thee was, leaning 'gainst thy cheek,
Which with my hand I now caress. And what
Shall I then do for thee ? Shall I receive
My father when grown old, and in my house
Cheer him with each fond office, to repay
The careful nurture which he gave my youth ?
These words are on my memory deep impress'd,
Thou hast forgot them, and wilt kill thy child.
By Pelops I entreat thee, by thy sire
Atreus, by this my mother, do not kill me.
If Paris be enamour'd of his bride,
His Helen, what concerns it me ? and how
Comes he to my destruction ?
   Look upon me,
Give me a smile, give me a kiss, my father,

That, if my words persuade thee not, in death
I may have this memorial of thy love.
My brother, small assistance canst thou give
Thy friends, yet for thy sister with thy tears
Implore thy father that she may not die :
E'en infants have a sense of ills : and see,
My father, silent though he be, he sues
To thee : be gentle to me, on my life
Have pity.   Thy two children by this beard
Entreat thee, thy dear children ; one is yet
An infant,* one to riper years arriv'd.
I will sum all in this, which shall contain
More than long speech ; to view the light of life
To mortals is most sweet, but all beneath
Is nothing : of his senses is he reft,
Who hath a wish to die ; for life, though ill,
Excels what'er there is of good in death.
   Aga. What calls for pity, and what not, I know :
I love my children, else I should be void
Of reason : to dare this is dreadful to me,
And not to dare is dreadful.   I perforce
Must do it.   What a naval camp is here
You see, how many kings for Greece array'd
In glitt'ring arms : to Ilium's towers are these
Denied t' advance, unless I offer thee
A victim, thus the prophet Calchas speaks,
Denied from her foundations to o'erturn
Illustrious Troy ; and through the Grecian host
Maddens the fierce desire to sail with speed
'Gainst the barbarians' land, and check their rage
For Grecian dames : my daughters these will slay
At Argos, you too will they slay, and me,
Should I, the goddess not revering, make
Of none effect her oracle.   To this
Not Menelaus, my child, hath wrought my soul,
Nor to his will am I a slave ; but Greece,
For which, will I, or will I not, perforce
Thee I must sacrifice : my weakness here

     * Orestes.

I feel, and must submit.   In thee, my child,
What lies, and what in me, Greece should be free,
Nor should her sons beneath barbarians bend,
Their household joys to ruffian force a prey.
    Clyt. Alas, my child!
How wretched in thy death! thy father flies thee,
He flies, but dooms thee to the realms beneath.
    Iph. My mother, hear ye now my words: for thee
Offended with thy husband I behold:
Vain anger! for where force will take its way,
To struggle is not easy.
                    Hear then what to my mind
Deliberate thought presents: it is decreed
For me to die: this then I wish, to die
With glory, all reluctance banish'd far.
My mother, weigh this well, that what I speak
Is honour's dictate: all the powers of Greece
Have now their eyes on me; on me depends
The sailing of the fleet, the fall of Troy,
And not to suffer, should a new attempt
Be dar'd, the rude barbarians from blest Greece
To bear in future times her dames by force,
This ruin bursting on them for the loss
Of Helena, whom Paris bore away.
By dying, all these things shall I achieve,
And blest, for that I have deliver'd Greece,
Shall be my fame.
                    To be too fond of life
Becomes not me; nor for thyself alone,
But to all Greece a blessing didst thou bear me.
Shall thousands, when their country's injur'd, lift
Their shields, shall thousands grasp the oar, and dare,
Advancing bravely 'gainst the foes, to die
For Greece? and shall my life, my single life
Obstruct all this? would this be just? what word
Can we reply?

        *   *   *   *   *   *   *

                                If me
The chaste Diana wills t' accept, shall I,

A mortal, dare oppose her heavenly will?
Vain the attempt: for Greece I give my life.
Slay me, demolish Troy: for these shall be
Long time my monuments, my children these,
My nuptials, and my glory.
  It is meet
That Greece should o'er barbarians bear the sway,
Not that barbarians lord it over Greece:
Nature hath form'd them slaves, the Grecians free.

IPHIGENIA and CHORUS.

Iph. Lead me: mine the glorious fate
To o'erturn the Phrygian state!
Ilium's towers their head shall bow.
With garlands bind my brow,
Bring them, be these tresses crown'd.
Round the shrine, the altar round
Bear the lavers, which you fill
From the pure translucent rill.
High your choral voices raise,
Tun'd to hymn Diana's praise,
Blest Diana, royal maid.
Since the fates demand my aid,
I fulfil their awful power
By my slaughter, by my gore.
 Chor. Reverenc'd, reverenc'd mother, now
Thus for thee our tears shall flow:
For unhallow'd would a tear
'Midst the solemn rites appear.
 Iph. Swell the notes, ye virgin train,
To Diana swell the strain,
Queen of Chalcis, adverse land,
Queen of Aulis, on whose strand,
Winding to a narrow bay,
Fierce to take its angry way,
Waits the war, and calls on me
Its retarded force to free.
O my country, where these eyes
Open'd on Pelasgic skies!

O ye virgins, once my pride,
In Mycenæ who reside!
 Chor. Why of Perseus name the town,
Which Cyclopean rampires crown?
 Iph. Me you rear'd a beam of light:
Freely now I sink in night.
 Chor. And for this, immortal fame,
Virgin, shall attend thy name.
 Iph. Ah, thou beaming lamp of day,
Jove-born, bright, etherial ray,
Other regions we await,
Other life, and other fate!
Farewell, beauteous lamp of day,
Farewell, bright etherial ray!
 Chor. See, she goes: her glorious fate
To o'erturn the Phrygian state:
Soon the wreaths shall bind her brow;
Soon the lustral waters flow;
Soon that beauteous neck shall feel
Piercing deep the fatal steel,
And the ruthless altar o'er
Sprinkle drops of gushing gore.
By thy father's dread command
There the cleansing lavers stand;
There in arms the Grecian powers
Burn to march 'gainst Ilium's towers.
But our voices let us raise,
Tun'd to hymn Diana's praise,
Virgin daughter she of Jove,
Queen among the gods above.
That with conquest and renown
Here the arms of Greece may crown.

Not Menelaus, but Greece, hath wrought my mind to this.—Not the persuasions of Menelaus, but the dreaded vengeance of the Greeks upon us, if by forbearing to sacrifice thee, I should frustrate their present designs, determines me to this unnatural act.

The Hebrew scriptures record a sacrifice similar to this in that of Jephtha's daughter.

The persuasive voice of Orpheus. Orpheus was a fabulous musician. It was pretended that the music of his voice and his lyre was so enchanting that rocks were animated, and rivers ceased to flow, at the sound.

Compel me not what is beneath to view. The pagan notion of death, as has been before observed, was that of descent, of darkness, and of doubt. It is the most welcome truth of Christianity, that it brings life and immortality to light ; and since the establishment of Christianity, the idea of the state after death includes that of purer elements than those of earth, and of powers to expatiate more extensively amidst the wonders of the universe.

Queen of Chalcis and of Aulis. Diana was the guardian goddess of these *adverse,* that is, opposite cities—the former on the coast of Euboea, and the latter on that of Greece.

SOUTHEY.

Robert Southey is among the most distinguished of living authors, in the various departments of Poetry, History, and Biography. His poetic talent has been chiefly displayed in the Epic.——Thalaba, Madoc, the Curse of Kehama, and Roderick, the Last of the Goths, are his principal poems. The last mentioned of these is the greatest favourite of the public, and deserves to be so.

The poem of Roderick, &c. is founded, as the name imports, upon the history of the last Gothic King of Spain, Upon the dismemberment of the Roman Empire, Hispania, the modern Spain, was taken by those northern barbarians called Goths. The Goths established a regal government, which subsisted from A. D. 411 to A. D. 712. Roderick, the Last of the Goths, had a private quarrel with a distinguished nobleman of his court, and the latter, indignant against the king, conspired with the Moors, a nation of the opposite shores of Africa, to dethrone Roderick and surrender the sovereignty to the Moors.

The authenticity of this statement of the origin of the Moorish conquest of Spain is disputed—but it is the tradition of the Moors and Spaniards, and upon the assumed fact, Mr. Southey has founded his poem. Many of Roderick's subjects remained faithful to him, but multitudes rebelled, and after a battle with the Moors and the rebels, Roderick is said to have disappeared, and never to have been found again, A. D. 712.

The most faithful adherent of Roderick was Pelayo, a prince of his blood, who became the founder of a new kingdom, that of Asturia. The following account of Pelayo, is taken from a French, *Abrégé de l' Histoire d' Espagn.* " Pelayo seeking liberty, and preferring a desert to a state of bondage, led a few faithful followers to a sequestered spot enclosed by rocks in the interior of Asturia. Being a man of talent and integrity, he acquired an absolute ascendancy over his friends, and they appointed him their king. His subjects were few, and his territory barren rocks ; but the men were faithful and courageous.—Their asylum was discovered and invaded by the Moors, but the refugees defended themselves; and from this commencement originated the kingdom of Asturia, long one of the most powerful in Spain. Pelayo died in A. D. 737."

It may here be remarked that under the Moors, Spain was divided into several sovereignties. Kings of Asturia, of Oviedo, of Arragon, of Castile and Leon, are numbered among the Princes of Spain. From the extinction of the Gothic kingdom to the accession of Philip II. A. D. 1555, these separate principalities subsisted, but all Spain acknowledged Philip, and received the laws of Madrid.

Mr. Southey supposes that immediately after his defeat Roderick sought a profound solitude, and in this situation he describes him. Roderick was accompanied in his concealment by Romano, an old man, who died and left the unhappy king alone.—Roderick had been guilty of a crime, and his self-reproach aggravated his affliction.

RODERICK IN SOLITUDE.

The fourth week of their painful pilgrimage
Was full, when they arrived where from the land
A rocky hill, rising with steep ascent,
O'erhung the glittering beach; there on the top
A little lowly hermitage they found,
And a rude cross, and at its foot a grave,
Bearing no name nor other monument.
Where better could they rest than here, where faith
And secret penitence and happiest death
Had blest the spot, and brought good angels down,
And opened as it were a way to Heaven?
Behind them was the desert, offering fruit
And water for their need; on either side
The white sand sparkling to the sun; in front
Great Ocean with its everlasting voice,
As in perpetual jubilee, proclaim'd
The wonders of the Almighty, filling thus
The pauses of their fervent orisons.

Where better could the wanderers rest than here?
Twelve months they sojourn'd in their solitude,
And then beneath the burden of old age
Romano sunk.   No brethren were there
To spread the sackcloth, and with ashes strew
That penitential bed, and gather round
To sing his requiem, and with prayer and psalm
Assist him in his hour of agony.
He lay on the bare earth, which long had been
His only couch ; beside him Roderick knelt,
Moisten'd from time to time his blacken'd lips,
Received a blessing with his latest breath,
Then closed his eyes, and by the nameless grave
Of the fore-tenant of that holy place
Consign'd him earth to earth.
Two graves are here,
And Roderick transverse at their feet began
To break the third.   In all his intervals
Of prayer, save only when he search'd the woods
And fill'd the water-cruise, he labour'd there ;
And when the work was done, and he had laid
Himself at length within its narrow sides
And measured it, he shook his head to think
There was no other business now for him.
Poor wretch, thy bed is ready, he exclaim'd,
And would that night were come ! . . . It was a task,
All gloomy as it was, which had beguiled
The sense of solitude ; but now he felt
The burthen of the solitary hours :—
The silence of that lonely hermitage
Lay on him like a spell ; and at the voice
Of his own prayers, he started, half aghast.
Then too, as on Romano's grave he sate
And pored upon his own, a natural thought
Arose within him, . . well might he have spared
That useless toil : the sepulchre would be
No hiding-place for him ; no Christian hands
Were here who should compose his decent corpse
And cover it with earth.   There he might drag

24

His wretched body at its passing hour,
And there the sea-birds of her heritage
Would rob the worm, or peradventure seize,
Ere death had done its work, their helpless prey.
Even now they did not fear him : when he walk'd
Beside them on the beach, regardlessly
They saw his coming ; and their whirring wings
Upon the height had sometimes fann'd his cheek,
As if, being thus alone, humanity
Had lost its rank, and the prerogative
Of man was done away.
    For his lost crown
And sceptre never had he felt a thought
Of pain : repentance had no pangs to spare
For trifles such as these,—the loss of these
Was a cheap penalty :—that he had fallen
Down to the lowest depth of wretchedness,
His hope and consolation. But to lose
His human station in the scale of things,—
To see brute Nature scorn him, and renounce
Its homage to the human form divine ;—
Had then almighty vengeance thus reveal'd
His punishment, and was he fallen indeed
Below fallen man.
    Oh for a voice
Of comfort,—for a ray of hope from heaven !
A hand that from these billows of despair
May reach and snatch him ere he sink engulph'd !
At length, as life when it hath lain long time
Opprest beneath some grievous malady,
Seems to rouse up with re-collected strength,
And the sick man doth feel within himself
A second spring ; so Roderick's better mind
Arose to save him. Lo ! the western sun
Flames o'er the broad Atlantic ; on the verge
Of glowing ocean rests ; retiring then
Draws with it all its rays, and sudden night
Fills the whole cope of heaven. The penitent
Knelt by Romano's grave, and, falling prone,

Claspt with extended arms the funeral mould.
   Father! he cried; companion, only friend,
When all beside was lost! thou too art gone,
And the poor sinner whom from utter death
Thy providential hand preserved, once more
Totters upon the gulf.   I am too weak
For solitude,—too vile a wretch to bear
This everlasting commune with myself.

*   *   *   *   *   *   *   *   *

   Despair hath laid the nets
To take my soul, and Memory, like a ghost,
Haunts me, and drives me to the toils. O Saint,
While I was blest with thee, the hermitage
Was my sure haven! Look upon me still ;
For from thy heavenly mansion thou canst see
The suppliant ; look upon thy child in Christ.
   Romano! Father! let me hear thy voice
In dreams, O sainted soul! or from the grave
Speak to thy penitent ; even from the grave
Thine were a voice of comfort.
   Thus he cried,
Easing the pressure of his burthen'd heart
With passionate prayer ; thus pour'd his spirit forth,
Till the long effort had exhausted him,
His spirit fail'd, and laying on the grave
His weary head, as on a pillow, sleep
Fell on him. He had pray'd to hear a voice
Of consolation, and in dreams a voice
Of consolation came. Roderick, it said,—
Roderick, my poor, unhappy, sinful child,
Jesus have mercy on thee !—Not if heaven
Had open'd, and Romano, visible
In his beatitude, had breath'd that prayer ;—
Not if the grave had spoken, had it pierced
So deeply in his soul, nor wrung his heart
With such compunctious visitings, nor given
So quick, so keen a pang.   It was that voice
Which sung his fretful infancy to sleep
So patiently ; which sooth'd his childish griefs ;

4

Counsell'd with anguish and prophetic tears,
His headstrong youth. And lo ! his *mother* stood
Before him in the vision.

PELAYO AND HIS CHILDREN.

  The ascending vale,
Long straitened by the narrowing mountains, here
Was closed. In front a rock, abrupt and bare,
Stood eminent, in height exceeding far
All edifice of human power, by king
Or caliph, or barbaric sultan reared,
Or mightier tyrants of the world of old,
Assyrian or Egyptian, in their pride :
Yet far above, beyond the reach of sight,
Swell after swell, the heathery mountain rose.
Here, in two sources, from the living rock
The everlasting springs of Deva gushed.
Upon a smooth and grassy plat below,
By Nature there as for an altar drest,
They joined their sister stream, which from the earth
Welled silently. In such a scene rude man
With pardonable error might have knelt,
Feeling a present Deity, and made
His offering to the fountain nymph devout.
The arching rock disclosed above the springs
A cave, where hugest son of giant birth,
That e'er of old in forest of romance
'Gainst knights and ladies waged discourteous war,
Erect within the portal might have stood.
No holier spot than Covadonga, Spain
Boasts in her wide extent, though all her realms
Be with the noblest blood of martyrdom
In elder or in later days enriched,
And glorified with tales of heavenly aid
By many a miracle made manifest ;
Nor in the heroic annals of her fame
Doth she show forth a scene of more renown.
Then, save the hunter, drawn in keen pursuit

Beyond his wonted haunts, or shepherd's boy,
Following the pleasure of his straggling flock,
None knew the place.
  Pelayo, when he saw
Those glittering sources and their sacred cave,
Took from his side the bugle silver-tipt,
And with a breath long drawn and slow expired
Sent forth that strain, which, echoing from the walls
Of Cangas, wont to tell his glad return
When from the chase he came.   At the first sound
Favila started in the cave, and cried,
My father's horn!——A sudden flame suffused
Hermesind's cheek, and she with quickened eye
Looked eager to her mother silently;
But Gaudiosa trembled and grew pale,
Doubting her sense deceived.   A second time
The bugle breathed its well-known notes abroad;
And Hermesind around her mother's neck
Threw her white arms, and earnestly exclaimed,
'Tis he!——But when a third and broader blast
Rung in the echoing archway, ne'er did wand,
With magic power endued, call up a sight
So strange, as sure in that wild solitude
It seemed, when from the bowels of the rock
The mother and her children hastened forth.
  She in the sober charms and dignity
Of womanhood mature, nor verging yet
Upon decay: in gesture like a queen,
Such inborn and habitual majesty
Ennobled all her steps,——or priestess, chosen
Because within such faultless work of heaven
Inspiring Deity might seem to make
Its habitation known.——Favila such
In form and stature as the Sea Nymph's son,
When that wise Centaur from his cave well-pleased
Beheld the boy divine his growing strength
Against some shaggy lionet essay,
And fixing in the half-grown mane his hands,
Roll with him in fierce dalliance intertwined.

24*

But like a creature of some higher sphere
His sister came ; she scarcely touched the rock,
So light was Hermesind's aërial speed.
Beauty and grace and innocence in her
In heavenly union shone.   One who had held
The faith of elder Greece, would sure have thought
She was some glorious nymph of seed divine,
Oread or Dryad, of Diana's train
The youngest and the loveliest : yea she seemed
Angel, or soul beatified, from realms
Of bliss, on errand of parental love
To earth re-sent,—if tears and trembling limbs
With such celestial natures might consist.

Favila such
In form and stature as the Sea Nymph's son,
When that wise Centaur, &c.

Achilles, the son of Thetis, a sea nymph, was educa-
ted in Thessaly by Chiron the Centaur. Favila, the son
and successor of Pelayo, is here compared with the
young Achilles.
The faith of elder Greece. This religion has been
described with considerable effect by Mr. Percival, an
American poet.

RELIGION OF GREECE.

There was a time, when the o'erhanging sky,
And the fair earth with its variety,
Mountain and valley, continent and sea,
Were not alone the unmoving things that lie
Slumbering beneath the sun's unclouded eye ;
But every fountain had its spirit then,
That held communion oft with holy men,
And frequent from the heavenward mountain came
Bright creatures, hovering round on wings of flame,
And some mysterious sybil darkly gave
Responses from the dim and hidden cave :—
Voices were heard waking the silent air,

A solemn music echoed from the wood,
And often from the bosom of the flood
Came forth a sportive Naiad passing fair,
The clear drops twinkling in her braided hair ;
And as the hunter through the forest strayed,
Quick-glancing beauty shot across the glade,
Her polished arrow levelled on her bow,
Ready to meet the fawn or bounding roe.
   Each lonely spot was hallowed then—the oak
That o'er the village altar hung, would tell
Strange hidden things ;—the old remembered well,
How from its gloom a spirit often spoke.
There was not then a fountain or a cave,
But had its reverend oracle, and gave
Responses to the fearful crowd, who came
And called the indwelling deity by name ;
Then every snowy peak, that lifted high
Its shadowy cone to meet the bending sky,
Stood like a heaven of loveliness and light :—
And as the gilt cloud rolled its glory by,
Chariots and steeds of flame stood harnessed there,
And gods came forth and seized the golden reins,
Shook the bright scourge, and through the boundless air
Rode over starry fields and azure plains.
   It was a beautiful and glorious dream,
Such as would kindle high the soul of song.
All seemed one bright enchantment then ;—but now,
Since the long sought for goal of truth is won,
Nature stands forth unveiled with cloudless brow,
On earth ONE SPIRIT OF LIFE, in heaven ONE.

HEAVENLY LOVE.

They sin who tell us Love can die.
   With life all other passions fly,
      All others are but vanity.
In heaven Ambition cannot dwell,
   Nor Avarice in the vaults of hell ;
Earthly these passions of the earth,

They perish where they have their birth ;
  But Love is indestructible.
    Its holy flame for ever burneth,
From heaven it came, to heaven returneth ;
  Too oft on earth a troubled guest,
  At times deceiv'd, at times opprest,
    It here is tried and purified,
  Then hath in heaven its perfect rest ;
    It soweth here with toil and care,
But the harvest time of Love is there.

SOUTHEY.

LORD BYRON.

George Gordon, Lord Byron, was an English nobleman, descended from Commodore Byron, the celebrated navigator. Lord Byron died at Missolonghi in Greece, April 1824, at the age of thirty-seven. He was distinguished at an early period of his life for his poetical talents ; and his genius, if it has not made men better, has opened a source of pleasure to the readers of poetry, which once enjoyed is never forgotten. .

Lord Byron had not a well governed mind, and, though he was born to great opulence, and possessed all the resources of knowledge, taste, and cultivated society, he was not happy. His serious poetry is sad and bitter, and his gayer productions are immoral ; but there are many parts of his writings of a high character. His strong passions, and his dark views of human nature, cannot be understood by young readers, but his better feelings, and his fine descriptive talent, afford some passages which are highly improving and interesting to them.

The passages of Lord Byron's poetry which immediately succeed, have as much life as sentiment, and on that account they are best adapted to the comprehension and sympathies of young persons. Two only, Night at Corinth, and Turkey, are purely descriptive.

NIGHT AT CORINTH.

In 1715, Corinth, situated on the Isthmus of that name, being in possession of the Venetians, was besieged by the Turks. Lord Byron describes the delicious nights of that fine climate in his poem, the Siege of Corinth. The night described is that previous to the taking of Corinth, while the Turkish army surrounded its walls.

"'Tis midnight : on the mountains brown
   The cold round moon shines deeply down ;
   Blue roll the waters, blue the sky
   Spreads like an ocean hung on high,

Bespangled with those isles of light,*
So wildly, spiritually bright ;
Who ever gazed upon them shining,
And turned to earth without repining,
Nor wish'd for wings to flee away,
And mix with their eternal ray ?
The waves on either shore lay there
Calm, clear, and azure as the air ;
And scarce their foam the pebbles shook,
But murmured meekly as the brook.
The winds were pillowed on the waves ;
The banners drooped along their staves,
And, as they fell around them furling,
Above them shone the crescent curling ;
And that deep silence was unbroke,
Save where the watch his signal spoke,
Save where the steed neighed oft and shrill,
And echo answered from the hill,
And the wild hum of that wild host
Rustled like leaves from coast to coast,
As rose the Muezzin's voice in air
In midnight call to wonted prayer."

———

The Muezzin's voice. 'The Turks do not use bells to
summon the religious to their devotions.   They have an
appointed person, whose function it is to send forth to the
extent of his voice, the *call to wonted prayer.*

———

DECAPITATION OF HUGO.

The marquis of Este, the sovereign of Ferrara in
Italy, had a son named Hugo, and a beautiful young wife
called Parasina.   This lady loved Hugo better than his
father, and was equally beloved by the young man.
When the marquis was fully convinced of this fact, he or-
dered Hugo and Parasina to be beheaded, and the sen-
tence was executed, according to Lord Byron's authori-

* The stars.

ty, about 1405. The execution of Hugo is described in the poem of Parasina.

"The Convent bells are ringing,
    But mournfully and slow ;
In the gray square turret swinging,
    With a deep sound, to and fro.
Heavily to the heart they go !
    Hark ! the hymn is singing—
The song for the dead below,
    Or the living who shortly shall be so !
For a departing being's soul
The death-hymn peals and the hollow-bells knoll ;
He is near his mortal goal
Kneeling at the Friar's knee ;
Sad to hear—and piteous to see
Kneeling on the bare cold ground,
With the block before and the guards around—
While the crowd in a speechless circle gather
To see the Son fall by the doom of the Father !

    It is a lovely hour as yet
Before the summer sun shall set,
Which rose upon that heavy day,
And mocked it with his steadiest ray ;
And his evening beams are shed
Full on Hugo's fated head,
As his last confession pouring
To the monk, his doom deploring
In penitential holiness
He bends to hear his accents bless
With absolution such as may
Wipe our mortal stains away.
That high sun on his head did glisten
As he there did bow and listen—
And the rings of chestnut hair
Curled half down his neck so bare ;
But brighter still the beam was thrown
Upon the axe which near him shone
With a clear and ghastly glitter——
    Oh ! that parting hour was bitter !

Even the stern stood chilled with awe :
Dark the crime, and just the law —
Yet they shuddered as they saw.
   The parting prayers are said and over
Of that false son and daring lover!
His beads and sins are all recounted,
His hours to their last minute mounted—
His mantling cloak before was stripped,
His bright brown locks must now be clipped ;
'Tis done—all closely are they shorn—
The vest which till this moment worn—
The scarf which Parasina gave—
Must not adorn him to the grave.
Even that must now be thrown aside,
And o'er his eyes the kerchief tied ;
But no—that last indignity
Shall ne'er approach his haughty eye.
'No—yours my forfeit blood and breath—
These hands are chained—but let me die
At least with an unshackled eye—
'Strike :'—and as the word he said,
Upon the block he bowed his head ;
These the last accents Hugo spoke :
'Strike'—and flashing fell the stroke—
Rolled the head—and, gushing, sunk
Back the stained and heaving trunk,
In the dust, which each deep vein
Slacked with its ensanguined rain ;
His eyes and lips a moment quiver,
Convulsed and quick—then fix for ever.''

THE PRISONER OF CHILLON.

The Prisoner of Chillon is a sweet and touching poem.
"Chillon is a ruined castle on the lake of Geneva in
Switzerland, in the dungeon of which three gallant bro-
thers were confined, each chained to a separate pillar,
till, after years of anguish, the two younger died, and
were buried under the cold floor of the prison.   The el-

dest was at length liberated, when worn out with age and
misery—and is supposed, in his joyless liberty, to tell, in
this poem, the sad story of his imprisonment.

The annexed verses describe the sympathy of the un-
happy brothers, the peculiar loveliness of the youngest,
and the bitterness of sorrow with which the survivor de-
plored the fate of this "blooming Benjamin of the fa-
mily."

> "We could not move a single pace,
> We could not see each other's face,
> But with that pale and livid light
> That made us strangers in our sight;
> And thus together—yet apart
> Fettered in hand, but pined in heart;
> 'Twas still some solace in the dearth
> Of the pure elements of earth,
> To hearken to each other's speech,
> And each turn comforter to each,
> With some new hope, or legend old,
> Or song heroically bold;
> But even these at length grew cold.
> Our voices took a dreary tone,
> An echo of the dungeon-stone,
>   A grating sound—not full and free
>   As they of yore were wont to be:
>   It might be fancy—but to me
> They never sounded like our own.
>
>   *   *   *   *   *   *
>
> I was the eldest of the three,
> And to uphold and cheer the rest
> I ought to do—and did my best—
> And each did well in his degree.
> The youngest, whom my father loved,
> Because our mother's brow was given
> To him—with eyes as blue as heaven,
> For him my soul was sorely moved;
> And truly might it be distrest
> To see such bird in such a nest;

25

He was the favourite and the flower,
Most cherish'd since his natal hour,
His mother's image in fair face,
The infant love of all his race,
His martyred father's dearest thought,
My latest care, for whom I sought
To hoard my life, that his might be
Less wretched now, and one day free;
He, too, who yet had held untired
A spirit natural or inspired—
He, too, was struck, and day by day
Was withered on the stalk away.

    Oh God! it is a fearful thing
To see the human soul take wing
In any shape, in any mood :—
I've seen it rushing forth in blood,
I've seen it on the breaking ocean
Strive with a swoln convulsive motion ;
I've seen the sick and ghastly bed
Of sin delirious with its dread :
But these were horrors—This was wo
Unmix'd with such—but sure and slow :
He faded, and so calm and meek,
So softly worn, so sweetly weak,
So tearless, yet so tender— kind,
And grieved for those he left behind ;
With all the while a cheek whose bloom
Was as a mockery of the tomb,
Whose tints as gently sunk away
As a departing rainbow's ray—
An eye of most transparent light
That almost made the dungeon bright.
And not a word of murmur—not
A groan o'er his untimely lot.

    A little talk of better days,
A little hope my own to raise,
For I was sunk in silence—lost
In this last loss, of all the most ;
And then the sighs he would suppress

Of fainting nature's feebleness,
More slowly drawn; grew less and less :
I listened but I could not hear—
I called, for I was wild with fear ;
I knew 'twas hopeless, but my dread
Would not be thus admonished ;
I called, and thought I heard a sound—
I burst my chain with one strong bound,
And rush'd to him :—I found him not,
I only stirr'd in this black spot,
I only lived—*I* only drew
The accursed breath of dungeon dew."

TURKEY.

Know ye the land where the cypress and myrtle
Are emblems of deeds that are done in their clime?
Where the rage of the vulture, the love of the turtle,
Now melt into sorrow, now madden to crime ?
Know ye the land of the cedar and vine,
Where the flowers ever blossom, the beams ever shine ;
Where the light wings of Zephyr, oppress'd with perfume,
Wax faint o'er the gardens of Gúl* in her bloom ;
Where the citron and olive are fairest of fruit,
And the voice of the nightingale never is mute :
Where the tints of the earth, and the hues of the sky,
In colour though varied, in beauty may vie,
And the purple of Ocean is deepest in dye ;
Where the virgins are soft as the roses they twine,
And all, save the spirit of man, is divine ?
'Tis the clime of the east ; 'tis the land of the Sun—
Can he smile on such deeds as his children have done ?
Oh ! wild as the accents of lover's farewell   [tell.
Are the hearts which they bear, and the tales which they

VISION OF BELSHAZZAR.

The king was on his throne,
    The satraps throng'd the hall ;

* *Gul*—The rose.

A thousand bright lamps shone
   O'er that high festival.
A thousand cups of gold,
   In Judah deem'd divine—
Jehovah's vessels hold
   The godless heathen's wine !

In that same hour and hall,
   The fingers of a hand
Came forth against the wall,
   And wrote as if on sand :
The fingers of a man ;—
   A solitary hand
Along the letters ran,
   And traced them like a wand.

The monarch saw, and shook,
   And bade no more rejoice ;
All bloodless wax'd his look,
   And tremulous his voice.
" Let the men of lore appear,
   The wisest of the earth,
And expound the words of fear,
   Which mar our royal mirth."

Chaldea's seers are good,
   But here they have no skill ;
And the unknown letters stood
   Untold and awful still.
And Babel's men of age
   Are wise and deep in lore ;
But now they were not sage,
   They saw—but knew no more.

A captive in the land,
   A stranger and a youth,
He heard the king's command,
   He saw that writing's truth,
The lamps around were bright,
   The prophecy in view ;
He read it on that night,—
   The morrow proved it true.

" Belshazzar's grave is made,
His kingdom pass'd away,
He, in the balance weigh'd,
Is light and worthless clay.
The shroud his robe of state,
His canopy the stone ;
The Mede is at his gate !
The Persian on his throne !''

In the fifth chapter of the prophecy of Daniel, the feast of Belshazzar, and the end of the Babylonian empire, which terminated in him, are recorded ; but there is a vividness in Lord Byron's imitation of that passage which gives new power to the original scene.

BATTLE OF WATERLOO.

To comprehend the verses which the following facts are designed to illustrate, it is necessary they should be known. The verses relate especially to the memorable battle of Waterloo—a battle which put an end to the military career of Napoleon Bonaparte, and gave peace to Europe. Bonaparte was a native of the island of Corsica, and, in his early life, an officer of engineers in the French service : his military talents at length raised him to the chief command of the French armies.

Bonaparte subjected all the civil affairs of France to military power, caused himself to be declared First Consul, and afterwards Emperor of France, and King of Italy. He did not limit his ambition to the government of France and Italy, but actually conquered Switzerland, Holland, and the greater part of Germany. He united the Netherlands to France, made one of his brothers King of Holland, another of Naples, a third of Westphalia, and bestowed upon princes of Germany the titles of Kings of Bavaria, Saxony, and Wirtemburg. He invited the King of Spain to visit him, made him a prisoner, and in 1808 placed his brother Joseph on the throne of Spain.

25*

Bonaparte's insatiable thirst of dominion prompted him in 1812 to invade Russia at the head of 500,000 troops ; but the severity of a Russian winter, and the defensive power of the Russians, gave the first check to his conquering spirit.   100,000 men of the French army were made prisoners, and 200,000 perished by cold, famine, and the sword, in this campaign.

The different independent governments of Europe took advantage of these disasters in order to restore independence and political liberty to the subjugated countries.   The monarchs of Great Britain, Russia, Prussia, Austria, and Sweden, formed a confederacy to dethrone Bonaparte, and to restore to the several usurped thrones, members of families which had formerly held the sovereignty of the different states.   This alliance is often called the Holy Alliance—as a compact of defenders of the *rights of kings,* and, as the allied powers professed, of protectors of religion and morals.   The armies of these sovereigns—the combined forces which acted under the command of generals from each of the allied states, was called the Allied Army.

The allied army entered Paris and took possession of it on the 18th March, 1814.   Bonaparte consequently fled, and retired to the island of Elba in the Mediterranean ; but he quitted his retreat on the 1st March, 1815, and at the head of the French army which flocked to his standard he re-entered Paris amidst acclamations of *Vive l'Empereur.*   The allied army was prepared to defend the *rights of the Bourbons.*—During the absence of Bonaparte, Louis XVIII, brother to Louis XVI, (a King of France beheaded in 1793,) was placed on the throne of France, and to restore him to his late assumed dignity was an immediate purpose of the allied powers.

Bonaparte encountered the allied army near Brussels in Belgium.   On the 15th of June he defeated the Prussians ; on the 16th he obtained some advantages over the British ; but on the 18th his army was completely defeated in the BATTLE OF WATERLOO.   The French army under Bonaparte consisted of 75,000

Frenchmen. The troops under Lord Wellington, 35,000 English and Scots, and the rest, of German contingents, formed, in point of numbers, a nearly equal force.

"The loss on the British side during this dreadful battle," to borrow the words of Sir Walter Scott, was, "immense.—One hundred officers slain, five hundred wounded, many of them to death, fifteen thousand men killed and wounded, threw half Britain into mourning." It is supposed that about 35,000 French perished at Waterloo,—or in consequence of the battle. It was said that the English officers, when news came to them of the advance of Bonaparte, were at a ball at Brussels. Lord Byron has commemorated this circumstance in Childe Harolde.

THE BALL OF BRUSSELS.

There was a sound of revelry by night,
And Belgium's capital had gather'd then
Her beauty and her chivalry, and bright
The lamps shone o'er fair women and brave men ;
A thousand hearts beat happily ; and when
Music arose with its voluptuous swell,
Soft eyes look'd love to eyes which spake again,
And all went merry as a marriage-bell ;
But hush ! hark ! a deep sound strikes likes a rising knell !

Did ye not hear it ?—No ; 'twas but the wind,
Or the car rattling o'er the stony street ;
On with the dance ! let joy be unconfined ;
No sleep till morn, when Youth and Pleasure meet
To chase the glowing Hours with flying feet—
But, hark !—that heavy sound breaks in once more,
As if the clouds its echo would repeat ;
And nearer, clearer, deadlier than before !
Arm ! Arm ! it is—it is—the cannon's opening roar !

Within a window'd niche of that high hall
Sate Brunswick's fated chieftain ; he did hear
That sound the first amidst the festival,
And caught its tone with Death's prophetic ear

And when they smil'd because he deem'd it near,
His heart more truly knew that peal too well
Which stretched his father on a bloody bier,
And roused the vengeance blood alone can quell :
He rush'd into the field, and, foremost fighting, fell.

Ah! then and there was hurrying to and fro,
And gathering tears, and tremblings of distress,
And cheeks all pale, which but an hour ago
Blush'd at the praise of their own loveliness ;
And there were sudden partings, such as press
The life from out young hearts, and choking sighs
Which ne'er might be repeated ; who could guess
If ever more should meet those mutual eyes,
Since upon nights so sweet such awful-morn could rise ?

And there was mounting in hot haste : the steed,
The mustering squadron, and the clattering car,
Went pouring forward with impetuous speed,
And swiftly forming in the ranks of war ;
And the deep thunder peal on peal afar ;
And near, the beat of the alarming drum
Roused up the soldier ere the morning star ;
While throng'd the citizens with terror dumb,
Or whispering, with white lips—" The foe ! they come !
　　they come !"

And wild and high the " Cameron's gathering" rose!
The war-note of Lochiel, which Albyn's hills
Have heard, and heard, too, have her Saxon foes :—
How in the noon of night that pibroch thrills,
Savage and shrill ! But with the breath which fills
Their mountain-pipe, so fill the mountaineers
With the fierce native daring which instils
The stirring memory of a thousand years,
And Evan's, Donald's fame rings in each clansman's
　　ears !

And Ardennes waves above them her green leaves,
Dewy with nature's tear-drops, as they pass,
Grieving, if aught inanimate e'er grieves,
Over the unreturning brave,—alas !

Ere evening to be trodden like the grass
Which now beneath them, but above shall grow
In its next verdure, when this fiery mass
Of living valour, rolling on the foe
And burning with high hope, shall moulder cold and low.

Last noon beheld them full of lusty life,
Last eve in Beauty's circle proudly gay,
The midnight brought the signal-sound of strife,
The morn the marshalling in arms,—the day
Battle's magnificently-stern array !
The thunder-clouds close o'er it, which when rent
The earth is cover'd thick with other clay,
Which her own clay shall cover, heap'd and pent,
Rider and horse,—friend, foe,—in one red burial blent !

Brunswick's fated chieftain. The Duke of Brunswick, a German Prince, killed in the action.

The " Cameron's gathering" rose. This alludes to the music of the Scottish troops. They distinguish themselves always as soldiers, for they bring the most noble principles of duty and patriotism into the service. An interesting moral view of the Highland soldiery is afforded by Mrs. Grant, in her Essay on the Superstitions of the Highlanders.

Evan's and Donald's fame. Sir Evan Cameron and his descendant Donald, chiefs of the Camerons, beloved and cherished in the memory of their clansmen.

Ardennes waves above them her green leaves.

" The wood of Soignies, near the field of Waterloo, is supposed to be a remnant of the ' forest of Ardennes,' famous in Boiardo's Orlando, and immortal in Shakspeare's ' As you like it.' It is also celebrated in Tacitus as being the spot of successful defence by the Germans against the Roman encroachments."

WORDSWORTH.

Of living poets there is not one whose moral feelings, as they are exhibited in his poetry, more entitle him to the respect of mankind than Mr. Wordsworth. This gentleman resides in the North of England. He loves the rural life, and exhibits it delightfully in his poetry; and the benevolence of his heart is as remarkably connected with his poetic talent, as the purest spirit of devotion, and the finest enjoyment of external nature. The Bee, the Solitary Reaper, and the Deserted Indian Woman, are the only extracts from Wordsworth's poetry which there is room to insert in this volume.

THE BEE.

"—— the soft murmur of the vagrant Bee.
—A slender sound! yet hoary Time
Doth to the soul exalt it with the chime
Of all his years;—a company
Of ages coming, ages gone;
(Nations from before them sweeping,
Regions in destruction steeping,)
But every awful note in unison
With that faint utterance, which tells
Of treasure sucked from buds and bells
For the pure keeping of those waxen cells;
Where she, a prudent statist to confer
Upon the public weal; a warrior bold—
Radiant all over with unburnished gold;
And armed with living spear for mortal fight;
A cunning forager
That spreads no waste;—a social builder; one
In whom all offices unite
With all fine functions that afford delight,
Safe through the winter storm in quiet dwells!
And is she brought within the power
Of vision?—o'er this tempting flower
Hovering until the petals stay
Her flight, and take its voice away!

Observe each wing—a tiny van!
The structure of her laden thigh
How fragile!—yet of ancestry
Mysteriously remote and high—
High as the imperial front of man,
The roseate bloom on woman's cheek ;
The soaring eagle's curved beak;
The white plumes of the floating swan ;
Old as the tyger's paws, the lion's mane
Ere shaken by that mood of stern disdain
At which the desert trembles.
  · Humming Bee!
Thy sting was needless then, perchance unknown :
The seeds of malice were not sown ;
All creatures met in peace from fierceness free,
And no pride blended with their dignity.
    Tears had not broken from their source ;
Nor anguish strayed from her Tartarian den,
The golden years maintained a course
Not undiversified, though smooth and even ;
We were not mocked with glimpse and shadow then,
Bright seraphs mixed familiarly with men ;
And earth and stars composed a universal heaven.

In these verses Mr. Wordsworth suggests a comparison between the history of mankind, and the lower animals. Regarding particular races of men, in respect to the countries they once inhabited—*nations* truly are swept away, and *regions* are steeped in destruction. The glories of ancient Greece, and the misery and degradation of that country under the Turkish government —the military prowess and political power of republican Rome, and the feebleness and anarchy of modern Italy, afford awful contrasts of former elevation and present degeneracy of national character. But animal life exhibits no such gloomy views—the same faculties and enjoyments now exist in the lower orders of life as " When the eagle from the ark" exulted in the reconciled face of Heaven. Ages roll away, and neither improvement nor corruption modify the powers and pleasures of those humbler objects of God's goodness, who partake with us in all the luxuries of earthly elements; and, if we believe the scriptures, the date of whose existence is coeval with ours—therefore their voices speak to us of all antiquity, and the past years of *hoary Time* are commemorated by the *faint utterance* of an insect's hum—for that very sound has been propagated by innumerable multiplications ever since Adam gave names to every living creature.

The beautiful economy of bees has always been a theme for admiration to the lovers of nature. The symmetry and excellent contrivance of their cells, their order and agreement in carrying on their work, the presiding function of the queen bee, their apparent forecast, and their perseverance in accumulating their sweet food, exhibits an image of happy human society, and has often been held up as a model for the imitation of rational beings.

The suggestion that bees were once stingless, is a poetic superstition. According to the Bible, man was happy and innocent in the first days of his existence, but when he disobeyed God he became subject not only to misery but to violent passions. Some poets have represented that brute animals exhibited a sort of sympathy with the fate of man, and that different tribes began to prey upon others when human beings became liable to sin and its punishment. Of that time, Milton says,

" ————nature first gave signs, impress'd
On bird, beast, air,
The bird of Jove, stoop'd from his aëry tour,
Two birds of gayest plume before him drove;
Down from a hill the beast that reigns in woods,
First hunter then, pursu'd a gentle brace,
Godliest of all the forest, hart and hind."

But before this " all creatures met in peace from fierceness free," says Mr. Wordsworth—A Golden Age is the pretty fiction of more ancient poets than Mr.

Wordsworth—It never existed—it supposes universal peace in nature's realm; but in respect to brutes, it could not possibly be, because those which subsist on animal food, have organs to seize and to destroy other animals, and appetites given to them by the Author of nature which demand animal food to sustain their life.

THE FORSAKEN INDIAN WOMAN.

It is said by Mr. Hearne, a traveller among the Indian tribes who inhabit the northern regions of North America, that when the Indians, in considerable companies, undertake journeys on foot, if one of their number becomes unable through illness or fatigue to proceed with the travellers, that individual is left behind with a fire and a few articles of sustenance, and in this state languishes and dies. Mr. Wordsworth supposes a poor Indian woman to have been left thus, and in these pathetic verses has expressed what might be her distressed feelings in this situation.

"Before I see another day,
Oh let my body die away!
In sleep I heard the northern gleams;
The stars were mingled with my dreams;
In rustling conflict through the skies,
I heard, and saw the flashes drive;
And yet they are upon my eyes,
And yet I am alive.
Before I see another day,
Oh let my body die away!

My fire is dead: it knew no pain;
Yet is it dead, and I remain.
All stiff with ice the ashes lie;
And they are dead, and I will die.
When I was well, I wished to live,
For clothes, for warmth, for food, and fire;
But they to me no joy can give,
No pleasure now, and no desire.

26

Then here contented will I lie !
Alone I cannot fear to die.

Alas ! ye might have dragged me on
Another day, a single one !
Too soon I yielded to despair ;
Why did ye listen to my prayer ?
When ye were gone my limbs were stronger
And oh how grievously I rue,
That afterwards a little longer,
My friends, I did not follow you !
For strong and without pain I lay,
My friends, when ye were gone away.

My child ! they gave thee to another,
A woman who was not thy mother.
When from my arms my babe they took,
On me how strangely did he look !
Through his whole body something ran,
A most strange working did I see ;
—As if he strove to be a man,
That he might pull the sledge for me,
And then he stretch'd his arms, how wild !
Oh mercy ! like a helpless child.

My little joy ! my little pride !
In two days more I must have died.
Then do not weep and grieve for me ;
I feel I must have died with thee.
Oh wind, that o'er my head art flying
The way my friends their course did bend,
I should not feel the pain of dying,
Could I with thee a message send !
Too soon, my friends, ye went away ;
For I had many things to say.

I'll follow you across the snow ;
Ye travel heavily and slow ;
In spite of all my weary pain,
I'll look upon your tents again.
—My fire is dead, and snowy white
The water which beside it stood ;

The wolf has come to me to-night,
And he has stolen away my food.
For ever left alone am I,
Then wherefore should I fear to die?"

In sleep I heard the northern gleams. This alludes to the Aurora Borealis—in English, the Morning of the North. In countries which lie far north, as Lapland, Greenland, &c., the heavens on the north side, often exhibit a brilliant white light, which is sometimes the same in lustre for many hours, and at other times throws up long jets of light, which vanish, and are succeeded by others. It is sometimes imagined that these *northern gleams* are accompanied by explosive sounds,—these are what the dying Indian woman fancies she heard.

THE SOLITARY REAPER.

In the Highlands of Scotland, women perform some of the lighter labours of the field. They beguile their labour by singing in the Gaelic tongue—sometimes, as Mr. Wordsworth supposes, of *battles long ago*, and sometimes *familiar matter of to-day.*

"Behold her, single in the field,
Yon solitary Highland lass!
Reaping and singing by herself;
Stop here, or gently pass!
Alone she cuts, and binds the grain,
And sings a melancholy strain;
Oh listen! for the vale profound
Is overflowing with the sound.

No nightingale did ever chaunt
So sweetly to reposing bands
Of travellers in some shady haunt
Among Arabian sands:
No sweeter voice was ever heard
In spring-time from the cuckoo-bird,
Breaking the silence of the seas
Among the farthest Hebrides.

Will no one tell me what she sings?
Perhaps the plaintive numbers flow
For old, unhappy, far-off things,
And battles long ago:
Or is it some more humble lay,
Familiar matter of to-day?
Some natural sorrow, loss, or pain
That has been, or may be again?

Whate'er the theme the maiden sung.
As if her song could have no ending:
I saw her singing at her work
And o'er her sickle bending;
I listened—motionless and still:
And as I mounted up the hill,
The music in my heart I bore
Long after it was heard no more.

ANDREW MARVELL.
Born 1620—*Died* 1678.

Andrew Marvell is little known as a poet, but the poetry which he left, is, according to Mr. Campbell, worthy of higher consideration than has been bestowed upon it. He lived in the time of Oliver Cromwell, and was a sincere republican, but he held a seat in the British parliament after the restoration of the Stuarts, and is remarkable for the independence and honesty with which he avowed his sentiments. He had visited foreign countries, had studied and meditated much : thus his conversation was adorned with original thought and various knowledge ; and as his manners were simple but polished, he was in his private intercourse singularly agreeable. Charles II. once met with this respectable man, and being struck with him, thought he would be a valuable acquisition to the royalists.—To gain Marvell's favour the King sent him a present of money, which was refused, and Mr. Marvell giving a rational and dignified exposition of his sentiments, preferred his poverty with integrity to the favour of princes.

This excellent man loved poetry, and vindicated Milton when his character was aspersed. His religious sentiments, like those of Milton, were in favour of liberty, and he sympathized with those who were compelled to emigrate to foreign lands that they might enjoy freedom of conscience. In 1620, the famous emigration to New-England took place. One year before that time a small company of religious persons, who were not permitted to worship God in England in the manner which seemed to them right, removed to the Bermuda islands. These islands are in a healthful and pleasant climate, but they have never had many inhabitants—still the first English who went thither, anticipated much satisfaction in their retreat. Mr. Marvell wrote a song which may be supposed to express the grateful emotions of these voyagers as they entered their desired haven.

26*

THE EMIGRANTS.

Where the remote Bermudas ride,
In the ocean's bosom unespied ;
From a small boat, that row'd along,
The list'ning winds received this song.

What should we do but sing his praise,
That led us through the wat'ry maze,
Unto an isle so long unknown,
And yet far kinder than our own ?

Where he the huge sea-monsters wracks,
That lift the deep upon their backs.
He lands us on a grassy stage,
Safe from the storms, and prelate's rage.

He gave us this eternal spring,
Which here enamels every thing ;
And sends the fowls to us in care,
On daily visits through the air.

He hangs in shades the orange bright,
Like golden lamps in a green night.
And does in the pomegranates close
Jewels more rich than Ormus shows.

He cast (of which we rather boast)
The gospel's pearl upon our coast.
And in these rocks for us did frame
A temple where to sound his name.

Oh ! let our voice his praise exalt,
Till it arrive at heaven's vault :
Which, thence (perhaps) rebounding, may,
Echo beyond the Mexique Bay.

Thus sung they, in the English boat,
An holy and a cheerful note ;
And all the way, to guide their chime,
With falling oars they kept the time.

HENRY VAUGHAN.

"Henry Vaughan was a Welsh gentleman, born on the banks of the Uske, in Brecknockshire, who was bred to the law, but relinquished it for the profession of physic." The extraordinary beauty of Vaughan's poetry makes it desirable that the few remains of it which follow should become popular.

EARLY RISING AND PRAYER.

When first thy eyes unveil, give thy soul leave
To do the like ; our bodies but forerun
The spirit's duty : true hearts spread and heave
Unto their God as flowers do to the sun ;
Give him thy first thoughts then, so shalt thou keep
Him company all day, and in him sleep.

Yet never sleep the sun up; prayer should
Dawn with the day : there are set awful hours
'Twixt heaven and us ; the manna was not good
After sun-rising ; for day sullies flowers :
Rise to prevent the sun; sleep doth sins glut,
And heaven's gate opens when the world's is shut.

Walk with thy fellow creatures : note the hush
And whisperings amongst them.   Not a spring
Or leaf but hath his morning hymn ; each bush
And oak doth know I AM.——Canst thou not sing ?
O leave thy cares and follies ! go this way,
And thou art sure to prosper all the day.

Serve God before the world ; let him not go
Until thou hast a blessing ; then resign
The whole unto him, and remember who
Prevail'd by wrestling ere the sun did shine ;
Pour oil upon the stones, weep for thy sin,
Then journey on, and have an eye to heav'n.

Mornings are mysteries : the first, world's youth,
Man's resurrection, and the future's bud,

Shrowd in their births; the crown of life, light, truth,
Is styl'd their star; the stone and hidden food:
Three blessings wait upon them, one of which
Should move—they make us holy, happy, rich.

When the world's up, and every swarm abroad,
Keep well thy temper, mix not with each clay;
Dispatch necessities; life hath a load
Which must be carried on, and safely may:
Yet keep those cares without thee: let the heart
Be God's alone, and choose the better part.

THE TIMBER.

Sure thou didst flourish once, and many springs,
  Many bright mornings, much dew, many showers,
Past o'er thy head; many light hearts and wings,
  Which now are dead, lodg'd in thy living towers.

And still a new succession sings and flies,
  Fresh groves grow up, and their green branches shoot,
Towards the old and still enduring skies,
  While the low violet thrives at their root.

* · * * * * · * * * ·

THE RAINBOW.

Still young and fine, but what is still and in view
We slight as old and soil'd, though fresh and new.
How bright wert thou when Shem's admiring eye
Thy burnish'd flaming arch did first descry;
When Zerah, Nahor, Haran, Abram, Lot,
The youthful world's gray fathers, in one knot
Did with intentive looks watch every hour
For thy new light, and trembled at each shower!
When thou dost shine, darkness looks white and fair;
Forms turn to music, clouds to smiles and air;
Rain gently spends to honey-drops, and pours
Balm on the cleft earth, milk on grass and flowers.
Bright pledge of peace and sunshine, the sure tye
Of thy Lord's hand, the object of his eye!

When I behold thee, though my light be dim,
Distant and low, I can in thine see him,
Who looks upon thee from his glorious throne,
And minds the covenant betwixt all and One.

* * * * * * *

How bright wert thou, &c. · The reader who is acquainted with Mr. Campbell's verses to The Rainbow, will perceive that he has imitated Vaughan :

 " When o'er the green undeluged earth
  Heaven's covenant thou didst shine,
 How came the world's gray fathers forth
  To watch thy sacred sign."

THE WREATH. (TO THE REDEEMER.)

 Since I in storms most us'd to be,
  And seldom yielded flowers,
 How shall I get a wreath for thee
  From those rude barren hours ?

The softer dressings of the spring,
 Or summer's later store,
I will not for thy temples bring,
 Which thorns, not roses, wore :
But a twin'd wreath of grief and praise,
 Praise soil'd with tears, and tears again
Shining with joy, like dewy days,
 This day I bring for all thy pain,
Thy causeless pain ; and as sad death,
 Which sadness breeds in the most vain,
O not in vain ! now beg thy breath,
 Thy quick'ning breath, which gladly bears
Through saddest clouds to that glad place
 Where cloudless quires sing without tears,
 Sing thy just praise, and see thy face.

JAMES THOMSON.
Born in 1700.—Died in 1748.

This admirable poet was born in Scotland, but he removed to London while young, and devoted himself to poetry.   The sweetness of Thomson's disposition, and the purity and elegance of his taste, procured him patrons and he spent his life surrounded by discerning friends and generous benefactors."

Thomson's principal, and most popular work, is the Seasons.   A descriptive poem like the Seasons, was unknown in ancient literature.   It was impossible under the system of paganism that the sentiment of piety could have the tender and pervading influence which sweetens and sanctifies the poetry of Thomson and Cowper. " The religion of the ancients had not taught poetry," says Mr. Campbell, " to contemplate nature as one great image of the Divine benignity, or all created beings as the objects of comprehensive human sympathy. Before popular poetry could assume this character, Christianity, Philosophy, and Freedom, must have civilized the human mind."

The Castle of Indolence is less read than Thomson's Seasons ; but to the genuine and cultivated lover of poetry, the refinement and beautiful expression of this exquisite poem perhaps exalts it above all other of Thomson's poetry. The following extract from the Castle of Indolence is full of instruction. The happiest use that its blameless and benevolent author could have desired should be made of it, is, that it should awaken in young minds the consciousness of their own power, and stimulate them to the natural and energetic exertion of faculties designed for all high and holy purposes.

INTELLECTUAL LABOUR.

" The Knight of Arts and Industry,
And his achievements fair."

" It was not by vile loitering in ease
That Greece obtain'd the brighter palm of art,
That soft yet ardent Athens learn'd to please,
To keen the wit, and to sublime the heart,
In all supreme! complete in every part!
It was not thence majestic Rome arose,
And o'er the nations shook her conquering dart:
For sluggard's brow the laurel never grows;
Renown is not the child of indolent repose.

" Had unambitious mortals minded nought,
But in loose joy their time to wear away;
Had they alone the lap of dalliance sought,
Pleas'd on her pillow their dull heads to lay;
Rude nature's state had been our state to-day:
No cities e'er their towery fronts had rais'd,
No arts had made us opulent and gay;
With brother-brutes the human race had graz'd:
None e'er had soar'd to fame, none honour'd been, none
prais'd.

" Great Homer's song had never fir'd the breast
To thirst of glory, and heroic deeds,
Sweet Maro's Muse, sunk in inglorious rest,
Had silent slept mid the Mincian reeds:
The wits of modern time had told their beads,
And monkish legends been their only strains;
Our Milton's Eden had lain wrapt in weeds,
Our Shakspeare stroll'd and laugh'd with Warwick
swains,
Nor had my master Spencer charm'd his Mulla's plains.

" Dumb too had been the sage historic Muse,
And perish'd all the sons of ancient fame;
Those starry lights of virtue, that diffuse
Through the dark depth of time, their vivid flame,
Had all been lost with such as have no name.

Who then had scorn'd his ease for others' good ?
Who then had toil'd rapacious men to tame ?
. Who in the public breach devoted stood,
And for his country's cause been prodigal of blood ?

    " Come, follow me, I will direct you right,
Where pleasure's roses, void of serpents, grow ;
Sincere as sweet ; come, follow this good knight,
And you will bless the day that brought him to your sight.

    " Some he will lead to courts, and some to camps ;
To senates some, and public sage debates,
Where, by the solemn gleam of midnight lamps,
The world is pois'd, and manag'd mighty states ;
To high discovery some, that new-creates
The face of earth ; some to the thriving mart ;
Some to the rural reign, and softer fates ;
To the sweet Muses some, who raise the heart ;
All glory shall be yours, all nature, and all art.

    " There are, I see, who listen to my lay,
Who wretched sigh for virtue, but despair.
All may be done (methinks I hear them say)
Ev'n death despis'd by generous actions fair ;
All, but for those who to these bowers repair,
Their every power dissolv'd in luxury.
To quit of torpid sluggishness the lair,
And from the powerful arms of sloth get free,
'Tis rising from the dead—Alas!—It cannot be !

    " Would you then learn to dissipate the band
Of these huge threatening difficulties dire,
That in the weak man's way like lions stand,
His soul appal, and damp his rising fire !
Resolve, resolve, and to be men aspire.
Exert that noblest privilege, alone,
Here to mankind indulg'd : control desire :
Let godlike reason, from her sovereign throne,
Speak the commanding word—*I will*—and it is done."

COLLINS.

William Collins died at the age of thirty-five, 1756. The latter years of his life were clouded by melancholy. In this state Dr. Johnson describes him as having lost all relish for books—*except one.* This was the best of books, and it may be presumed that he who had lost all interest in temporal things, as his sad eye explored the pages of the Gospel, enjoyed a foretaste of heavenly happiness. Collins's verses on the death of Thomson are tender and pastoral. The poet supposes the author of the Seasons to repose on the banks of the Thames, in a delightful spot, suitable to a lover of nature; and he fancies that the living will long connect the memory of *his gentle spirit* with the beauty of that quiet and charming scene.

"In yonder grave a Druid lies,
  Where slowly winds the stealing wave !
The year's best sweets shall duteous rise,
  To deck the poet's sylvan grave !

In yon deep bed of whispering reeds
  His airy harp shall now be laid,
That he, whose heart in sorrow bleeds,
  May love through life the soothing shade.

The maids and youths shall linger here,
  And, while its sounds at distance swell,
Shall sadly seem in pity's ear
  To hear the woodland pilgrim's knell.

Remembrance oft shall haunt the shore,
  When Thames in summer wreaths is drest ;
And oft suspend the dashing oar,
  To bid his gentle spirit rest!

And oft as ease and health retire
  To breezy lawn, or forest deep,
The friend shall view yon whitening spire,
  And mid the varied landscape weep.

27

But, thou, who own'st that earthly bed,
   Ah! what will every dirge avail?
Or tears, which love and pity shed,
   That mourn beneath the gliding sail!

Yet lives there one, whose heedless eye
   Shall scorn thy pale shrine glimmering near?
With him, sweet bard, may fancy die,
   And joy desert the blooming year.

But thou, lorn stream, whose sullen tide
   No sedge-crown'd sisters now attend,
Now waft me from the green hill's side,
   Whose cold turf hides the buried friend!

And see, the fairy valleys fade,
   Dun night has veil'd the solemn view!
Yet once again, dear parted shade,
   Meek nature's child, again adieu!

The genial meads, assign'd to bless
   Thy life, shall mourn thy early doom!
Their hinds and shepherd girls shall dress
   With simple hands thy rural tomb.

Long, long, thy stone, and pointed clay
   Shall melt the musing Briton's eyes.
O! vales, and wild woods, shall he say,
   In yonder grave a Druid lies!

HASSAN, THE CAMEL-DRIVER.

In silent horror o'er the boundless waste
The driver Hassan with his camels pass'd;
One cruse of water on his back he bore,
And his light scrip contain'd a scanty store;
A fan of painted feathers in his hand,
To guard his shaded face from scorching sand.
The sultry sun had gain'd the middle sky,
Nor tree, nor tree and not an herb was nigh;

The beasts with pain their dusty way pursue,
Shrill roared the winds, and dreary was the view.
With desp'rate sorrow wild, th' affrighted man
Thrice sigh'd, thrice struck his breast, and thus began :
" Sad was the hour, and luckless was the day,
When first from Shiraz' walls I bent my way !

" Ah ! little thought I of the blasting wind,
The thirst or pinching hunger that I find !
Bethink thee, Hassan, where shall thirst assuage,
When fails this cruse, his unrelenting rage ?
Soon shall this scrip its precious load resign,
Then what but tears and hunger shall be thine ?
Ye mute companions of my toils, that bear
In all my griefs a more than equal share !
Here, where no springs in murmurs break away,
Or moss-crown'd fountains mitigate the day,
In vain ye hope the green delights to know
Which plains more blest or verdant vales bestow.
Here rocks alone and tasteless sands are found,
And faint and sickly winds for ever howl around.

O cease, my fears ! all frantic as I go,
When thought creates unnumber'd scenes of wo,
What if the lion in his rage I meet ?
Oft in the dust I view his printed feet :
And fearful ! oft when day's declining light
Yields her pale empire to the mourner night,
By hunger rous'd he scours the groaning plain,
Gaunt wolves and sullen tigers in his train.
At that dead hour the silent asp shall creep,
If aught of rest I find, upon my sleep ;
Or some swollen serpent twist his scales around,
And wake to anguish with a burning wound.
Thrice happy they, the wise contented poor,
From lust of wealth and dread of death secure !
They tempt no deserts, and no griefs they find ;
Peace rules the day where reason rules the mind.
Sad was the hour, and luckless was the day,
When first from Shiraz' walls I bent my way."

It is well known that in the wide tract which intervenes between the Mediterranean and Persia, there are vast tracts, lonely, sandy, and parched by the absence of water and shade, which men, tempted by the love of gain, are induced to traverse ; and that some inland commerce is thus carried on between the western Asiatics and those of the interior. The merchants or their agents, usually travel in caravans, or large companies, but Mr. Collins supposes his Camel-Driver to undertake a journey alone, and he describes his fears and his actual sufferings, in a manner which is intelligible and affecting.

GAY.

Born A. D. 1688—*Died* 1732.

No great importance is now attached to the name of Gay, and he would not probably have been known to readers of the present age, if he had not been a favourite of his contemporaries. Pope was his friend, he survived him, and wrote an Epitaph in honour of his memory. In the Epitaph he is described as '*a safe companion, and an easy friend.*' This faint, and common-place praise, seemed to Dr. Johnson, the biographer and critic of English poets, to be very insignificant, but it records the amiableness of Mr. Gay's disposition and manners, and leads us to remember his goodness when we are forced to confess his want of talent in any elevated sense, for he possessed the talent to amuse the public of his own time. He wrote a dramatic piece called the Beggar's Opera, which was often exhibited, and extremely admired during the author's life, but it has now fallen into oblivion. Gay's Fables have been very popular. They were written for a young prince, are mostly political, and not very plain or pointed in their meaning. Two only are selected for this volume.

THE BUTTERFLY AND SNAIL.

" All upstarts, insolent in place,
Remind us of their vulgar race.
As in the sunshine of the morn
A butterfly (but newly born)
Sat proudly perking on a rose,
With pert conceit his bosom glows ;
His wings (all glorious to behold)
Bedropt with azure, jet, and gold,
Wide he displays ; the spangled dew
Reflects his eyes and various hue.
His now-forgotten friend, a snail,
Beneath his house, with slimy trail,

27*

Crawls o'er the grass ; whom when he spies,
In wrath he to the gardener cries :
  " What means yon peasant's daily toil,
From choking weeds to rid the soil?
Why wake you to the morning's care ?
Why with new arts correct the year ?
Why grows the peach with crimson hue ?
And why the plum's inviting blue ?
Were they to feast his taste design'd,
That vermin of voracious kind !
Crush then the slow, the pilfering race,
So purge thy garden from disgrace.'
  " What arrogance !" the snail reply'd ;
" How insolent is upstart pride !
Hadst thou not thus, with insult vain,
Provok'd my patience to complain,
I had conceal'd thy meaner birth,
Nor trac'd thee to the scum of earth :
For scarce nine suns had wak'd the hours,
To swell the fruit, and paint the flowers,
Since I thy humbler life survey'd,
In base, in sordid guise array'd ;
A hideous insect, vile, unclean,
You dragg'd a slow and noisome train ;
And from your spider bowels drew
Foul film, and spun the dirty clue.
I own my humble life, good friend ;
Snail was I born, and snail shall end.
And what's a butterfly at best ?
He's but a caterpillar drest ;
And all thy race (a numerous seed)
Shall prove of caterpillar breed."

————

 This fable is intended for a satire upon such persons as being born in humble circumstances, and forming friendships suitable to their station, are afterwards in their own estimation exalted by wealth, and disdain their early and poorer friends.

The butterfly state, is the last stage of that insect's life. She is hatched from an egg, and is at first an unsightly caterpillar; after a certain time she weaves herself a little envelope, in which she appears to sleep : in this state the insect is a chrysalis, but at length in her last formation she forces her way out of this case—she is then a butterfly. She " sports and flutters in the fields of air" for a few days, lays her eggs, and dies. Gay's butterfly is supposed, in his caterpillar shape, to have been the friend and companion of the snail, which he afterwards despises.

THE HARE AND MANY FRIENDS.

A hare who, in a civil way,
Comply'd with every thing, like Gay,
Was known by all the bestial train
Who haunt the wood or graze the plain ,
Her care was never to offend ;
And every creature was her friend.
   As forth she went at early dawn,
To taste the dew-besprinkled lawn,
Behind she hears the hunter's cries,
And from the deep-mouth'd thunder flies,
She starts, she stops, she pants for breath ;
She hears the near advance of death ;
She doubles to mislead the hound,
And measures back her mazy round ;
Till, fainting in the public way,
Half dead with fear she gasping lay.
   What transport in her bosom grew,
When first the horse appear'd in view !
   " Let me," says she, " your back ascend,
And owe my safety to a friend.
You know my feet betray my flight ;
To friendship every burden's light."
   The horse reply'd, " Poor honest puss,
It grieves my heart to see you thus :
Be comforted, relief is near ;
For all your friends are in the rear."

She next the stately bull implor'd,
And thus reply'd the mighty lord :
" Since every beast alive can tell
That I sincerely wish you well,
I may, without offence, pretend
To take the freedom of a friend.
Love calls me hence ; a favourite cow
Expects me near yon barley-mow ;
And, when a lady's in the case,
You know, all other things give place.
To leave you thus might seem'd unkind ;
But see the goat is just behind."
    The goat remark'd " her pulse was high,
Her languid head, her heavy eye :
My back, says he, may do you harm ;
The sheep's at hand, and wool is warm."
    The sheep was feeble, and complain'd
" His sides a load of wool sustain'd ;"
Said he was slow, confess'd his fears ;
" For hounds eat sheep as well as hares."
    She now the trotting calf address'd,
To save from death a friend distress'd.
" Shall I," says he, " of tender age,
In this important care engage ?
Older and abler pass'd you by ;
How strong are those ! how weak am I !
Should I presume to bear you hence,
Those friends of mine may take offence.
Excuse me, then ; you know my heart ;
But dearest friends, alas must part.
How shall we all lament ! Adieu ;
For see the hounds are just in view."

   This fable is meant to afford a lesson in what is called
a *knowledge of the world.*—To show that the feeble and
dependant are too often *deserted at their utmost need.* To
be feeble, and to need protection is an unhappy state ;
but it is necessary that some men should exist in it, that

the benevolence of others may have objects to employ itself upon. We should avoid the state of dependance by all the means in our power, but we should never forsake others when we can afford them protection and favour.

EXTRACT FROM THE PLEASURES OF MEMORY.

Oft may the spirits of the dead descend,
To watch the silent slumbers of a friend ;
To hover round his evening walk unseen,
And hold sweet converse on the dusky green ;
To hail the spot where once their friendship grew,
And heaven and nature opened to their view !
Oft when he trims his cheerful hearth and sees
A social circle emulous to please ;
There may these gentle guests delight to dwell,
And bless the scene they loved in life so well !
   Oh thou with whom my heart was wont to share
From reason's dawn each pleasure and each care !
With whom, alas ! I fondly hoped to know
The humble walks of happiness below ;
If thy blest nature now unites above
An angel's pity with a brother's love ;
Still o'er my life preserve thy mild control,
Correct my views, and elevate my soul :
Grant me thy peace and purity of mind,
Devout yet cheerful, active yet resigned ;
Grant me like thee whose heart knew no disguise,
Whose blameless wishes never aimed to rise,
To meet the changes time and chance present,
With modest dignity, and calm content.
When thy last breath, ere nature sunk to rest
Thy meek submission to thy God expressed, —
When thy last look, ere thought and feeling fled,
A mingled gleam of hope and triumph shed ;
What to thy soul its glad assurance gave
Its hope in death, its triumph o'er the grave.
The sweet remembrance of unblemished youth,
   The inspiring voice of innocence and truth.
      Hail memory, hail ! in thy exhaustless mine
From age to age, unnumbered treasures shine !

'Thought and her shadowy brood thy call obey,
And place and time are subject to thy sway !
Thy pleasures most we feel when most alone,
The only pleasures we can call our own.
Lighter than air, Hope's summer visions fly,
If but a fleeting cloud obscure the sky ;
If but a beam of sober reason play,
Lo ! Fancy's fairy frostwork melts away !
But can the wiles of Art, the grasp of Power,
Snatch the rich relics of a well spent hour ?
These when the trembling spirit takes her flight,
Pour round her path a stream of living light ,
And gild those pure and perfect realms of rest,
Where virtue triumphs, and her sons are blest.

The' Pleasures of Memory, a very agreeable poem,
was written by Samuel Rogers, Esq.   Mr. Rogers still
lives (1827) in England, at a very advanced age ; he is
a banker and a man of fortune, and is now, considered
as a father of living English poets.   Lord Byron, Mr.
Fox, Thomas Moore, and many other eminent men,
have regarded his friendship as a high privilege.   The
tenderness of Mr. Rogers' heart is manifest throughout
the preceding lines from the Pleasures of Memory.
They are principally addressed to a deceased brother—
by the sentiments they express the heart is made better.
    The reader well knows that Memory is that faculty of
the mind by which knowledge acquired at one time, is
preserved; and may be brought up in the mind at all
times future to that in which it was first acquired.—
Without memory man would be like an infant all his
days.   Memory is not only of infinite use, but is a source
of infinite pleasure.—The memory of good actions, may
be called the " testimony of a good conscience.—The
memory of good friends is sometimes a consolation for
the loss of them.—The memory, or the remembrance
of the just," who are no more, " is blest " by those
who survive them.   Many have believed that the good,
when they are removed to another life still remember

those they loved in this, and that they are permitted to
exert a watchful care over the friends they knew in this
world.   The author of The Pleasures of Memory
expresses such a belief.

THE ALPS AT DAY BREAK.

The sun-beams strike the azure skies,
And line with light the mountain's brow :
With hounds and horns the hunters rise,
And chase the roe-buck through the snow.

From rock to rock with giant bound,
High on their iron poles they pass :
Mute, lest the air convulsed by sound,
Rend from above, a frozen mass.

The goats wind slow their wonted way,
Up craggy steeps, and ridges rude ;
Marked by the wild wolf for his prey,
From desert cave or hanging wood.

And while the torrent thunders loud,
And as the echoing cliffs reply,
The hut peeps o'er the morning cloud,
Perched like an eagle's nest on high.

The region of the Alps is the abode of a secluded but
vigorous and adventurous race of men, whose favourite
occupations are hunting and scaling their snow covered
mountains.   In the ascent of these they are assisted by
poles pointed with iron, which aid them in their danger-
ous passages.   Mr. Gray says " there are passes in the
Alps, where the guides tell you to move on with speed,
and *say nothing*, lest the air agitated by the voice should
loosen the snows above," and the detached masses
should instantly destroy the travellers.

SIR JOHN MOORE.

General Sir John Moore was the son of Dr. John Moore, the author of Zeluco, and of several other excellent novels. General Moore was killed at Corunna, in Spain, January 1808. He was sent into Spain by the British government, at the head of a large military force, in order to assist the Spaniards against the French. At that period Ferdinand II., king of Spain, was a prisoner in France, and Joseph Bonaparte, (a brother of the Emperor Napoleon, now resident in the United States,) was the "intrusive king" of the country. Bonaparte had resolved to establish his family in Spain, and the English government intended to defend what they call *legitimate power*—meaning by this, the continued authority of European sovereigns, whose ancestors have governed before them. The English, upon this principle, sent an army to expel the French from Spain; but their army was forced to leave Spain without accomplishing their purpose. General Moore was a man of great courage and military skill, and his want of success in this enterprize was owing to circumstances which he could not control. When he was about to embark his troops, in order to return to England, he was overtaken by the French general, Marshal Soult, and a battle took place between them.

"The attack was made by the French on the 16th January, in heavy columns, and with their usual vivacity; but it was sustained and repelled on all hands. The gallant general was mortally wounded in the action, just as he called on the 42d Highland regiment to 'remember Egypt,' and reminded the same brave mountaineers that though ammunition was scarce, 'they had their bayonets!'"

"Thus died on the field of victory, which atoned for previous misfortunes, one of the bravest and best officers of the British army. His body was wrapped in his military cloak, instead of the usual vestments of the tomb; it was deposited in a grave hastily dug on the ramparts of Co-

28

runna ; and the army completing its embarkation on the subsequent day, their late general was left 'alone with his glory.' "   *Sir Walter Scott's life of Napoleon.*

A few verses written upon this occasion were admired by the readers of poetry long before their author was discovered : he is now known to have been a clergyman by the name of Wolfe—a man of fine genius, but destined to an obscure station in the church somewhere in England or Ireland.

"Not a drum was heard, nor a funeral note,
As his corse to the ramparts we hurried ;
Not a soldier discharged his farewell shot
O'er the grave where our hero was buried.

We buried him darkly at dead of night,
The sods with our bayonets turning,—
By the struggling moonbeam's misty light,
And the lantern dimly burning.

No useless coffin confined his breast,
Nor in sheet nor in shroud we bound him,
But he lay like a warrior taking his rest
With his martial cloak around him.

Few and short were the prayers we said,
And we spoke not a word of sorrow ;
But we steadfastly gazed on the face of the dead,
And we bitterly thought of the morrow.

We thought as we heaped his narrow bed,
And smooth'd down his lonely pillow,
That the foe and the stranger would tread o'er his
And we far away on the billow.   [head,

Lightly they'll talk of the spirit that's gone,
And o'er his cold ashes upbraid him ;
But nothing he'll reck, if they let him sleep on
In the grave where a Briton has laid him.

But half of our heavy task was done,
When the clock told the hour of retiring ;

And we heard by the distant and random gun,
That the foe was suddenly firing.

Slowly and sad we laid him down
From the field of his fame fresh and gory,
We carved not a line, we raised not a stone,
But we left him alone with his glory."

COWPER.

Born 1731—Died 1800.

The Biographers of Cowper are fond of tracing his origin to nobles, and even to kings. "His mother was descended," says the poet's relative, the reverend Mr. Johnson, "by four different lines from Henry the Third, king of England." Cowper says of himself,

> " My boast is not that I deduce my birth
> From loins enthroned, and rulers of the earth,
> But *higher far* my proud pretensions rise."

The *proud pretensions* thus asserted by this truly humble man were the merits of his excellent parents, but we shall exalt these pretensions above every other consideration should we refer them to himself alone.——To him

> " Whose virtues formed the magic of his song,"

whose genius was so informed by piety and goodness, so devoted to the contemplation of God and his works, that he has left one of the most lovely examples upon record of what a high and holy gift the talent of the true poet is. The first extract from his works which shall be inserted here, is his own sketch of the poetical character, which, however, is limited to the peculiar moral character of the poet, without touching upon the excursive and inventive powers of his imagination, of which Shakspeare says,

> " The Poet's eye in a fine phrenzy rolling
> Doth glance from heaven to earth, from earth to heaven.
> And, as imagination bodies form,
> The forms of things unseen, the poet's pen
> Turns them to shapes, and gives to airy nothing
> A local habitation and a name."

THE POET.

————The mind that feels indeed the fire
The muse imparts, and can command the lyre,

Acts with a force and kindles with a zeal,
Whate'er the theme, that others never feel.
If human woes her soft attention claim,
A tender sympathy pervades the frame ;
She pours a sensibility divine
Along the nerve of ev'ry feeling line.
But if a deed not tamely to be borne
Fire indignation, and a sense of scorn,
The strings are swept with such a power, so loud
The storm of music shakes the astonished crowd.
So when remote futurity is brought
Before the keen inquiry of her thought,
A terrible sagacity informs
The Poet's heart, he looks to distant storms,
He hears the thunder, ere the tempest lowers,
And armed with strength, surpassing human powers,
Seizes events as yet unknown to man,
And darts his soul into the dawning plan.
Hence, in a Roman mouth, the graceful name
Of poet, and of prophet was the same ;
Hence British poets in the priesthood shared
And every hallowed poet was a bard.

CRAZY KATE.

There often wanders one, whom better days
Saw better clad, in cloak of satin trimm'd
With lace, and hat with splendid ribbon bound.
A serving maid was she, and fell in love
With one who left her, went to sea, and died.
Her fancy follow'd him through foaming waves
To distant shores ; and she would sit and weep
At what a sailor suffers ; fancy too,
Delusive most where warmest wishes are,
Would oft anticipate his glad return,
And dream of transports she was not to know.
She heard the doleful tidings of his death—
And never smil'd again ! and now she roams

28*

The dreary waste; there spends the livelong day.
And there, unless when charity forbids,
The livelong night.   A tatter'd apron hides,
Worn as a cloak, and hardly hides, a gown
More tatter'd still ; and both but ill conceal
A bosom heav'd with never ceasing sighs.
She begs an idle pin of all she meets,
And hoards them in her sleeve ; but needful food,
Though press'd with hunger oft, or comelier clothes,
Though pinch'd with cold, asks never—Kate is craz'd.

A TALE.

In Scotland's realm where trees are few,
   Nor even shrubs abound ;
But where, however bleak the view,
   Some better things are found.

For husband there and wife may boast
   Their union undefil'd,
And false ones are as rare almost
   As hedge-rows in the wild.

In Scotland's realm forlorn and bare,
   This hist'ry chanc'd of late—
The hist'ry of a wedded pair,
   A chaffinch and his mate.

The spring drew near, each felt a breast
   With genial instinct fill'd ;
They pair'd, and would have built a nest,
   But found not where to build.

The heaths uncover'd, and the moors,
   Except with snow and sleet,
Sea-beaten rocks, and naked shores
   Could yield them no retreat.

Long time a breeding-place they sought,
   Till both grew vex'd and tir'd ;
At length, a ship arriving, brought
   The good so long desir'd.

A ship! could such a restless thing
  Afford them place of rest?
Or was the merchant charg'd to bring
  The homeless birds a nest?

Hush—silent hearers profit most—
  This racer of the sea
Prov'd kinder to them than the coast,
  It serv'd them with a tree.

But such a tree! 'twas shaven deal,
  The tree they call a mast,
And had a hollow with a wheel
  Through which the tackle pass'd.

Within that cavity aloft,
  Their roofless home they fix'd,
Form'd with materials neat and soft,
  Bents, wool, and feathers mix'd.

Four iv'ry eggs soon pave its floor,
  With russet specks bedight—
The vessel weighs, forsakes the shore,
  And lessens to the sight.

The mother-bird is gone to sea,
  As she had changed her kind;
But goes the male! Far wiser, he
  Is doubtless left behind?

No—Soon as from ashore he saw
  The winged mansion move,
He flew to reach it, by a law
  Of never-failing love.

Then perching at his consort's side,
  Was briskly borne along,
The billows and the blast defied,
  And cheer'd her with a song.

The seaman with sincere delight,
  His feather'd shipmates eyes,

Scarce less exulting in the sight
   Than when he tows a prize.

For seamen much believe in signs,
   And from a chance so new,
Each some approaching good divines,
   And may his hopes be true !

Hail, honour'd land ! a desert where
   Not even birds can hide,
Yet parent of this loving pair
   Whom nothing could divide.

And ye who, rather than resign
   Your matrimonial plan,
Were not afraid to plough the brine
   In company with Man.

For whose lean country much disdain
   We English often show,
Yet from a richer nothing gain,
   But wantonness and wo.

Be it your fortune year by year,
   The same resource to prove,
And may ye, sometimes landing here,
   Instruct us how to love.

" This tale is founded on an article of intelligence which
the author found in the Buckinghamshire Herald, for
Saturday, June 1, 1793, in the following words.
                    "Glasgow, May 23.

   " In a block, or pulley, near the head of the mast of a
gabert, now lying at the Bromeslaw, there is a chaffinch's
nest and four eggs.   The nest was built while the vessel
lay at Greenock, and was followed hither by both birds.
Though the block is occasionally lowered for the inspec-
tion of the curious, the birds have not forsaken the nest.
The cock, however, visits the nest but seldom, while the
hen never leaves it but when she descends to the hull for
food."

On a Spaniel, called Beau, killing a young Bird.

A spaniel, Beau, that fares like you,
  Well fed, and at his ease.
Should wiser be than to pursue
  Each trifle that he sees.

But you have kill'd a tiny bird,
  Which flew not till to day.
Against my orders, whom you heard
  Forbidding you the prey.

Nor did you kill that you might eat,
  And ease a doggish pain,
For him, though chas'd with furious heat,
  You left where he was slain.

Nor was he of the thievish sort,
  Or one whom blood allures,
But innocent was all his sport
  Whom you have torn for yours.

My dog! what remedy remains,
  Since, teach you all I can,
I see you, after all my pains,
  So much resemble Man?

Beau's Reply.

Sir, when I flew to seize the bird
  In spite of your command,
A louder voice than yours I heard,
  And harder to withstand.

You cried—forbear—but in my breast
  A mightier cried—proceed—
'Twas Nature, Sir, whose strong behest
  Impell'd me to the deed.

Yet much as nature I respect,
  I ventur'd once to break,

(As you, perhaps, may recollect)
Her precept for your sake;

And when your linnet on a day,
Passing his prison door,
Had flutter'd all his strength away,
And panting press'd the floor.

Well knowing him a sacred thing,
Not destin'd to my tooth,
I only kiss'd his ruffled wing,
And lick'd the feathers smooth.

Let my obedience *then* excuse
My disobedience *now*,
Nor some reproof yourself refuse
From your aggriev'd Bow-wow;

If killing birds be such a crime,
(Which I can hardly see,)
What think you sir of killing Time
With verse address'd to me?"

Beau was Mr. Cowper's favourite Dog, and often accompanied him in his walks. Those who possess Cowper's entire works, will find Beau celebrated in the verses, the Dog and the Water Lily.

The verses to Mrs. Anne Bodham, on receiving from her, a net-work purse, made by herself, are lively, and epigrammatic; expressive of the cordiality and sportiveness with which Cowper treated the friends whom he loved.

My gentle Anne, whom heretofore,
When I was young, and thou no more
Than plaything for a nurse,
I danc'd and fondled on my knee
A kitten both in size and glee,
I thank thee for my purse.

Gold pays the worth of all things here ;
But not of love ;—that gem's too dear
  For richest rogues to win it ;
I, therefore, as a proof of love,
Esteem thy present far above
  The best things kept within it."

THE CASTAWAY.

The date of this piece is March 20, 1799. It is the last original effort of Cowper, and as such, a melancholy interest is attached to it. The Castaway is founded upon an incident recorded in Lord Anson's voyage. A sailor fell overboard, but the force of the wind, and the roughness of the sea, frustrated every effort which could be made to save his life, and he was drowned.

Obscurest night involv'd the sky ;
  Th' Atlantic billows roar'd,
When such a destin'd wretch as I,
  Wash'd headlong from on board,
Of friends, of hope, of all bereft,
His floating home for ever left.

No braver chief could Albion boast,
  Than he, with whom he went,
Nor ever ship left Albion's coast,
  With warmer wishes sent.
He lov'd them both, but both in vain,
Nor him beheld, nor her again.

Not long beneath the whelming brine,
  Expert to swim, he lay ;
Nor soon he felt his strength decline,
  Or courage die away ;
But wag'd with death a lasting strife,
Supported by despair of life.

He shouted ; nor his friends had fail'd
  To check the vessel's course,
But so the furious blast prevail'd,
  That, pitiless, perforce,

They left their outcast mate behind,
And scudded still before the wind.

Some succour yet they could afford ;
   And such as storms allow,
The cask, the coop, the floated cord,
   Delay'd not to bestow,
But he (they knew) nor ship nor shore,
Whate'er they gave, should visit more.

Nor, cruel as it seem'd, could he
   Their haste himself condemn,
Aware that flight, in such a sea,
   Alone could rescue them ;
Yet bitter felt it still to die
Deserted, and his friends so nigh.

He long survives, who lives an hour
   In ocean, self-upheld :
And so long he, with unspent pow'r
   His destiny repell'd :
And ever as the minutes flew,
Entreated help, or cried—'Adieu !'

At length his transient respite past,
   His comrades, who before
Had heard his voice in ev'ry blast,
   Could catch the sound no more.
For then, by toil subdu'd, he drank
The stifling wave, and then he sank.

No poet wept him : but the page
   Of narrative sincere,
That tells his name, his worth, his age,
   Is wet with Anson's tear.
And tears by bards or heroes shed,
Alike immortalize the dead.

I therefore purpose not, or dream,
Descanting on his fate,
   To give the melancholy theme
   A more enduring date.

But misery still delights to trace
Its semblance in another's case.

ON THE LOSS OF THE ROYAL GEORGE.

The Royal George, was a British vessel belonging to
the navy. While she was in harbour, and undergoing some
repair, with Admiral Kempenfelt, and eight hundred
persons, officers and men, on board, the vessel, and all
in it suddenly sunk, and every individual, perished Sep-
tember, 1782.

Toll for the brave !
  The brave that are no more !
All sunk beneath the wave,
  Fast by their native shore.

Eight hundred of the brave,
  Whose courage well was tried,
Had made the vessel heel,
  And laid her on her side.

A land breeze shook the shrouds,
  And she was overset ;
Down went the Royal George,
  With all her crew complete.

Toll for the brave !
  Brave Kempenfelt is gone ;
His last sea-fight is fought ;
  His work of glory done.

It was not in the battle ;
  No tempest gave the shock ;
She sprang no fatal leak ;
  She ran upon no rock.

His sword was in his sheath ;
  His fingers held the pen,
When Kempenfelt went down,
  With twice four hundred men.

29

Weigh the vessel up,
 Once dreaded by our foes !
And mingle with our cup,
 The tear that England owes.

Her timbers yet are sound,
 And she may float again,
Full charg'd with England's thunder,
 And plough the distant main.

But Kempenfelt is gone,
 His victories are o'er ;
And he and his eight hundred,
 Shall plough the wave no more.

GRAY.

Born 1716—Died 1771.

Mr. Gray was accounted in his time, according to Dr. Johnson, the most *learned man* in Europe—doubtless he was *among* the most learned ; but his learning dignifies ░ memory less than his genius and his taste. Gray's ░░░, which give short sketches of the places and cu-░░░░ which he visited as a traveller, and express the ░░░░░ of a good son, and an affectionate friend, ex-░░░the elegance of an accomplished mind, and the ░░░ments of a sincere and pure heart. The Elegy in a Country Church Yard, is the most popular of Gray's poems : it is not inserted here because it may be found in every miscellaneous collection. The less admired and exalted, but more sprightly and happy toned Ode to Spring, and verses on the Drowned Cat, are suitable to the design of these specimens.

ODE ON THE SPRING.

Lo ! where the rosy-bosom'd Hours,
　　Fair Venus' train, appear,
Disclose the long-expected flowers,
　　And wake the purple year !
The attic warbler* pours her throat,
Responsive to the cuckoo's note,
　　The untaught harmony of Spring :
While, whispering pleasure as they fly,
Cool Zephyrs through the clear blue sky
　　Their gather'd fragrance fling.

Where'er the oak's thick branches stretch
　　A broader browner shade,
Where'er the rude and moss-grown beech
　　O'er canopies the glade.
Beside some water's rushy brink
With me the Muse shall sit, and think
　　(At ease reclin'd in rustic state)
How vain the ardour of the croud,

*The Swallow.

How low, how little are the proud,
　How indigent the great !

Still is the toiling hand of Care ;
　The panting herds repose :
Yet hark, how through the peopled air
　The busy murmur glows !
The insect youth are on the wing,
Eager to taste the honied spring,
　And float amid the liquid noon :
Some lightly o'er the current skim,
Some show their gaily-gilded trim
　Quick-glancing to the sun.

To Contemplation's sober eye
　Such is the race of Man :
And they that creep, and they that fly,
　Shall end where they began.
Alike the busy and the gay
But flutter through life's little day,
　In Fortune's varying colours dress'd :
Brushed by the hand of rough Mischance,
Or chill'd by Age, their airy dance
　They leave, in dust to rest.

ON THE DEATH OF A FAVOURITE CAT,
Drowned in a tub of Gold Fishes.

'Twas on a lofty vase's side,
Where China's gayest art had dy'd
　The azure flowers that blow ;
Demurest of the tabby kind,
The pensive Selima, reclin'd,
　Gaz'd on the lake below.

Her conscious tail her joy declar'd ;
The fair round face, the snowy beard,
　The velvet of her paws,

Her coat, that with the tortoise vies,
Her ears of jet, and emerald eyes,
  She saw ; and púrr'd applause.

Still had she gaz'd : bút mìdst the tide
Two angel forms were seen to glide,
  The Genii of the stream :
Their scaly armour's Tyrian hue
Though richest purple, to the view
  Betray'd a golden gleam.

The hapless Nymph with wonder saw
A whisker first, and then a claw :
  With many an ardent wish,
She stretch'd, in vain, to reach the prize :
What female heart can gold despise ?
  What cat's averse to fish ?

Presumptuous Maid ! with looks intent
Again she stretch'd, again she bent,
  Nor knew the gulf between :
(Malignant Fate sat by, and smil'd)
The slippery verge her feet beguil'd,
  She tumbled headlong in.

Eight times emerging from the flood,
She mew'd to ev'ry wat'ry god,
  Some speedy aid to send.
No Dolphin came, no Nereid stir'd :
Nor cruel Tom, nor Susan heard.
  A fav'rite has no friend !

From hence, ye Beauties, undeceiv'd,
Know, one false step is ne'er retreiv'd,
  And be with caution bold.
Not all that tempts your wand'ring eyes
And heedless heart, is lawful prize :
  Nor all that glistens gold.

CAMPBELL.

Thomas Campbell, the author of the Pleasures of Hope, of Gertrude of Wyoming, &c., is among the most popular of living writers. As a poet and a critic, he ranks with the first of the age. Mr. Campbell is now principal of the university of Glasgow. Lochiel's Warning, one of Campbell's shorter pieces, is often read and recited in schools, but it cannot be comprehended without some acquaintance with Scottish history and character.

England and Scotland were governed by separate kings till 1603. In that year Elizabeth of England died, and named as her successor James VI of Scotland. James was the son of Mary, Queen of Scots, and Henry Stuart, Lord Darnley. James was descended from Henry VII of England, and among his ancestors was a long line of Scottish kings : as *their* descendants, the people of Scotland cherished an ardent affection for James and his posterity. The Scots are remarkable for their attachment to power. The heads of the Clans, and the hereditary prince, were to the people objects of the highest enthusiasm ; and they esteemed it a duty, and even a privilege, to die in their service.

James was succeeded by his son Charles I, who did not know how to govern, and was beheaded by his subjects. After Charles' death, England was a commonwealth, or republic, governed for nine years by Oliver Cromwell. In 1668, Charles Stuart, the second of that name, was made king of England, as the legitimate successor of his father, Charles I. Charles II died 1685, and his brother James, duke of York, was immediately proclaimed king; but by the laws of England he was incapacitated for the sovereignty.

In the reigns of Edward VI, and his sister Elizabeth, the Protestant faith became the foundation of what is called the Established Church of England; and it was made a law that the king, and all persons holding places under the government, should acknowledge themselves to be Protestants, and worship according to the forms prescribed by the national Church. James II was a Catholic. When the people were convinced of this fact, and of the king's inclination to restore Popery in Britain, they sent over to Holland to William, prince of Orange, a grandson of Charles I, and to his wife, Mary, daughter of the English king, James II, to come over to England, and take the government upon themselves. William and Mary were crowned king and queen 1689. A party in Scotland, attached to the Stuarts, refused to acknowledge them; but in the same year the Scottish army was defeated at Killycrankie in Perthshire.

The banished James endeavoured to make friends in Ireland, but his adherents were defeated by king William, at the battle of the Boyne, and he was forced to retire into France. The Jacobites (the friends of James) long continued their machinations to restore the Stuarts to the throne of Britain, but all their plans were ultimately frustrated.

James Stuart died in France in 1701, and his daughter, the princess Anne, succeeded William III. She was proclaimed queen in April 1702, and died in 1714. Anne was succeeded by George I of the house of Brunswick. George was a German prince, descended in the female line from James I of England. This new family were destined for ever to exclude the Stuarts from the throne of Britain; but one of that race, sometimes called the Pretender, and sometimes the chevalier St. George, went from France to Scotland in 1715, and there, assisted by the favourers of his unfortunate pretensions, made some attempts to recover his forfeited inheritance. These were unavailing; he was forced to return to France, and many of his adherents were executed as traitors to their king and country.

The rebellion of the Stuarts did not end here. The following narrative details its progress and termination.

" In 1745 the son of the old pretender resolved to make an effort at gaining the British crown. Being furnished with some money, and still larger promises from

France, he embarked for Scotland on board a small frigate, accompanied by the Marquis Tullibardine, and a few other desperate adventurers. For the conquest of the whole British empire, he brought with him seven officers, and arms for 2000 men. He landed on the coast of Lochabar, July 27, and was in a little time joined by some Highland chiefs, and their vassals. He soon saw himself at the head of 1500 men, and invited others to join him by manifestoes, which were dispersed throughout all the highlands. The English ministry was no sooner informed of the truth of his arrival, than Sir John Cope was ordered to oppose his progress. In the mean time, the young adventurer marched to Perth, where his father, the chevalier de St. George, had been proclaimed king of Great Britain. The rebel army advanced towards Edinburgh, which they entered without opposition. Here, too the pageantry of proclamation was performed. But, though he was master of the capital, yet the citadel or castle, with a good garrison, under the command of General Guest, braved all his attempts. Sir John Cope, who was now reinforced by two regiments of dragoons, resolved to march towards Edinburgh, and give him battle The young adventurer attacked him near Preston Pans, and in a few minutes totally routed him and his troops. In this victory the king lost about 500 men, and the rebel not above 80.

In the mean time, the pretender went forward with vigour; and having advanced to Penrith, continued his irruption till he came to Manchester, where he established his head-quarters; from thence he prosecuted his route to Derby; but he determined once more to return to Scotland. He effected his retreat to Carlisle without any loss, and, having reinforced the garrison of the place, crossed the rivers Eden and Solway into Scotland.

After many attacks and skirmishes, the duke of Cumberland, son of George II, the reigning king, put himself at the head of the troops of Edinburgh, which consisted of about 14,000 men. He resolved to come to a battle soon as possible, and marched forward, while the young adventurer retired at his approach. The duke advanced to Aberdeen, where he was joined by the duke of Gordon, and some other lords. The Highlanders were drawn up in order of battle, on the plain of Culloden, to the number of 8000 men. The duke marched thither, and the battle began about one o'clock in the afternoon, April 16. In less than thirty minutes, the rebels were totally routed, and the field was covered with their dead bodies. The duke immediately after the battle, ordered thirty-six deserters to be executed."

The adventure of Prince Charles-Edward in his perilous undertaking, and his escape out of the British dominions, form a most extraordinary romance of real life. The novel of Waverley gives some interesting sketches of this Prince's enterprize, and particularly of the generosity and devotedness of his adherents. The British government made a most severe example of the misguided men, who sacrificed themselves to their principles of loyalty, but so elevated were their motives that it is impossible not to deplore their fate. The principal chiefs engaged in this rebellion were executed at Carlisle, Culloden, and other places, and thousands of inferior condition were transported to foreign countries.

Lochiel, the chief of the warlike clan of the Camerons, engaged in this unhappy cause. "His memory is still cherished among the Highlanders, by the appellation of the gentle Lochiel, for he was famed for his social virtues as much as for his martial and magnanimous (though mistaken) loyalty."

Before Lochiel had led his followers to the standard of the Pretender, it is related that a *Seer* forewarned him of the catastrophe which awaited the rebels. This remonstrance is the foundation of Lochiel's Warning. The less informed of the Scots, from time immemorial, have cherished a belief in the gift of *second sight*—more properly *first sight*. The second sight, say those who believe in it, is an actual perception which the gifted person has of things absent and future, which he can afterwards describe to others, and which usually intimates some important event. Ellen, in the Lady of the Lake, tells the stranger Knight,

> " Old Allan-bane foretold your plight,—
> A gray-haired sire, whose eye intent,
> Was on the visioned future bent."

LOCHIEL'S WARNING.

Wizard. Lochiel! Lochiel, beware of the day
When the Lowlands shall meet thee in battle array !
For a field of the dead rushes red on my sight,
And the clans of Culloden are scattered in fight :
They rally, they bleed, for their kingdom and crown ;
Wo, wo to the riders that trample them down !
Proud Cumberland prances, insulting the slain,
And their hoof-beaten bosoms are trod to the plain.
But hark ! through the fast-flashing lightning of war,
What steed to the desert flies frantic and far?
'Tis thine, oh Glenullin ! whose bride shall await,
Like a love-lighted watchfire, all night at the gate.
A steed comes at morning : no rider is there ;
But its bridle is red with the sign of despair.
Weep, Albin ! to death and captivity led !
Oh weep ! but thy tears cannot number the dead :
For a merciless sword on Culloden shall wave,
Culloden ! that wreaks with the blood of the brave.
 Lochiel. Go, preach to the coward, thou death-telling
  seer !
Or, if gory Culloden so dreadful appear,
Draw, dotard, around thy old wavering sight
This mantle, to cover the phantoms of fright.
 Wizard. Ha ! laugh'st thou, Lochiel, my vision to
  scorn ?
Proud bird of the mountain, thy plume shall be torn !
Say, rushed the bold eagle exultingly forth,
From his home, in the dark rolling clouds of the north ?
Lo ! the death-shot of foemen outspeeding, he rode
Companionless, bearing destruction abroad ;

But down let him stoop from his havoc on high !
Ah ! home let him speed—for the spoiler is nigh.
Why flames the far summit ?   Why shoot to the blast
Those embers, like stars from the firmament cast ?
'Tis the fire-shower of ruin all dreadfully driven
From his eyrie, that beacons the darkness of heaven.
Oh, crested Lochiel ! the peerless in might,
Whose banners arise on the battlements' height,
Heaven's fire is around thee, to blast and to burn ;
Return to thy dwelling ! all lonely return !
For the blackness of ashes shall mark where it stood,
And a wild mother scream o'er her famishing brood.

    Lochiel. False Wizard avaunt ! I have marshalled my
      clan :
Their swords are a thousand, their bosoms are one !
They are true to the last of their blood and their breath,
And like reapers descend to the harvest of death.
Then welcome be Cumberland's steed to the shock !
Let him dash his proud foam like a wave on the rock !
But wo to his kindred, and wo to his cause,
When Albin her claymore indignantly draws ;
When her bonneted chieftains to victory crowd,
Clanranald the dauntless, and Moray the proud ;
All plaided and plumed in their tartan array—

    Wizard. —Lochiel, Lochiel, beware of the day !
For, dark and despairing, my sight I may seal,
But man cannot cover what God would reveal :
'Tis the sunset of life gives me mystical lore,
And coming events cast their shadows before.
I tell thee, Culloden's dread echoes shall ring
With the bloodhounds, that bark for thy fugitive king.
Lo ! anointed by heaven with vials of wrath,
Behold, where he flies on his desolate path !
Now, in darkness and billows, he sweeps from my sight :
Rise ! rise ! ye wild tempests, and cover his flight !
'Tis finished.   Their thunders are hushed on the moors
Culloden is lost, and my country deplores ;
But where is the iron-bound prisoner ? Where ?
For the red eye of battle is shut in despair.

Say, mounts he the ocean-wave, banished, forlorn,
Like a limb from his country cast bleeding and torn ?
Ah no ! *for a darker departure is near,*
The war-drum is muffled, and black is the bier ;
His death-bell is tolling ; oh ! mercy dispel
Yon sight, that it freezes my spirit to tell !
Life flutters convulsed in his quivering limbs,
And his blood-streaming nostril in agony swims.
Accursed be the faggots, that blaze at his feet,
Where his heart shall be thrown ere it ceases to beat,
With the smoke of its ashes to poison the gale——

   Lochiel. ——Down, soothless insulter ! I trust not
     the tale :
Though my perishing ranks should be strewed in their
     gore,
Like ocean-weeds heaped on the surf-beaten shore,
Lochiel, untainted by flight or by chains,
While the kindling of life in his bosom remains,
Shall victor exult, or in death be laid low,
With his back to the field and his feet to the foe !
And leaving in battle no blot on his name,
Look proudly to heaven from the death-bed of fame.

   Weep, Albin—Scotland, or literally, people of Scot-
land.
   Proud bird of the mountain. The Wizard here addres-
ses Lochiel figuratively, and speaks of the ruin which is
impending over his house, as a *fire shower* destined to
consume the *eyrie* or eagle's nest—that signifies the
chief's home and his family.
   A darker departure is near. The agonizing description
given in the lines which follow to the end of the passage
refer to a fact. " The brother of Lochiel returned to
England ten years after the rebellion, though he acted
only as a surgeon in the rebel army, suffered the dread-
ful fate here predicted, by a sentence which happily has
no parallel for needless severity in the modern history
of state trials in this humane age."

ODE TO WINTER.

When first the fiery-mantled sun
His heavenly race began to run,
Round the earth and ocean blue,
His children four, the Seasons, flew.

First, in green apparel dancing,
  The young Spring smiled with angel grace ;
Rosy Summer next advancing,
  Rushed into her sire's embrace :
Her bright-hair'd sire, who bade her keep
  For ever nearest to his smiles,
On Calpe's olive-shaded steep,
  On India's citron-covered isles :
More remote and buxom-brown,
  The queen of vintage bowed before his throne ;
A rich pomegranate gemmed her crown,
  A ripe sheaf bound her zone.
But howling Winter fled afar,
To hills that prop the polar star,
And loves on deer borne car to ride,
With barren darkness by his side.
Round the shore where loud Lofoden
  Whirls to death the roaring whale,
Round the halls where Runic Odin
  Howls his war-song to the gale.

Oh, sire of storms ! whose savage ear
The Lapland drum delights to hear,
When Frenzy, with her bloodshot eye,
Implores thy dreadful deity.
Archangel ! power of desolation !
  Fast descending as thou art,
Say, hath mortal invocation
  Spells to touch thy stony heart ?
Then, sullen Winter, hear my prayer,
And gently rule the ruined year ;

30

Nor chill the wand'rer's bosom bare,
Nor freeze the wretch's falling tear ;—
To shuddering want's unmantled bed,
    Thy horror-breathing agues cease to lend,
And gently on the orphan head
    Of innocence descend.—
But chiefly spare, O king of clouds!
The sailor on his airy shrouds :
When wrecks and beacons strew the steep,
    And spectres walk along the deep.
Milder yet thy snowy breezes
    Pour on yonder tented shores,
Where the Rhine's broad billow freezes,
    Or the dark-brown Danube roars.
Oh, winds of Winter ! list ye there
    To many a deep and dying groan ;
Or start, ye demons of the midnight air,
    At shrieks and thunders louder than your own.
Alas ! e'en your unhallowed breath
    May spare the victim, fallen low ;
But man will ask no truce to death,—
    No bounds to human wo*.

THE SOLDIER'S DREAM,

Our bugles sang truce—for the night cloud had lowered,
    And the sentinel stars set their watch in the sky ;
And thousands had sunk on the ground overpowered,
    The weary to sleep, and the wounded to die.

When reposing that night on my pallet of straw,
    By the wolf-scaring faggot that guarded the slain ;
At the dead of the night a sweet vision I saw,
    And thrice ere the morning I dreamt it again.

Methought from the battle-field's dreadful array,
    Far, far I had roamed on a desolate track ;
'Twas autumn—and sunshine arose on the way
    To the home of my fathers, that welcomed me back.

*This ode was written in Germany, at the close of 1800, before
the conclusion of hostilities.

I flew to the pleasant fields traversed so oft
 In life's morning march, when my bosom was young ;
I heard my own mountain-goats bleating aloft,
 And knew the sweet strain that the corn-reapers sung.

Then pledged we the wine-cup, and fondly I swore
 From my home and my weeping friends never to part ;
My little ones kissed me a thousand times o'er,
 And my wife sobbed aloud in her fulness of heart.

Stay, stay with us—rest, thou art weary and worn :
 And fain was their war-broken soldier to stay ;
But sorrow returned with the dawning of morn,
 And the voice in my dreaming ear melted away,

AMERICAN POETRY.

The three articles next in course, are from the pen of **Mr. Bryant.** Of living poets of our native country, it is **unnecessary to** give information—the public regards them **with curiosity** which is generally gratified, and when they **deserve it, they** are objects of favour which is freely expressed. The individual whose name is attached to Autumn **Woods, to the Song of the Stars, and to Rizpah, enjoys a reputation** never attached to mediocrity, **and it becomes his countrymen and his contemporaries to furnish a pledge of the sure honours which late posterity will pay to his genius by the manner in which they cherish and requite that genius.**

AUTUMN WOODS.

Ere, in the northern gale,
The summer tresses of the trees are gone,
The woods of Autumn, all around our vale,
  Have put their glory on.

The mountains that infold
In their wide sweep, the coloured landscape round,
Seem groups of giant kings in purple and gold,
  That guard the enchanted ground.

I roam the woods that crown
The upland, where the mingled splendours glow,
Where the gay company of trees look down
  On the green fields below.

My steps are not alone
In these bright walks ; the sweet southwest, at play,
Flies, rustling, where the painted leaves are strown
  Along the winding way.

And far in heaven, the while,
The sun that sends that gale to wander here,
Pours out on the fair earth his quiet smile,—
  The sweetest of the year.

Where now the solemn shade,
Verdure and gloom, where many branches meet;
So grateful, when the noon of summer made
   The valleys sick with heat?

Let in through all the trees
Come the strange rays; the forest depths are bright;
Their sunny-coloured foliage, in the breeze,
   Twinkles, like beams of light.

The rivulet, late unseen,
Where bickering through the shrubs its waters run,
Shines with the image of its golden screen,
   And glimmerings of the sun.

But, 'neath yon crimson tree,
Lover to listening maid might breathe his flame,
Nor mark within its roseate canopy,
   Her blush of maiden shame.

Oh, Autumn! why so soon
Depart the hues that make thy forests glad;
Thy gentle wind and thy fair sunny noon,
   And leave thee wild and sad!

Ah! 'twere a lot too blest
For ever in thy coloured shades to stray;
Amidst the kisses of the soft southwest
   To rove and dream for aye;

And leave the vain low strife   [power,
That makes men mad—the tug for wealth and
The passions and the cares that wither life,
   And waste its little hour.

The variable climate of the eastern states, affords
grounds of complaint to sensitive people, but the beauti-
ful Autumn of that region is congenial to every consti-
tution and taste. The aspect of nature at that season in
New-England, inspires the most tranquil and happy

emotions, and the peace of its scenes disposes every heart to sympathize with the sentiments which the preceding verses express. The appearance of the American woods in autumn is peculiar to this country. Mr. Tudor, in his Letters on the Eastern States, gives this description of it:

"The rich and mellow tints of the forest at that season of the year, have often furnished subjects for the painter and the poet in Europe; but the woods of Europe never exhibit the appearance of ours. Besides all the shades of brown and green, which the forests of Europe display in the decay of their foliage, the American woods in the same stage of vegetation put on "the most glaring and brilliant colours—bright yellow, scarlet, orange and purple—not merely on single leaves, but masses of whole trees have their foliage thus tinged."

"I do not know that it has ever been accounted for; but it may perhaps be owing to the frosts coming earlier here than in Europe, and falling on the leaves while the sap is yet copious, before they have begun to dry and fall off. However this may be, the colouring is wonderful;—the walnut is turned to the brightest yellow, the maple to scarlet, &c. Our trees put on this dress about the first of October." At this time of the year the effect of the atmosphere upon our scenery and upon the sensations of the beholder, induce sentiments of sober cheerfulness, and pure enjoyment of this breathing life, and this beautiful world, such as we never feel at other seasons.

Mr. Tudor observes that "the reader who has any relic of veneration for Pomona and the Hamadryads," (I hope my young readers are acquainted with Pomona and the Hamadryads) will take an interest in the history of certain celebrated trees of New-England, and he proceeds to enumerate the more remarkable of these.

"In Salem, (Mass.) there is a pear tree still producing fruit, that was planted by Governor Endicott in his garden in 1630, and which is now owned by his descendants. At Sagadahoc, in Maine, when the French had a footing in 1689, there is an apple tree with some remains of life, amidst the ruins of their dwellings. The trunk is nearly the size of a hogshead, and entirely hollow. It was almost a century after before any apple trees were planted in the neighbouring country. In Hartford (Connecticut,) the oak yet stands, in which the Connecticut charter was secreted, during the disastrous administration of Andross, when all the New-England charters were taken away. Governor Andross went to Hartford to obtain the charter of Connecticut; when the Council were assembled with Andross in the evening, while the destined victim was lying on the table, the lights were suddenly extinguished, Captain Wadsworth seized the Charter and hid it in this tree, which even then, in 1692, was hollow with age. This tree forms an appropriate counterpart to the " royal oak" of England. The most celebrated of all our trees, however, was the *Liberty-tree* in Boston, which fell a sacrifice to party vengeance, and was cut down when the British troops got possession of the town. It was an elm of vast size, of which only the stump remains. Many transactions leading to the revolution took place beneath it. Trees in various places in this country and Europe, were named after it: in France at one time every municipality had one; but in that country they never flourished, and finally perished root and branch under Napoleon."

SONG OF THE STARS.

When the radiant morn of creation broke,
And the world in the smile of God awoke,
And the empty realms of darkness and death
Were moved through their depths by his mighty breath,
And orbs of beauty, and spheres of flame,
From the void abyss by myriads came,
In the joy of youth, as they darted away,
Through the widening wastes of space to play,
Their silver voices in chorus rung,
And this was the song the bright ones sung:

Away, away, through the wide, wide sky,
The fair blue fields that before us lie :
Each sun with the worlds that round us roll,
Each planet poised on her turning pole,
With her isles of green, and her clouds of white,
And her waters that lie like fluid light.

For the source of glory uncovers his face,
And the brightness o'erflows unbounded space ;
And we drink, as we go, the luminous tides
In our ruddy air and our blooming sides ;
Lo, yonder the living splendours play !
Away, on our joyous path away !

Look, look, through our glittering ranks afar,
In the infinite azure, star after star,
How they brighten and bloom as they swiftly pass !
How the verdure runs o'er each rolling mass !
And the path of the gentle winds is seen,
Where the small waves dance, and the young woods lean.

And see where the brighter day-beams pour,
How the rainbows hang in the sunny shower ;
And the morn and eve, with their pomp of hues,
Shift o'er the bright planets and shed their dews ;
And 'twixt them both, o'er the teeming ground,
With her shadowy cone, the night goes round.

Away, away !—in our blossoming bowers,
In the soft air wrapping those spheres of ours,
In the seas and fountains that shine with morn,
See, love is brooding, and life is born,
And breathing myriads are breaking from night,
To rejoice, like us, in motion and light.

Glide on in your beauty, ye youthful spheres !
To weave the dance that measures the years.
Glide on in the glory and gladness sent
To the farthest wall of the firmament,
The boundless visible smile of him
To the vale of whose brow our lamps are dim.

RIZPAH.

And he delivered them into the hands of the Gibeonites, and they hanged them in the hill before the Lord; and they fell all seven together, and were put to death in the days of the harvest, in the first days, in the beginning of barley-harvest.

And Rizpah, the daughter of Aiah, took sackcloth and spread it for her upon the rock, from the beginning of harvest until the water dropped upon them out of heaven, and suffered neither the birds of the air to rest upon them by day, nor the beasts of the field by night.

2 Samuel, xxi. 9, 10.

Hear what the desolate Rizpah said,
As on Gibeah's rocks she watched the dead.
The sons of Michal before her lay,
And her own fair children, dearer than they;
By a death of shame they all had died,
And were stretched on the bare rock, side by side.
And Rizpah, once the loveliest of all
That bloomed and smiled in the court of Saul,
All wasted with watching and famine now,
And scorched by the sun her haggard brow,
Sat, mournfully guarding their corpses there,
And murmured a strange and solemn air;
The low, heart-broken, and wailing strain
Of a mother that mourns her children slain.

I have made the crags my home, and spread
On their desert backs my sackcloth bed;
I have eaten the bitter herb of the rocks,
And drank the midnight dew in my locks;
I have wept till I could not weep, and the pain
Of my burning eyeballs went to my brain.
Seven blackened corpses before me lie,
In the blaze of the sun and the winds of the sky.
I have watched them through the burning day,
And driven the vulture and raven away;

And the cormorant wheeled in circles round,
Yet feared to alight on the guarded ground.
And, when the shadows of twilight came,
I have seen the hyena's eyes of flame,
And heard at my side his stealthy tread,
But aye at my shout the savage fled !
And I threw the lighted brand, to fright
The jackal and wolf that yelled in the night.

Ye were foully murdered, my hapless sons,
By the hands of wicked and cruel ones ;
Ye fell in your fresh and blooming prime,
All innocent, for your father's crime.
He sinned—but he paid the price of his guilt,
When his blood by a nameless hand was spilt ;
When he strove with the heathen host in vain,
And fell with the flower of his people slain,
And the sceptre his children's hands should sway,
From his injured lineage passed away.

But I hoped that the cottage roof would be
A safe retreat for my sons and me ;
And that while they ripened to manhood fast,
They should wean my thoughts from woes of the past:
And my bosom swelled with a mother's pride,
As they stood in their beauty and strength by my side,
Tall like their sire, with the princely grace
Of his stately form, and the bloom of his face.

Oh, what an hour for a mother's heart,
When the pitiless ruffians tore us apart !
When I clasped their knees and wept and prayed,
And struggled and shrieked to heaven for aid,
And clung to my sons with desperate strength,
Till the murderers loosed my hold at length,
And bore me breathless and faint aside,
In their iron arms, while my children died.
They died—and the mother that gave them birth
Is forbid to cover their bones with earth.

The barley harvest was nodding white,
When my children died on the rocky height,
And the reapers were singing on hill and plain,
When I came to my task of sorrow and pain.
But now the season of rain is nigh,
The sun is dim in the thickening sky,
And the clouds in sullen darkness rest.
When he hides his light at the doors of the west,
I hear the howl of the wind that brings
The long drear storm on its heavy wings;
But the howling wind, and the driving rain
Will beat on my houseless head in vain :
I shall stay, from my murdered sons to scare
The beasts of the desert, and fowls of the air.

When the Israelites took possession of the land of Canaan, they were commanded to extirpate the occupants of the country. This was but imperfectly fulfilled : in Israel and its borders there always remained some of the descendants of the primitive inhabitants. About a thousand years before Christ, Saul, king of Israel, slew some of the Gibeonites, a remnant of the Amorites. A few years after, the Gibeonites, like other savages, demanded of David, as a satisfaction for the injury they had sustained from his predecessor, *life for life.* They required that seven men of the posterity of Saul should be delivered to them to be hanged, and David consented to this cruel proposition. The king took two sons of Saul and Rizpah, and five sons of Michal, Saul's daughter, and delivered them to the Gibeonites.—The fearful vengeance executed upon these men, and the constant heart-rending fondness of Rizpah, are already known from the words of the scripture and the pathetic verses of the poet.

FRISBIE.

The author of the two hymns inserted below, was a professor of Moral Philosophy in Harvard University, Cambridge, Massachusetts. Professor Frisbie died in 1821. He was almost entirely deprived of sight, but it happened to him, as to the divine Milton, and to many other highly gifted men, that Providence made him amends for the imperfection of external vision by a more profound insight of holy and heavenly things. Human happiness and virtue, were the subjects of Professor Frisbie's habitual and anxious inquiries; "but all his serious thoughts had rest in Heaven"—Piety was the constant frame of his mind, and his conversation and example afforded uniform illustrations of the Christian temper and faith. His death was a loss to the young particularly, and his worth as a man, a scholar, and a Christian, was duly appreciated and felt by those of his college who looked up to him for the exposition of duty and of truth. Perhaps the good seed which he scattered in many minds, is now expanded to fruit, and it may be that the devotional pieces here annexed will yet serve to awaken gratitude to God, and to strengthen resolutions of virtue.

MORNING HYMN.

While nature welcomes in the day,
My heart its earliest vows would pay
To him whose care has kindly kept
My life from danger while I slept.

His genial rays the sun renews;
How bright the scene with glittering dews!
The blushing flowers more beauteous bloom,
And breathe more sweet their rich perfume.

So may the sun of righteousness,
With kindliest beams my bosom bless,
Warm into life each heavenly seed,
To bud and bear some generous deed.

So may the dews of grace distil,
And gently soften all my will ;
So may my morning sacrifice
To heaven like grateful incense rise.

Wilt thou this day my footsteps guide,
And kindly all I need provide ;
With strength divine my bosom arm,
Against temptation's powerful charm ?

Where'er I am, oh, may I feel
That God is all around me still ;
That all I say, or do, or mean,
By his all-searching eye is seen.

Oh may each day my heart improve !
Increase my faith, my hope, my love ;
And thus its shades around me close
More wise and holy than I rose.

EVENING HYMN.

My soul, a hymn of evening praise
To God, thy kind preserver, raise,
Whose hand this day hath guarded, fed,
And thousand blessings round thee shed.

Forgive my sins this day, O Lord,
In thought or feeling, deed or word ;
And if in aught thy law I've kept,
My feeble efforts, Lord, accept.

While nature round is hush'd to rest,
Let no vain thought disturb my breast;
Shed o'er my soul religion's power,
Serenely solemn as the hour.

Oh, bid thy angels o'er me keep
Their watch, to shield me while I sleep !
Till the fresh morn shall round me break,
Then with new vigour may I wake !

31

Yet think, my soul, another day
Of thy short course has roll'd away :
Ah, think how soon in deep'ning shade
The day of life itself shall fade !

How soon death's sleep my eyes must close,
Lock every sense in dread repose,
And lay amid the awful gloom
And solemn silence of the tomb !

This very night, Lord, should it be,
Oh may my soul repose on thee,
Till the glad morn in heaven shall rise,
Then wake to triumph in the skies !

JERUSALEM.

————Like a queen,
Arme'd with a helm in virgin loveliness,
Her heaving bosom in a bossy cuirass,
She sits aloft, begirt with battlements
And bulwarks swelling from the rock, to guard
The sacred courts, pavilions, palaces,
Soft gleaming through the umbrage of the woods
Which tuft the summit, and like raven tresses,
Wave their dark beauty round the tower of David.
Resplendent with a thousand golden bucklers,
The embrasures of alabaster shine ;
Hailed by the pilgrims of the desert, bound
To Judah's mart with orient merchandise.

Hillhouse.

Jerusalem, a city of modern Palestine, and the capital
of Judea, was more anciently Jebus, and was taken by
David, incorporated into his dominions, and consecrated
to the worship of the God of Israel.   David fortified and
embellished Jerusalem, and his son Solomon erected the
temple, whither the Jews repaired annually to celebrate

the feast of the Passover. Jerusalem was ever an object of attachment and veneration to the Jews, and in the time of Christ was the resort and residence of many foreigners. Jerusalem was at that time subject to the Romans, but a spirit of revolt against their foreign masters exposed the Jews to their vengeance.—Christ foretold the destruction of this city, and his prophecy was accomplished by Titus, A. D. 70.

Modern Jerusalem is included in the Turkish dominions—none of the splendour which Mr. Hillhouse describes now remains, but there are many monuments of Christianity, and it is interesting to the traveller as the scene of the greatest splendour and dignity of that extraordinary nation, the Jews; and more particularly as the place where Jesus Christ performed many of his miracles, where he promulgated the doctrines of our religion, and where he was crucified and buried.

Mr. Milman is a British poet. He takes his subjects principally from scripture history. The following article is rendered intelligible by the XIVth chapter of Exodus.

SONG OF THE JEWS.
Chorus.

King of Kings! and Lord of Lords!
   Thus we move, our sad steps timing
   To our our cymbals' feeblest chiming,
Where thy house its rest accords.
Chas'd and wounded birds are we,
Through the dark air fled to thee;
To the shadow of thy wings,
   Lord of Lords! and King of Kings!

Behold, oh Lord! the Heathen tread
   The branches of thy fruitful vine,
That its luxurious tendrils spread
   O'er all the hills of Palestine.
And now the wild boar comes to waste
Even us, the greenest boughs, and last,

That, drinking of thy choicest dew,
On Zion's hill, in beauty grew.

No! by the marvels of thine hand,
Thou wilt save thy chosen land !
By all thine ancient mercies shown,
By all our fathers' foes o'erthrown ;
By the Egyptian's car-borne host,
Scattered on the Red Sea coast ;
By that wide and bloodless slaughter
Underneath the drowning water.

Like us in utter helplessness,
In their last and worst distress——
On the sand and sea-weed lying,
Israel poured her doleful sighing ;
While before the deep sea flow'd,
And behind fierce Egypt rode——
To their fathers' God they pray'd,
To the Lord of Hosts for aid.

On the margin of the flood
With lifted rod the Prophet stood ;
And the summon'd east wind blew,
And aside it sternly threw.
The gather'd waves, that took their stand
Like crystal rocks, on either hand,
Or walls of sea-green marble piled
Round some irregular city wild.

Then the light of morning lay
On the wonder-paved way,
Where the treasures of the deep
In their caves of coral sleep.
The profound abysses, where
Was never sound from upper air,
Rang with Israel's chanted words,
King of Kings ! and Lord of Lords !

Then with bow and banner glancing,
On exulting Egypt came,
With her chosen horsemen prancing,
And her cars on wheels of flame,

In a rich and boastful ring,
All around her furious king.

But the Lord from out his cloud,
The Lord look'd down upon the proud ;
And the host drave heavily
Down the deep bosom of the sea.

With a quick and sudden swell
Prone the liquid ramparts fell ;
Over horse, and over car,
Over every man of war,
Over Pharaoh's crown of gold
The loud thundering billows roll'd.

As the level waters spread
Down they sank, they sank like lead,
Down sank without a cry or groan.
And the morning sun, that shone
On myriads of bright-armed men,
Its meridian radiance then
Cast on a wide sea, heaving as of yore,
Against a silent, solitary shore.

This is a song of some Jews, who deplore the captivity of their nation, which they represent under the scripture figure which describes the Hebrew people as a vine, trodden down by the devastation of their enemies. The remembrance of God's mercies and promises always animated this unfortunate people ; and in their deepest affliction they celebrate their deliverance from their Egyptian bondage.

" And they took their journey from Succoth, and encamped in Etham, in the edge of the wilderness. And the Lord went before them by day in a pillar of a cloud, to lead them the way ; and by night in a pillar of fire, to give them light ; to go by day and night : He took not away the pillar of the cloud by day, nor the pillar of fire by night, from before the people.

" And it was told the king of Egypt that the people fled : and the heart of Pharaoh and of his servants was turned against the people, and they said, Why have we done this,

that we have let Israel go from serving us ? And he made
ready his chariot, and took his people with him ; and
he took six hundred chosen chariots, and all the chariots
of Egypt, and captains over every one of them.   And the
Lord hardened the heart of Pharaoh king of Egypt, and
he pursued after the children of Israel : and the children
of Israel went out with an high hand.   But the Egyp-
tians pursued after them, all the horses and chariots of
Pharaoh, and his horsemen, and his army, and overtook
them encamping by the sea, beside Pi-hahiroth, before
Baal-zephon.

    " And when Pharaoh drew nigh, the children of Israel
lifted up their eyes, and, behold, the Egyptians marched
after them ; and they were sore afraid : and the children
of Israel cried out unto the Lord.

    " And Moses said unto the people, Fear ye not, stand
still, and see the salvation of the Lord, which he will
show to you to-day : for the Egyptians whom ye have
seen to-day, ye shall see them again no more for ever.
The Lord shall fight for you, and ye shall hold your
peace.

    " And the Lord said unto Moses, Wherefore criest thou
unto me ? speak unto the children of Israel, that they go
forward : but lift up thy rod, and stretch out thine hand
over the sea, and divide it : and the children of Israel shall
go on dry ground through the midst of the sea.   And I,
behold, I will harden the hearts of the Egyptians, and
they shall follow them : and I will get me honour upon
Pharaoh, and upon all his host, upon his chariots, and
upon his horsemen.   And the Egyptians shall know that
I am the Lord, when I have gotten me honour upon Pha-
raoh, upon his chariots, and upon his horsemen.

    " And the angel of God, which went before the camp of
Israel, removed and went behind them ; and the pillar of
the cloud went from before their face, and stood behind
them :   And it came between the camp of the Egyptians
and the camp of Israel ; and it was a cloud and darkness
to them, but it gave light by night to these : so that the
one came not near the other all the night.   And Moses

stretched out his hand over the sea : and the Lord caused the sea to go back by a strong east wind all that night, and made the sea dry land, and the waters were divided. And the children of Israel went into the midst of the sea upon the dry ground : and the waters were a wall unto them on their right hand, and on their left.

"And the Egyptians pursued, and went in after them to the midst of the sea, even all Pharaoh's horses, his chariots, and his horsemen. And it came to pass, that in the morning watch the Lord looked unto the host of the Egyptians through the pillar of fire and of the cloud, and troubled the host of the Egyptians, and took off their chariot wheels, that they drave them heavily : so that the Egyptians said, Let us flee from the face of Israel ; for the Lord fighteth for them against the Egyptians.

"And the Lord said unto Moses, Stretch out thine hand over the sea, that the waters may come again upon the Egyptians, upon their chariots, and upon their horsemen : And Moses stretched forth his hand over the sea, and the sea returned to his strength when the morning appeared ; and the Egyptians fled against it ; and the Lord overthrew the Egyptians in the midst of the sea. And the waters returned, and covered the chariots, and the horsemen, and all the host of Pharaoh that came into the sea after them ; there remained not so much as one of them. But the children of Israel walked upon dry land in the midst of the sea , and the waters were a wall unto them on their right hand, and on their left. Thus the Lord saved Israel that day out of the hand of the Egyptians ; and Israel saw the Egyptians dead upon the sea-shore. And Israel saw that great work which the Lord did upon the Egyptians ; and the people feared the Lord, and believed the Lord, and his servant Moses."

TITUS BEFORE JERUSALEM.

Christ, when he was upon earth, admonished his countrymen to submit to the political circumstances in which they were placed. "Render," said he, " to Cæsar, the

things that are Cæsar's." The Roman Emperor's title was
Cæsar.   Our Saviour's exhortation amounted to this:
Pay the taxes imposed upon you, and conform patiently
to oppressions which you cannot remove.   But he knew
that to them his preaching was vain.   They knew not
what belonged to their peace, and Jesus foresaw that
they would at last provoke the severest punishment
which the Roman power could inflict.   He wept over
Jerusalem, and as he fixed his eyes upon the great tem-
ple of the Jews, declared that of it not one stone should
remain upon another.

During forty years which succeeded this prophecy,
the Roman Emperor and the provincials of Judea kept
up mutual ill-will, and frequent hostility, till the Emperor
Vespasian sent a powerful army under his son Titus
against this devoted city.   Mr. Milman, the author of
the Fall of Jerusalem, represents, according to history,
that Titus lamented the *necessity* he was under to destroy
Jerusalem, for he acted under the Emperor's orders,
which were, if the Jews would not peaceably submit to
the Roman arms, to take possession of the city at any
price of severity and destruction.

Mr. Milman fancies Titus, while his forces were in a
state of preparation for the attack of Jerusalem, to sur-
vey the city, and to express at once his admiration of her
beauty and splendour, and his deep regret that his pain-
ful duty was to destroy all the art and majesty of so fair
a scene.

"——————————————————— It must be !
And yet it moves me, Romans ! it confounds
The counsel of my firm philosophy,
That ruin's merciless ploughshare must pass o'er,
And barren salt be sowed on yon proud city.
As on our olive-crowned hill we stand,
Where Kedron at our feet its scanty waters
Distils from stone to stone with gentle motion,
As through a valley sacred to sweet peace,
How boldly doth it front us! how majestically !
Like a luxurious vineyard, the hill side

Is hung with marble fabrics, line o'er line,
Terrace o'er terrace, nearer still, and nearer
To the blue heavens.
    Here bright and sumptuous palaces,
With cool and verdant gardens interspers'd ;
Here towers of war, that frown in massy strength ;
While over all hangs the rich purple eve,
As conscious of its being her last farewell
Of light and glory to that faded city.
And, as our clouds of battle dust, and smoke
Are melted into air, behold the temple,
In undisturb'd and lone serenity,
Finding itself a solemn sanctuary
In the profound of heaven !
    It stands before us
A mount of snow fretted with golden pinnacles !
The very sun, as though he worshipp'd there,
Lingers upon the gilded cedar roofs :
And down the long and branching porticoes,
On every flowing-sculptur'd capital,
Glitters the homage of his parting beams.
By Hercules ! the sight might almost win
The offended majesty of Rome to mercy."

    Jerusalem was built upon two hills opposite to each
other, and divided by a valley ; the valley terminated at
the fountain of Siloam.   This fountain was celebrated
for the sweetness and abundance of its waters, which
flowed near the temple—Hence, Milton says,

        ————Siloa's brook which flowed
         Fast by the oracle of God.

    The brook Kedron, or Cedron, separated Jerusalem
from the mount of Olives, on which was Gethsemene,
and the garden where Jesus prayed and suffered so bit-
terly.

————

JAVAN'S LAMENTATION.

    Javan, a Christian soldier, after the siege of Jerusa-
lem, thus deplores its destruction :

" Oh ! fair and favour'd city, where of old
The balmy airs were rich with melody,
That led her pomp beneath the cloudless sky
In vestments flaming with the orient gold ;
Her gold is dim, and mute her music's voice,
The Heathen o'er her perish'd pomp rejoice.

How stately then was every palm-deck'd street,
Down which the maidens danc'd with tinkling feet !
How proud the elders in the lofty gate !
How crowded all her nation's solemn feasts !
With white-rob'd Levites and high-mitred Priests ;
How gorgeous all her Temple's sacred state !

Her streets are raz'd, her maidens sold for slaves,
Her gates thrown down, her elders in their graves ;
Her feasts are holden 'mid the Gentile's scorn ;
By stealth her Priesthood's holy garments worn ;
And where her Temple crown'd the glittering rock,
The wandering shepherd folds his evening flock."

SAMUEL.

The first chapter of the first book of Samuel relates
the domestic history of that venerable man's childhood.
It describes his father's and mother's mutual affection,
and the piety of Hannah. Hannah prayed to God for
this son, and promised that from his birth he should be
set apart for the services of religion ; and when God
had answered her prayer, and given her the child, as soon
as the young Samuel was old enough for the temple ser-
vice, his mother accompanied him to the Lord's house,
and presented him to Eli the high priest, saying, as she
offered him, " Oh my lord, as thy soul liveth, my lord, I
am the woman that stood by thee here, praying unto the
Lord. For this child I prayed ; and the Lord hath gi-
ven me my petition which I asked of him ; therefore
also I have lent him to the Lord ; as long as he liveth he
shall be lent to the Lord. And he worshipped the Lord
there." Mrs. Hemans has made an interesting picture
of this affecting transaction.

THE HEBREW MOTHER.

The rose was in rich bloom on Sharon's plain,
When a young mother with her first-born thence
Went up to Zion, for the boy was vow'd
Unto the Temple-service ;— by the hand
She led him, and her silent soul, the while,
Oft as the dewy laughter of his eye
Met her sweet serious glance, rejoic'd to think
That aught so pure, so beautiful was hers,
To bring before her God.   So pass'd they on,
O'er Judah's hills : and wheresoe'er the leaves
Of the broad sycamore made sounds at noon,
Like lulling rain-drops, or the olive-boughs,
With their cool dimness, cross'd the sultry blue
Of Syria's heaven, she paus'd, that he might rest ;
Yet from her own meek eyelids chas'd the sleep
That weigh'd their dark fringe down, to sit and watch
The crimson deepening o'er his cheek's repose,
As at a red flower's heart.
    And where a fount
Lay like a twilight-star 'midst palmy shades,
Making its banks green gems along the wild,
There too she linger'd, from the diamond wave
Drawing bright water for his rosy lips,
And softly parting clusters of jet curls
To bathe his brow.   At last the Fane was reach'd,
The Earth's One Sanctuary—and rapture hush'd
Her bosom, as before her, through the day,
It rose, a mountain of white marble, steep'd
In light, like floating gold.
    But when that hour
Wan'd to the farewell moment, when the boy
Lifted, through rainbow-gleaming tears, his eye
Beseechingly to hers, and half in fear
Turn'd from the white-rob'd priest, and round her arm
Clung as the ivy clings—the deep spring-tide
Of Nature then swell'd high, and o'er her child
Bending, her soul broke forth, in mingled sound
Of weeping and sad song.—"Alas," she cried,

"Alas! my boy, thy gentle grasp is on me,
The bright tears quiver in thy pleading eyes,
        And now fond thoughts arise,
And silver cords again to earth have won me;
And like a vine thou claspest my full heart—
        How shall I hence depart?

How the lone paths retrace where thou wert playing
So late, along the mountains, at my side?
        And I, in joyous pride,
By every place of flowers my course delaying
Wove, e'en as pearls, the lilies round thy hair,
        Beholding thee so fair!

And oh! the home whence thy bright smile hath parted,
Will it not seem as if the sunny day
        Turn'd from its door away?
While through its chambers wandering, weary-hearted,
I languish for thy voice, which past me still
        Went like a singing rill?

Under the palm-trees thou no more shalt meet me,
When from the fount at evening I return,
        With the full water-urn;
Nor will thy sleep's low dove-like breathings greet me,
As 'midst the silence of the stars I wake,
        And watch for thy dear sake.

And thou, will slumber's dewy cloud fall round thee,
Without thy mother's hand to smooth thy bed?
        Wilt thou not vainly spread
Thine arms, when darkness as a veil hath wound thee,
To fold my neck, and lift up, in thy fear,
        A cry which none shall hear?

What have I said. my child?—Will He not hear thee,
Who the young ravens heareth from their nest?
        Shall He not guard thy rest,
And, in the hush of holy midnight near thee,
Breathe o'er thy soul, and fill its dreams with joy?
        Thou shalt sleep soft, my boy!

I give thee to thy God—the God that gave thee,
A wellspring of deep gladness to my heart!
     And precious as thou art,
And pure as dew of Hermon, He shall have thee,
My own, my beautiful, my undefil'd!
     And thou shalt be His child.

Therefore, farewell!—I go, my soul may fail me,
As the hart panteth for the water-brooks,
     Yearning for thy sweet looks—
But thou, my first-born, droop not, nor bewail me;
Thou in the Shadow of the Rock shalt dwell,
     The Rock of Strength.—Farewell."

—————————— at last the Fane was reached,
    The earth's One Sanctuary.

    Fane means a place of worship. *Hence, ye profane, is
a poetic expression.* The word *profane*, thus used,
means the *unholy*—those who are not instructed in religion, or not capable of understanding and feeling any
thing beautiful.
    The earth's One Sanctuary. Other nations besides
the Hebrews observed religious worship, and had splendid temples in honour of their gods—but those were
false gods, and Mrs. Hemans supposes that the "house
of the Lord in Shiloh," was the only temple then upon
earth where the Lord had set his name, and where he
was worshipped in the spirit and purity which he had revealed to a chosen people.
    Mrs. Hemans has given a brief but delightful sketch
of the climate and scenery of Judea. The "olive
boughs," the "palmy shades," and the fountain by the
way side, according to Dr. Clarke, are still features of
a country where, though names, rulers, and religions
are changed, nature is still the same, and where the pastoral simplicity of ancient manners yet remains—where
Rachel still tends the flocks, and Rebecca bears her
pitcher to the well.

The Irish poet, Thomas Moore, describes the deli
cious climate of Syria and Palestine, with their produc
tions, in one of his poems.

SYRIA.

Now, upon Syria's land of roses
Softly the light of eve reposes,
And, like a glory, the broad sun
Hangs over sainted Lebanon;
Whose head in wintry grandeur towers,
   And whitens with eternal sleet,
While summer, in a vale of flowers,
   Is sleeping rosy at his feet.

To one, who looked from upper air
O'er all the enchanted regions there,
How beauteous must have been the glow,
The life, the sparkling from below!
Fair gardens, shining streams, with ranks
Of golden melons on their banks,
More golden where the sun-light falls;—
Gay lizards, glittering on the walls
Of ruined shrines, busy and bright
As they were all alive with light;—
   And, yet more splendid, numerous flocks
Of pigeons, settling on the rocks,
With their rich restless wings, that gleam
Variously in the crimson beam
Of the warm west,—as if inlaid
With brilliants from the mine, or made
Of tearless rainbows, such as span
The unclouded skies of Peristan!
And then, the mingling sounds that come,
Of shepherd's ancient reed, with hum
Of the wild bees of Palestine,
   Banquetting through the flowery vales;—
And, Jordan, those sweet banks of thine,
   And woods, so full of nightingales!

ODE TO THE SAVIOUR.

——For thou wert born of woman! thou didst come,
Oh Holiest! to this world of sin and gloom,
Not in thy dread omnipotent array,
   And not by thunders strew'd
   Was thy tempestuous road ;
Nor indignation burnt before thee on thy way.
  But thee, a soft and naked child,
   Thy mother undefil'd
In the rude manger laid to rest
   From off her virgin breast.

The heavens were not commanded to prepare
A gorgeous canopy of golden air ;
Nor stoop'd their lamps th' enthroned fires on high :
   A single silent star
   Came wandering from afar,
Gliding uncheck'd and calm along the liquid sky ;

   The Eastern sages leading on
    As at a kingly throne,
  To lay their gold and odours sweet
    Before thy infant feet.
The Earth and Ocean were not hush'd to hear
Bright harmony from every starry sphere ;
Nor at thy presence break the voice of song
   From all the cherub choirs,
   And seraphs' burning lyres,
Pour'd thro' the host of heaven the charmed clouds along.
  One angel-troop the strain began,
   Of all the race of man
  By simple shepherds heard alone,
   That soft Hosanna's tone.

And when thou didst depart, no car of flame
To bear thee hence in lambent radiance came ;
Nor visible angels mourn'd with drooping plumes :
   Nor didst thou mount on high
   From fatal Calvary
With all thy own redeem'd out-bursting from their tombs.

For thou didst bear away from earth
  But one of human birth,
The dying felon by thy side, to be
  In Paradise with thee.

Nor o'er thy cross the clouds of vengeance break ;
A little while the conscious earth did shake
At that foul deed by her fierce children done ;
  A few dim hours of day
  The world in darkness lay ;
Then bask'd in bright repose beneath the cloudless sun ;
  While thou didst sleep within the tomb,
    Consenting to thy doom ;
  Ere yet the white-rob'd angel shone
  Upon the sealed stone.

And when thou didst arise, thou didst not stand
With devastation in thy red right hand,
Plaguing the guilty city's murderous crew ;
  But thou didst haste to meet
  Thy mother's coming feet,
And bear the words of peace unto the faithful few.
  Then calmly, slowly didst thou rise
    Into thy native skies,
Thy human form dissolved on high
In its own radiancy.
                   Milman.

LINES,

*On seeing a clear stream which supplied the neighbour-
hood with water.*

  Gentle reader, see in me
  An emblem of true charity:
  For, while my bounty I bestow,
  I'm neither heard nor seen to flow ;
  And I have fresh supplies from heaven
  For every cup of water given.
              Bishop Hoadly.

THOMAS MOORE.

Mr. Moore is a native of Ireland, only a small portion of his poetry is of a serious character; but two of his hymns are selected as illustrative of his talent for sacred poetry.

THE UNIVERSE IS GOD'S TEMPLE.

To thee whose temple is all space,
    Whose altar earth, sea, skies,
One chorus let all beings raise,
    All nature's incense rise.   *Pope.*

The turf shall be my fragrant shrine,
My temple, Lord! that arch of thine;
My censer's breath the mountain airs,
And silent thoughts my only prayers*.

My choir shall be the moonlight waves,
When murmuring homeward to their caves,
Or when the stillness of the sea,
Even more than music, breathes of thee!

I'll seek, by day, some glade unknown,
All light and silence, like thy throne!
And the pale stars shall be, at night,
The only eyes that watch my rite.

Thy heaven, on which 'tis bliss to look,
Shall be my pure and shining book,
Where I shall read, in words of flame,
The glories of thy wond'rous name.

I'll read thy anger in the rack
That clouds awhile the day-beam's track;
Thy mercy in the azure hue
Of sunny brightness, breaking through!

*Pii orant tacite.

32*

There's nothing bright, above, below,
From flowers that bloom to stars that glow
But in its light my soul can see
Some feature of thy Deity.

There's nothing dark, below, above,
But in its gloom I trace thy Love,
And meekly wait that moment, when
Thy touch shall turn all-bright again!

THE KINGDOM COME.

These verses repeat the figures by which the Hebrew
Prophets, Isaiah, and others indicate the *reign of Christ.*
The Jews believed he would be their political ruler, and
the splendid oriental imagery by which the circumstances
of his power were illustrated, led them to presume that he
would be arrayed in all the magnificence of eastern mo-
narchs.

Those who know the history of the Christian religion,
know, that though the life of Jesus was humble, and his
death ignominious, yet *kings and princes,* " from every
nook of earth" have acknowledged the truth of this re-
ligion, and that every nation of civilized men is subject
in some measure to the blessed influences of Christiani-
ty.

Awake arise*! thy light is come!
  The nations that before outshone thee,
Now at thy feet lie dark and dumb—
  The glory of the Lord is on thee!

Arise—the Gentiles to thy ray,
  From every nook of earth shall cluster;
And kings and princes haste to pay
  Their homage to thy rising lustre.

Lift up thine eyes around, and see,
  O'er foreign fields, o'er farthest waters

* People of God.

Thy exiled sons returned to thee
   To thee return thy home-sick daughters.

And camels rich, from Midian's tents
   Shall lay their treasures down before thee,
And Saba bring her gold and scents,
   To fill thy air and sparkle o'er thee.

See who are these, that like a cloud,
   Are gath'ring from all-earth's dominions,
Like doves long absent, when allowed
   Homeward to shoot their trembling pinions !

Surely the isles shall wait for thee,—
   The ships of Tarshish round shall hover,
To bring thy sons across the sea,
   And waft their gold and silver over :

And Lebanon thy pomp shall grace—
   The fir, the pine, the palm victorious
Shall beautify thy holy place,
   And make the ground we tread on glorious.

No more shall discord haunt thy ways,
   Nor ruin waste thy cheerless nation ;
But thou shall call the portals *praise,*
   And thou shall name thy walls *salvation.*

The sun no more shall make thee bright,
   Nor moon shall lend her lustre to thee—
But God himself shall be thy light,
   And flash eternal glory through thee.

Thy sun shall never more go down ;
   A ray from heaven itself descended,
Shall light thy everlasting crown—
   Thy days of mourning all are ended.

My own elect and righteous land !
   Thy branch, for ever green and vernal,
Which I have planted with this hand,
   Live thou shalt, in life eternal.

This piece, throughout, is a personification of a people chosen by God for his own.—The Jews believe that they were this people, and that their city, Jerusalem, is the metropolis of this happy nation; but they, whose God is the Lord, form this people every where.—" He that worketh righteousness" of all nations, belongs to the great family of the just, and the place where he abides is holy, for he dwelleth in God, and God in him.

MRS. BARBAULD.

Anna Lætitia Barbauld was the daughter of Dr. Aikin: she is memorable for her happy talent in instructing the young, for her accomplishments, her elegant criticisms, her excellent moral writings in poetry and prose, and above all, for her sincere piety and exemplary conduct through life. This lady died at the age of eighty-one, near London, March, 1825.

In the third chapter of Habakkuk the prophet gives a sublime description of God's power, and of his displeasure against the wicked. The whole passage is highly *figurative*, only a small part of it can be literally understood. But the " terrors of the Lord" did not alarm the prophet; he knew that the meek, and they who seek righteousness, are safe in the day of God's anger; and though he trembled at the indignation of God against the transgressor, he trusted in the mercy which endureth for ever; and he says,

" Although the fig-tree shall not blossom, neither shall fruit be in the vines; the labour of the olive shall fail, and the fields shall yield no meat; the flock shall be cut off from the fold, and there shall be no herd in the stalls: Yet I will rejoice in the Lord, I will joy in the God of my salvation." Mrs. Barbauld has paraphrased this passage thus:

Praise to God, immortal praise,
For the love that crowns our days;
Bounteous source of every joy!
Let thy praise our tongues employ.

For the blessings of the field ;
For the stores the gardens yield ;
For the vine's exalted juice ;
For the generous olive's use.

Flocks that whiten all the plain ;
Yellow sheaves of ripened grain ;
Clouds that drop their fattening dews ;
Suns that temperate warmth diffuse :

All that spring with bounteous hand,
Scatters o'er the smiling land ;
All that liberal autumn pours
From her rich o'erflowing stores :

These to thee, our God ! we owe,
Source whence all our blessings flow
And for these our souls shall raise
Grateful vows and solemn praise.

Yet should rising whirlwinds tear
From its stem the ripening ear;
Should the fig tree's blasted shoot
Drop her green untimely fruit :

Should the vine put forth no more,
Nor the olive yield her store :
Though the sickening flocks should fall,
And the herds desert the stall :

Should thine altered hand restrain
Vernal showers and latter rain ;
Blast each opening bud of joy,
And the rising year destroy :

Still to thee our souls shall raise
Grateful vows and solemn praise ;
And, when every blessing's flown,
Love thee—for thyself alone !

MISS WILLIAMS.

Helen Maria Williams is an English lady, long resident in France. She has subsisted by the exertion of her talents, as a writer and translator, and has been considered an ornament to society from the elegance of her conversation, and the liberality of her sentiments. A single specimen of her poetry will serve to inspire reverence for her piety.

GOD SEEN IN ALL.

My God! all nature owns thy sway;
Thou giv'st the night and thou the day:
When all thy loved creation wakes,
When morning, rich in lustre, breaks,
And bathes in dew the opening flower,
To thee we owe her fragrant hour;
And when she pours her choral song,
Her melodies to thee belong.

Or, when in paler tints arrayed,
The evening slowly spreads her shade;
That soothing shade, that grateful gloom,
Can more than day's enlivening bloom,
Still every fond and vain desire,
And calmer, purer thoughts inspire;
From earth the pensive spirit free,
And lead the softened heart to thee.

In every scene thy hands have dressed,
In every form by thee impressed,
Upon the mountain's awful head,
Or where the sheltering woods are spread;
In every note that swells the gale,
Or tuneful stream that cheers the vale,
The cavern's depth, or echoing grove,
A voice is heard of praise and love.

As o'er thy works the seasons roll,
And soothe with change of bliss the soul,

O never may their smiling train
Pass o'er the human sense in vain !
But oft as on their charms we gaze,
Attune the wandering soul to praise ;
And be the joys that most we prize,
The joys that from thy favour rise.

BABYLON.

And now from out the watery floor
A city rose, and well she wore
Her beauty, and stupendous walls,
And towers that touched the stars, and halls
Pillar'd with whitest marble, whence
Palace on lofty palace sprung ;
And over all rich gardens hung,
Where, amongst silver waterfalls,
Cedars and spice-trees and green bowers,
And sweet winds playing with all the flowers
Of Persia and of Araby,
Walked princely shapes : some with an air
Like warriors, some like ladies fair
Listening, and, amidst all, the king
Nebuchadnezzar rioting
In supreme magnificence.
——This was famous Babylon.

Barry Cornwall.

Babylon was the capital of Chaldea or Babylonia. The
exact site of Babylon is disputed, and it is equally doubt-
ful who was its founder ; but Nebuchadnezzar, about six
centuries before Christ, repaired, extended, and adorned
it, so that its magnificence was the boast of this vainglo-
rious monarch.—" Is not this great babylon, that I have
built for the house of the kingdom, by the might of my
power, and for the honour of my majesty ?"

In scripture this magnificence is extolled in many pla-
ces—The " great Babylon ;" the " glory of kingdoms ;"
the " beauty of Chaldea's excellency ;" and " the praise
of the whole earth," besides many other appropriate ex-

pressions, are applied to this ancient city.   Babylon was
a square enclosed by walls, and each of its sides mea-
sured, according to some writers, fifteen miles; but it is
not presumed that it was wholly inhabited, or that the
houses were contiguous.   It was embellished by gardens
supported by arches, in terraces raised one above ano-
ther, on which the soil was sufficiently deep to permit the
growth of large trees; and the most luxuriant shrubs and
splendid flowers were disposed to produce the most bril-
liant effect.   These are usually called *hanging gardens*.

. Cyrus, king of Persia conquered Babylon B. C. 538;
and Xerxes, on his return from his Grecian expedition,
laid it in ruins.   Alexander of Macedon proposed to re-
build Babylon, but he did not live to effect that intention.
Soon after the death of Alexander B. C. 336, 500,000 of
the inhabitants of Babylon were withdrawn to Seleucia,
and after that time Babylon became that desolate place
described by the prophet Isaiah.

Isaiah's prophecies are dated from 760, to 798, B. C;
and though this was nearly two centuries before the cap-
tivity of his countrymen, and more than four previous to
the ruin of Babylon, the prophet foretelsl the restora-
tion of the Jews, and the desolation of their oppressors.

The 15th chapter of Isaiah contains a gracious promise
of God's mercy to his people, and a sublime and highly
poetical denunciation of divine vengeance against the
proud power which enslaved them.

" For the Lord will have mercy on Jacob, and will
yet choose Israel, and set them in their own land : and
the strangers shall be joined with them, and they shall
cleave to the house of Jacob.   And the people shall take
them, and bring them to their place : and the house of
Israel shall possess them in the land of the Lord for
servants and handmaids : and they shall take them cap-
tives, whose captives they were; and they shall rule
over their oppressors.   And it shall come to pass in the
day that the Lord shall give thee rest from thy sorrow,
and from thy fear, and from the hard bondage wherein
thou wast made to serve.

" That thou shalt take up this proverb against the king of Babylon, and say, How hath the oppressor ceased! the golden city ceased! The Lord hath broken the staff of the wicked, and the sceptre of the rulers. He who smote the people in wrath with a continual stroke, he that ruled the nations in anger, is persecuted, and none hindereth. The whole earth is at rest, and is quiet: they break forth into singing. Yea, the fir trees rejoice at thee, and the cedars of Lebanon, saying, Since thou art laid down, no feller is come up against us. Hell from beneath is moved for thee to meet thee at thy coming: it stirreth up the dead for thee, even all the chief ones of the earth; it raiseth up from their thrones all the kings of the nations. All they shall speak and say unto thee, Art thou also become weak as we ? art thou become like unto us ? Thy pomp is brought down to the grave, and the noise of thy viols : the worm is spread under thee, and the worms cover thee.

"How art thou fallen from heaven, O Lucifer, son of the morning ! how art thou cut down to the ground, which didst weaken the nations! For thou hast said in thine heart, I will ascend into heaven, I will exalt my throne above the stars of God : I will sit also upon the mount of the congregation, in the sides of the north : I will ascend above the heights of the clouds : I will be like the most High. Yet thou shalt be brought down to hell, to the sides of the pit. They that see thee shall narrowly look upon thee, and consider thee, saying, Is this the 'man that made the earth to tremble, that did shake kingdoms ; that made the world as a wilderness, and destroyed the cities thereof; that opened not the house of his prisoners ? All the kings of the nations, even all of them, lie in glory, every one in his own house.

" But thou art cast out of thy grave like an abominable branch, and as the raiment of those that are slain, thrust through with a sword, that go down to the stones of the pit ; as a carcase trodden under feet. Thou shalt not be joined with them in burial, because thou hast destroyed thy land, and slain thy people : the seed of evil-

33

doers shall never be renowned. Prepare slaughter for his
children for the iniquity of their fathers; that they do not
rise, nor possess the land, nor fill the face of the world
with cities.   For I will rise up against them, saith the
Lord of hosts, and cut off from Babylon the name, and
remnant, and son, and nephew, saith the Lord.   I will
also make it a possession for the bittern, and pools of
water: and I will sweep it with the besom of destruction,
saith the Lord of hosts.

" The Lord of hosts hath sworn, saying, Surely as I
have thought, so shall it come to pass; and as I have
purposed, so shall it stand: That I will break the Assy-
rian in my land, and upon my mountains tread him under
foot: then shall his yoke depart from off them, and his
burden depart from off their shoulders."

The consummateness of the destruction which was fore-
shown by Isaiah, is yet more impressively described in
the Apocalypse of St. John.

" That great city, Babylon, shall be thrown down, and
shall be found no more at all. And the voices of harpers,
and musicians, and of pipers, and trumpeters, shall be
heard no more at all in thee: and no craftsmen, of what-
soever craft he be, shall be found any more in thee; and
the sound of a millstone shall be heard no more at all in
thee; and the light of a candle shall shine no more at all
in thee; and the voice of the bridegroom and the bride
shall be heard no more at all in thee." *Rev. c.* 18, *v.* 21
—23.

It is proper to remark that St. John, who wrote this
passage, lived long after the destruction of Babylon,
and that it is supposed he did not intend to represent the
ruin of Babylon herself, but of *Rome.*   Rome, from her
magnitude and splendour, was sometimes called a
second Babylon: She was at the summit of her glory
when the apostle wrote the prophetic book of the Revela-
tions, and he foresaw that her fate nearly resembled that
of the Chaldean Babylon.

TO A FRIEND ON NEW YEAR'S DAY.

Sudden to cease, or gently to decline,
Oh, power of Mercy! may the lot be mine:
Let me not linger on the verge of fate,
Nor weary duty to its utmost date;.
Losing, in pain's impatient gloom confin'd,
Freedom of thought and dignity of mind;
Till pity views, untouch'd, the parting breath,
And cold indiff'rence adds a pang to death.
Yet if to suffer long my doom is cast,
Let me preserve this temper to the last.
Oh let me still from self my feelings bear,
To sympathize with sorrow's starting tear:
Nor sadden at the smile which joy bestows,
Though far from me her beam ethereal glows.
Let me remember in the gloom of age,
To smile at follies happier youth engage;
See them fallacious, but indulgent spare
The fairy dreams experience cannot share;
Nor view the rising morn with jaundic'd eye,
Because *for me*, no more the sparkling moments fly.

The amiable and sensible writer of the preceding ver-
ses, was Mrs. John Hunter, the wife of the celebrated
anatomist.

A RIDDLE.

From rosy lips we issue forth,
From east to west, from north to south,
Unseen, unfelt, by night, by day,
Abroad we take our airy way.
We fasten love, we kindle strife
The bitter and the sweet of life.
Piercing and sharp, we wound like steel,
Now smooth as oil, those wounds we heal.
Not strings of pearl are valued more,
Nor gems enchased in golden ore;
Yet thousands of us every day
Worthless and vile are thrown away.

Ye wise! secure with gates of brass
The double doors through which we pass,—
For once escaped, back to our cell
No art of man can us compel.   *Barbauld.*

"Riddles are of high antiquity, and were the employ-
ment of grave men formerly.   The first riddle that we
have on record was proposed by Sampson at a wedding
feast to the young men of the Philistines, who were invi-
ted upon the occasion.   The feast lasted seven days;
and if they found it out within the seven days, Sampson was
to give them thirty suits of clothes and thirty sheets; and if
they could not guess it, they were to forfeit the same to
him.   The riddle was: 'Out of the eater came forth
meat, and out of the strong came forth sweetness.'   He
had killed a lion, and left its carcase; on returning soon
after, he found a swarm of bees had made use of the
skeleton as a hive, and it was full of honey-comb. Struck
with the oddness of the circumstance, he made a riddle
of it."

LUCY AIKIN.

Miss Aikin is a niece of the late Mrs. Barbauld.   She
is known as the historian of the British Queen, Elizabeth,
and her successor, James I; but she has not confined her
attention to such high themes, she has composed books
for the young, and her little work, Poetry for Children, is
among the best *initiatory* collections. Many of the sub-
sequent pieces are extracted from it.

THE BEGGAR MAN.

Around the fire one wintry night
The farmer's rosy children sat;
The faggot lent its blazing light,
And jokes went round and careless chat.

When, hark! a gentle hand they hear
Low tapping at the bolted door,
And thus, to gain their willing ear,
A feeble voice was heard to implore.

" Cold blows the blast across the moor,
The fleet drives hissing in the wind ;
Yon toilsome mountain lies before,
A dreary treeless waste behind.

My eyes are weak, and dim with age,
No road, no path, can I descry,
And these poor rags ill stand the rage
Of such a keen inclement sky.

So faint I am—these tottering feet
No more my palsied frame can bear ;
My freezing heart forgets to beat,
And drifting snows my tomb prepare.

Open your hospitable door,
And shield me from the biting blast :
Cold, cold it blows across the moor,
The weary moor that I have pass'd !"

With hasty step the farmer ran,
And close beside the fire they place
The poor half frozen beggar man,
With shaking limbs and blue-pale face.

The little children flocking came
And chafed his frozen hands in theirs,
And busily the good old dame
A comfortable mess prepares.

Their kindness cheered his drooping soul,
And slowly down his wrinkled cheek
The big round tears were seen to roll,
And told the thanks he could not speak.

The children too began to sigh,
And all their merry chat was o'er ;
And yet they felt, they knew not why,
More glad than they had done before.

Lucy Aikin.

33*

INDIA.

Where sacred Ganges pours along the plain,
And Indus rolls to swell the eastern main,
What awful scenes the curious mind delight,
What wonders burst upon the dazzled sight!
There giant palms lift high their tufted heads,
The plantain wide his graceful foliage spreads ;
Wild in the woods the active monkey springs,
The chattering parrot claps his painted wings :
'Mid tall bamboos lies hid the deadly snake,
The tiger couches in the tangled brake ;
The spotted axis bounds in fear away,
The leopard darts on his defenceless prey,
'Mid reedy pools and ancient forests rude,
Cool, peaceful haunts of awful solitude!
The huge rhinoceros rends the crashing boughs,
And stately elephants untroubled browse.
Two tyrant seasons rule the wide domain,
Scorch with dry heat, or drench with floods of rain :
Now feverish herds rush madding o'er the plains,
And cool in shady streams their throbbing veins,
The birds drop lifeless from the silent spray,
And nature faints beneath the fiery day ;
Then bursts the deluge on the sinking shore,
And teeming Plenty empties all her store.

Lucy Aikin

THE SWALLOW.

Swallow ! that on rapid wing
Sweep'st along in sportive ring,
Now here, now there, now low, now high,
Chasing keen the painted fly,—
Could I skim away with thee
Over land and over sea,
What streams would flow, what cities rise,
What landscapes dance before mine eyes !
First from England's southern shore
'Cross the channel we would soar,

And our vent'rous course advance
To the lively plains of France;
Sport among the feather'd choir
On the verdant banks of Loire,
Skim Garonne's majestic tide,
Where Bordeaux adorns his side;
Cross the towering Pyrenees,
'Mid orange groves and myrtle trees;
Entering then the wild domain
Where wolves prowl round the flocks of Spain,
Where silk-worms spin, and olives grow,
And mules plod surely on and slow.
Steering then for many a day
Far to south our course away,
From Gibraltar's rocky steep,
Dashing o'er the foaming deep,
On sultry Afric's fruitful shore
We'd rest at length, our journey o'er,
Till vernal gales should gently play
To waft us on our homeward way.

Lucy Aikin.

THE TRAVELLER'S RETURN.

Sweet to the morning traveller
  The sky-lark's earliest song,
Whose twinkling wings are seen at fits
  The dewy lights among.

And cheering to the traveller
  The gales that round him play,
When faint and wearily he drags
  Along his noontide way.

And when beneath th' unclouded sun
  Full wearily toils he,
The flowing water makes to him
  Most pleasant melody.

And when the evening light decays,
  And all is calm around,
There is sweet music to his ear
  In the distant sheep-bell's sound.

And sweet the neighbouring church's bell
  That marks his journey's bourn;
But sweeter is the voice of love
  That welcomes his return!

Anthology.

THE PIEDMONTESE AND HIS MARMOT.

From my dear native moorlands, for many a day
Thro' fields and thro' cities I've wander'd away.
Tho' I merrily sing, yet forlorn is my lot;
I'm a poor Piedmontese, and I show a marmot.
This pretty marmot in a mountain's steep side
Made a burrow, himself and his young ones to hide.
The bottom they covered with moss and with hay,
And stopp'd up the entrance, and snugly they lay.
They carelessly slept till the cold winter blast,
And the hail, and the deep drifting snow-shower was
      past.
But the warbling of April awoke them again
To crop the young plants, and to frisk on the plain.
Then I caught this poor fellow, and taught him to dance,
And we liv'd by his tricks as we rambled through France,
But he droops and grows drowsy as onward we roam,
And he and his master both pine for their home.
Let your charity then hasten back to his cot
The poor Piedmotese with his harmless marmot.

Lucy Aikin.

The marmot is a little animal somewhat like a squirrel;
he is taken in Alpine countries, is susceptible of educa-
tion, and may be taught tricks, which are exhibited for
the emolument of some poor fellow who carries him
about through European cities. The marmot is a *torpid*
animal—falling into a long sleep on the approach of win-
ter.

THE ORANGE TREE.

In the soft bosom of Campania's vale,
When now the wintry tempests all are fled,
And genial summer breathes her gentle gale,
The verdant orange lifts its beauteous head ;
From every branch the balmy flow'rets rise,
On every bough the golden fruits are seen ;
With odours sweet it fills the smiling skies :
But, in the midst of all its blooming pride,
A sudden blast from Apenninus blows,
    Cold with perpetual snows ;
The tender blighted plant shrinks up its leaves, and
    dies.

*Lord **Lyttleton**.*

GENERATIONS OF MAN.

Like leaves on trees the race of man is found,
Now green in youth, now withering on the ground.
Another race the following spring supplies,
They fall successive, and successive rise :
So generations in their course decay,
So flourish these when those are pass'd dway.

Pope's Homer.

TO A BEE.

Thou wert out betimes, thou busy busy Bee !
    When around I took my early way,
Before the cow from her resting-place
Had risen up, and left her trace
    On the meadow with dew so gray,
I saw thee, thou busy busy Bee ?

Thou wert alive, thou busy busy Bee !
    When the crowd in their sleep were dead,
Thou wert abroad in the freshest hour,
When the sweetest odour comes from the flower.
    Man will not learn to leave his lifeless bed,
And be wise and copy thee, thou busy busy Bee !

Thou wert working late, thou busy busy Bee !
　　After the fall of the cistus flower,
I heard thee last as I saw thee first,
When the primrose tree blossom was ready to burst.
　　In the coolness of the ev'ning hour,
I heard thee, thou busy busy Bee !

Thou art a miser, thou busy busy Bee !
　　Late and early at employ ;
Still on thy golden stores intent,
Thy youth in heaping and hoarding is spent
　　What thy age will never enjoy.
I will not copy thee, thou miserly Bee !

Thou art a fool, thou busy busy Bee,
　　Thus for another to toil !
Thy master waits till thy work is done,
Till the latest flowers of the ivy are gone,
　　And then he will seize the spoil,
And will murder thee, thou poor little Bee !

Anthology.

RECOVERY FROM SICKNESS.

See the wretch that long has tost
　　On the thorny bed of pain,
At length repair his vigour lost,
　　And breathe and walk again :

The meanest flow'ret of the vale,
　　The simplest note that swells the gale,
The common sun, the air, the skies,
　　To him are op'ning paradise.

Gray.

TO A HEDGE-SPARROW.

Little flutt'rer ! swiftly flying,
　　Here is none to harm thee near.
Kite nor hawk, nor schoolboy prying ;
　　Little flutt'rer ! cease to fear.

One who would protect thee ever
  From the schoolboy, kite and hawk,
Musing, now obtrudes, but never
  Dreamt of plunder in his walk.

He no weasel stealing slily
  Would permit thy eggs to take ;
Nor the polecat, nor the wily
  Adder, nor the writhed snake.

May no cuckoo wander near thee
  Lay her eggs within thy nest,
Nor thy young ones, born to cheer thee,
  Be destroy'd by such a guest !

Little flutt'rer ! swiftly flying,
  Here is none to harm thee near ;
Kite nor hawk, nor schoolboy prying ;
  Little flutt'rer ! cease to fear.

Anthology.

ARABIA.

O'er Arabia's desert sands
  The patient camel walks,
'Mid lonely caves and rocky lands
  The fell hyæna stalks.
On her cool and shady hills
  Coffee-shrubs and tam'rinds grow,
Headlong fall the welcome rills
  Down the fruitless dells below.

The fragrant myrrh and healing balm
  Perfume the passing gale ;
Thick hung with dates the spreading palm
  Tow'rs o'er the peopled vale.
Locusts oft, a living cloud,
  Hover in the darken'd air,
Like a torrent dashing loud,
  Bringing famine and despair :

And often o'er the level waste
   The stifling hot winds fly;
Down falls the swain with trembling haste,
   The gasping cattle die.
Shepherd-people on the plain
   Pitch their tents and wander free,
Wealthy cities they disdain,
   Poor—yet blest with liberty.

Lucy Aikin.

THE COCK.

Within a homestead lived, without a peer
For crowing loud, the noble Chanticleer.
More certain was the crowing of this cock
To number hours than is an abbey clock;
And sooner than the morning bell was rung
He clapp'd his wings upon his roost, and sung.
High was his comb, and coral-red withal,
In dents embattled like a castle wall:
His bill was raven black, and shone like jet;
Blue were his legs, and orient were his feet;
White were his nails, like silver to behold;
His body glitter'd like the burnish'd gold.

Dryden

Check Out More Titles From HardPress Classics Series In this collection we are offering thousands of classic and hard to find books. This series spans a vast array of subjects – so you are bound to find something of interest to enjoy reading and learning about.

Subjects:
Architecture
Art
Biography & Autobiography
Body, Mind &Spirit
Children & Young Adult
Dramas
Education
Fiction
History
Language Arts & Disciplines
Law
Literary Collections
Music
Poetry
Psychology
Science
…and many more.

Visit us at www.hardpress.net

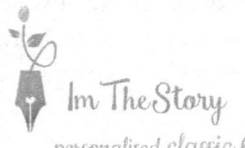

CPSIA information can be obtained
at www.ICGtesting.com
Printed in the USA
BVHW081808220819
556561BV00019B/4235/P

9 781406 997125